2004

In the Wake of Terror

Basic Bioethics
Glenn McGee and Arthur Caplan, series editors

In the Wake of Terror

Medicine and Morality in a Time of Crisis

edited by Jonathan D. Moreno

A Bradford Book
The MIT Press
Cambridge, Massachusetts
London, England

This book was set in Sabon by SNP Best-set Typesetter Ltd., Hong Kong and was printed and bound in the United States of America.

Library of Congress Cataloging-in-Publication Data
In the wake of terror : medicine and morality in a time of crisis / edited by Jonathan D. Moreno.
    p. cm.—(Basic bioethics)
  "A Bradford book."
  Includes bibliographical references and index.
  ISBN 0-262-13428-4 (hc. : alk. paper)
  1. Medical ethics. 2. Bioethics. 3. Medical ethics—Miscellanea.
4. Crisis management—Health aspects. 5. Terror. I. Moreno, Jonathan D.
II. Series.
R725.5 .I5 2003
174′.2—dc21
                                                        2002043132

10 9 8 7 6 5 4 3 2 1

Contents

Series Foreword

We are pleased to present the seventh volume in the series Basic Bioethics. The series presents innovative book-length manuscripts in bioethics to a broad audience and introduces seminal scholarly manuscripts, state-of-the-art reference works, and textbooks. Such broad areas as the philosophy of medicine, advancing genetics and biotechnology, end of life care, health and social policy, and the empirical study of biomedical life will be engaged.

Glenn McGee
Arthur Caplan

Basic Bioethics Series Editorial Board
Tod S. Chambers
Susan Dorr Goold
Mark Kuczewski
Herman Saatkamp

Foreword

This valuable collection is designed not just to make you think but to help us act. The committed enemies of Western society—including home-grown ones—have new capacity to strike terror and spread death. To cope with these threats we must respond ethically and build a consensus around appropriate policies and procedures.

I first heard Jonathan Moreno speak about how the threat of bioter-rorism is challenging the field of bioethics at a meeting of the Critical Incident Analysis Group at the University of Virginia in April 2002. The group included current and former law enforcement, defense and intel-ligence officers, medical specialists, and experts in a variety of fields. His discussion of past episodes—the CIA's MKULTRA experiments and the Army's secret LSD tests—evoked memories of how appalled I felt when I first heard of them in the mid-1970s. I was an NBC News correspon-dent covering congressional investigations of past abuses by intelligence and law enforcement agencies.

To put it in perspective, authorities in decades past were responding to a national emergency, the Cold War and Vietnam, and were trying to protect America. As a Pentagon news correspondent I was shocked by the extent of United States research into chemical and biological weapons; but the rationale—to defend against attack—seemed com-pelling to those in a position to order such activities. Keeping people in the dark, including those unwittingly participating in research studies, appeared justified in facing an "evil empire."

Military programs that in peaceful times may seem grossly exagger-ated can appear prudent in times of great stress. After 9/11 we find our-selves wondering how to protect against newly apprehended risks. Ethical norms in public health that seemed very appropriate in normal times may have to be reconsidered for emergency conditions. This volume suggests several areas that require careful consideration.

One that is highest on my list is determining before the event how our society will protect itself against an attack using a contagious disease. For example, if enemies use smallpox as a weapon, our health system will be extraordinarily taxed. Triage may be necessary at hospitals. The demand for vaccinations will be great. Public health and law enforcement will have to impose restrictions, including quarantine. Health care personnel will be overwhelmed. People will be urged to stay home or be quartered in institutions that are not designed for health care. Society urgently has to develop a consensus around the best policies. We must communicate with the public before another attack.

I have had the advantage of thinking about these challenges from more than one perspective. After I left the news profession I practiced law and consulted for corporations on public health issues. As a society we must consider whether the current market in health care is adequate, whether medicines can be made available widely and affordably. The fairness of resource allocation has to be evaluated in the light of the hostile threat of a biological or chemical attack.

For most people, medical information is so complex it is hard to comprehend in a time of stress. For those concerned about security—national, local, or corporate—secrecy is usually the default mode. In emergencies law enforcement personnel are used to ordering, not explaining. But the biggest challenge is to involve the general public as participants in developing norms and procedures for worst-case situations. This will require specialists unlearning familiar behaviors that thwart communication. The threshold requirement is for clear, understandable, and candid discussion of the risks, objectives, problems, options, and underlying values at stake.

I have become convinced that the key to effective risk communication is to identify the values that are perceived by the public to be at risk. These may not be the same as the ones experts quantify. Good risk communication requires an interactive process that involves people in decision making, preferably before urgent conditions demand action.

The need for preparation and communication was demonstrated for me last November when one of my clients, a large financial institution, decided to test for anthrax spores in mailrooms at major facilities on the East Coast. No one in the offices had reported symptoms of anthrax but the company was concerned because it had received mail from contaminated post offices. On a Friday afternoon we received word that one test was positive at an employees' cafeteria in a downtown office building. There was instant concern among senior managers. Immediate questions had to be answered:

- Should the building be evacuated?
- Should employees be informed before they left for the weekend?
- Should employees be informed over the weekend or on Monday morning?
- If so, how should that be handled?
- Should employees be advised to start taking antibiotics?
- Should the company bring in medical professionals to treat employees?
- Should local police be notified?
- How about the FBI or CDC or local public health officials?
- What should be done about vendors, customers, and tenants in the building?
- Should the news media be informed?
- If so, what should the company say publicly?
- Should the company wait until additional tests were conducted on the suspected substance found in the cafeteria?

As it turned out, the company opted for the last choice and the results the next day showed that the initial, alarming finding was a false positive. If you think a false positive anthrax test is trivial, you should have felt the angst of Friday's deliberation. Imagine if it had caused the building to be decontaminated or, worse yet, if people had become sick. The best outcomes can inform our worst-case planning. The relief felt that autumn Saturday should not obscure the lesson from the near miss. The hurried debate over what to do on the previous evening showed the importance of planning ahead. Such situations and options for dealing with them should be considered now, when less adrenalin is flowing and when ethical and policy considerations can be carefully weighed in designing protocols for dealing with risky contingencies.

The dreadful events of autumn 2001 spurred new defensive programs. This collection of essays articulates some of the ethical issues that our society must consider. It serves a valuable purpose of stimulating public discussion and building consensus about how we should face the uncertainties of the future.

Ford Rowan

Acknowledgments

The idea for an anthology on the bioethical implications of terrorism came in a dinner conversation with Jeremy Sugarman. I am very grateful to Glenn McGee, co-editor of the MIT Press series in bioethics, and Clay Morgan of MIT Press for their instantaneous enthusiasm and support for this project. The contributors, busy people all, made special efforts to complete their manuscripts in an unusually short time, and I thank them for tolerating my harassment to stay on deadline.

One of the University of Virginia's talented undergraduates, Carrie Williams, helped me manage the traffic of manuscripts and communications with authors while on a Stacy Boyle Fellowship in the Center for Biomedical Ethics. I am most grateful for her exceptional organizational skills, efficiency, and good humor. My resourceful administrator, Carrie Gumm, never loses her cool amid the many demands made on her time. She gave me much-needed help in preparing the final manuscript.

The enthusiasm of my colleagues at the Center for Biomedical Ethics helps make it second to none as a locale for scholarship in bioethics. Their inspiration and support stand behind all my work.

Special thanks to my wife, Leslye Fenton, who adapted to my schedule and work habits without complaint, and to Jarrett and Jillian, who obliged both of us to adapt to theirs.

This book is dedicated to the emergency workers who lost their lives on September 11, 2001, and to their families.

Introduction: Bioethics and National Security before and after the Terror

Before the Terror

One week before the attacks on the World Trade Center and the Pentagon, the United States government confirmed press reports that the Defense Intelligence Agency was preparing to develop a new and more virulent strain of anthrax thought to be in possession of Russia. No contravention of the treaty permitting only defensive bioweapons research was admitted, for these projects were aimed at preventing a successful attack, and, government officials reasoned, research aimed at defense could be effective only if undertaken in light of the potential of actual offensive devices. Simultaneously, the CIA was reported to have built a replica of a biological weapons dispersal device or bomblet developed by the former Soviet Union, again for purposes of defensive studies.[1]

I confess to being somewhat taken aback by these revelations, not, I hope, out of naivete about the need for continued biodefense work, or by the thin line between defensive and offensive research. Rather, I recalled the many questions I was asked while promoting a book on the history and ethics of national security experiments; both sophisticated and simple-minded conspiracy theorists pressed me for my opinion about whether abusive secret experiments might still be going on.[2] My response: although I can't prove a negative, it seems quite unlikely that covert human experiments could continue today. Could I be so confident after the admission of research that stretched, if it did not break, the spirit of an international treaty obligation? Could I be so sure that secret human experiments were not now taking place under the sponsorship of U.S. national security entities?

After the attacks, this story, like so many others, understandably took a back seat to the national emergency. Yet I have wondered whether the outrage that greeted revelations of human experiments conducted without adequate consent and under risky circumstances, especially those sponsored by national security agencies, might be tempered by the change in certain objective conditions. After all, the original scandals concerning the CIA's MKULTRA program and the Army's LSD experiments came in the wake of Vietnam and Watergate. Twenty years later, the human radiation experiments controversy surfaced after a largely (for Americans) bloodless victory in the Persian Gulf, and in the context of medical problems after service in the Gulf that again undermined confidence in our government's concern with its men and women in uniform. In the weeks after September 11 and during the subsequent anthrax scare I came to see the apparently shifting perception of national security research as a case study in bioethics after terror. How will a field that emerged from the medical breakthroughs and cultural turbulence of the 1960s, with its emphasis on self-determination, respond to a new set of issues in an environment that may not presume civil liberties as a trump card? In this introduction, I explore this question in terms of rules that should govern classified human experiments.

Human Experiments and National Security

Counterfactuals being what they are, it is impossible to be certain that public outrage about abusive human experiments involving people in uniform, hospitalized patients, institutionalized children, prisoners, and others would have been lessened had the information not become available when it did. But it is hard to argue that, for example, new revelations about secret state experiments designed to minimize the effects of a terrorist attack would excite quite the public reaction that they would have before September 11. In the months after the anthrax scare the National Institutes of Health sponsored studies of stockpiled smallpox vaccine to see if supplies could be stretched by dilution. The vaccine itself presents a danger to those with compromised immune systems. Based on my reading of the protocol summary and consent form, the studies appear to have been carefully conducted. Yet surely tests of the vaccine on healthy volunteers, including students at St. Louis University, would not have passed a risk-benefit analysis before the anthrax scare and the war on terrorism.

Of interest, whereas the smallpox-dilution trials passed without public protest, even by those known to be critics of human experimentation, public concern about ethical standards in academic and commercial human subjects research has continued since the terrorist attacks. Summarizing results of a Harris poll of American attitudes toward research in 2002, the report's authors concluded with this laconic remark: "The good news is that relatively few people tend to be downright hostile toward participating in clinical trials."[3] Have we entered a period in which public concern about human experiments is reduced if the experiments are conducted at least partly for national security purposes, even if there is also the prospect of commercial gain? In that case, one can imagine private companies touting the national security implications of hair growth (promoting the morale of senior male officers), similar to the way the billions Congress spent on America's highway system was billed as a national defense measure in the 1950s.

That having been said, what can we expect if the United States and its allies are engaged in a struggle against terrorism that is years in duration, as the president and other leaders have indicated? Without suggesting that history will simply cycle back to a hands-off attitude with respect to covert government activity, it seems unlikely that a great deal of public energy would be expended on the kinds of investigations we have witnessed in the past, at least not with the same intensity. Would the American people today applaud spending tens of millions of dollars to investigate Cold War human radiation experiments, for example, as was the case in the mid-1990s?

In the early 1970s scandals about unethical human experiments by civilian organizations and widespread loss of public sympathy for the military preceded revelations of chemical weapons research by the Army and CIA. The country was prepared for outrages when they were discovered. What if, nearly thirty years later, the process were to reverse itself? New preoccupation with "homeland defense" and renewed respect for the professionals engaged in these efforts, including granting greater legal flexibility for espionage activities, could easily spill over into an enhanced image for civilian institutions whose mission is to protect our national survival. Medical organizations and health care professionals will play an important role in ameliorating the effects of a chemical or biological attack, and the public health system will be required to identify an outbreak as well as to organize the response. The regard in which the medical profession is held, so battered in recent years, could well be improved in the eyes of a jittery public through their identification with these initiatives.

Surely the tradition of civil libertarianism that has always influenced American political thinking will remain. But the strength of the rights orientation has waxed and waned, depending partly on perceptions of external threats. As we enter a new political and ideological framework, recent intense concerns about the rights and welfare of human research subjects could be blunted. This could come about not only because the public's attention would be focused mainly on matters of large national interest, with room to concentrate on a relatively small set of domestic problems, but also if continued scientific progress is given greater priority with increased momentum for the research imperative.

All this is not to assert, of course, that international and domestic conventions governing ethical human experimentation will be erased or even explicitly disavowed. Rather, the energy and dynamism behind the identification of questionable research practices are likely to lessen if a besieged society views science as an important ally and therefore sees occasional ethical improprieties as lapses in judgment rather than indicators of a larger crisis of humanism in the pursuit of knowledge.

One immediate test of national resolve to learn from the lessons of the past will be the nature of protections for human subjects in future experiments conducted behind the veil of government secrecy. The groundwork for such rules was laid by the Advisory Committee on Human Radiation Experiments (ACHRE), which issued a set of recommendations in 1995.[4] Noting that in an open society such classified experiments should be rare, the ACHRE went on to conclude that, when judged necessary, they should entail informed consent from all human subjects, including the identity of the sponsoring agency, and that the project involves classified research. To help ensure government accountability, permanent records should be established.

In 1997 the Clinton administration accepted these recommendations, and added:

The President is issuing a memorandum directing Federal agencies to jointly propose modifications to the Federal Policy for the Protection of Human Subjects (Common Rule) as it applies to classified research in order to implement these changes. Further, subjects will be informed of the sponsoring agency, except in limited, minimal-risk cases. In all secret studies, researchers will obtain informed consent, disclose that the project involves classified research, and keep permanent records.[5]

Yet by March 2002, five years after the presidential directive, the Common Rule amendments had not been adopted. The delay resulted from bureaucratic inertia and a change from Democratic to Republican administrations in an era in which secret human experiments were not a realistic policy option. In presentations to federal advisory groups and agency representatives in the fall and winter of 2001, I explained the situation and urged adoption of the Common Rule amendment as directed by the Clinton administration. As I write this introduction, it appears that there has been significant movement toward adoption by the federal agencies that are signatories of rules governing federally sponsored research involving human participants.

But the rules that are finally adopted will not in themselves solve the problems associated with secret research. For example, experience teaches that well-intentioned initiatives by federal agencies during the Cold War ran afoul of cultural resistance within the agencies, poor dissemination and understanding of the meaning of the rules, and failure to perceive some national security activity as falling under the rubric of medical experiments subject to rules. The classic example of these problems, as I described in *Undue Risk*, is secret adoption of the Nuremberg Code by the Department of Defense in 1953, an effort that the Army's inspector general later concluded was an abject failure. The legacy of distrust left by these and other episodes surely should not be extended by our generation.

After the Terror

Circumstances for future classified human experiments are hardly the only, and are probably not the most pressing, bioethical issue that faces us in the next several years. A basic concern has to do with the extent to which our legal and administrative public health frameworks are amenable to the requirements of preparedness for future bioterror attacks. Medical research questions that remain subconscious for most of us in peacetime burst into the headlines when the threat of war becomes patent. The potential for spread of infectious disease in military combat units, the importance of developing vaccines and other antidotes to forestall epidemics that could endanger those troops and by extension the countries they defend—such concerns give research for preventive strategies national security status. In the first chapter, Paul A. Lombardo explores how in wartime, vulnerable populations have sometimes played their part as unwitting recruits for science.

The remainder of part I is taken up with a proposal by James G. Hodge, Jr. and Lawrence O. Gostin for a statute for a Model State Emergency Health Powers Act (MSEHPA) and commentaries on the Act. A number of organizations of public officials asked public health scholars to develop a proposed law that would provide authorities with powers to respond to bioterror attacks without infringing on civil rights. Contrasting their position with that of many bioethicists, Hodge and Gostin contend that individual rights must often yield when social justification for doing so exists. The MSEHPA thus includes measures such as testing, treatment, vaccination programs, and isolation, although these are limited in scope and duration. The authors contend that their scheme preserves fundamental rights while giving society the tools to respond to an emergency of the sort contemplated in a bioterrorist event.

George J. Annas is highly critical of the MSEHPA and of the thinking behind it. He contests the assumption that the fight against terrorism requires sacrifice of civil liberties. Instead, he argues that seriously promoting the goal of health both at home and abroad is the best move that health care professionals can take to defeat terrorism and advance human well-being. Annas analyzes several examples in support of his conclusion that promoting human rights is our best defense against aggressors.

In their contribution, Ronald Bayer and James Colgrove begin by returning us to the history of American public health, one they characterize as typified by precisely the sort of conflict exemplified in this section: a series of controversies in which the police powers of the state confronts the antiauthoritarianism that is such a basic element of American political culture. The events of September 11, in their view, once more laid bare the latent tension among different public health ideologies. The controversy about the MEHPA is the centerpiece of this renewed debate.

How are standard conceptions of resource allocation and triage stressed in an era of bioterrorism? In part II, James F. Childress, and Kenneth Kipnis measure moral values for a health care system in catastrophic circumstances. Here the classroom debates about "lifeboat ethics" that I recall from my early years in bioethics are given a life they lacked in those days, calling to mind again the way that a bioethic after terror combines familiar issues with novel cases.

Jim Childress engages in a close examination of the ethics of medical triage. He considers what ethical standards are available for ascertaining justifiable inequities associated with allocation or rationing schemes in emergencies. After analysing utilitarian and egalitarian approaches, he urges that whatever criteria are developed, they must be part of a publicly accountable system. This is especially critical when maintaining the public's trust is a high priority, as it surely is in the aftermath of a bioterror event.

Ken Kipnis examines the techniques hospitals have developed for managing surging patient loads. He considers the nature of triage, its justifications, and—of importance—its limits. After considering the Tokyo sarin gas attack, the Bhopal disaster, and Hiroshima, he shows how hospitals become dysfunctional when the burden of patient need exceeds disaster-level carrying capacity. What is called for is a plan to implement a decentralized system of health care delivery under catastrophic conditions, health care without hospitals.

Part III begins with a chapter by Lisa A. Eckenwiler who explores ways in which the moral duties of health care workers may be transformed in extreme conditions. Here traditional bioethics principles such as self-determination, beneficence, and justice are put to an unfamiliar test, because, as Eckenwiler notes, bioterror emergencies involve organizations that are often hierarchal and sometimes secretive. Among specific problems she explores are the extent of emergency health care workers' duty to face dangers, and moral and epistemological difficulties raised by complicated terror incidents when there is little time to formulate an appropriate response.

Griffin Trotter offers the provocative suggestion that expanded concerns about bioterrorism create an opportunity to put the issue of health care reform back on the table for the first time since the early Clinton administration effort. National security, he coutrude, "is the new banner for health care reform." In turn, Trotter contends that the Emergency Medical Treatment and Active Labor Act (EMTALA) of 1986, which provides that every individual who comes to an emergency room is entitled to a medical screening examination, has created a systemic crisis that constitutes a national security risk.

The anthology continues with chapters by Evan G. DeRenzo and Ann E. Mills and Patricia H. Werhane. These authors consider the roles and obligations of those often neglected key players in the health care system in a war on terrorism: pharmaceutical firms and managed care organizations. Participants in a moral community have duties and obligations, and the pharmaceutical industry has its role to play. Yet it is difficult to determine exactly what that role should be. To reduce the complexity of the task, DeRenzo starts by stating that the rightful focus of a for-profit corporation is not the mere pursuit of profits but rather production and exchange of goods and services useful to members of society, from which activity profits naturally flow. She proposes that the special products and services pharmaceutical companies produce give rise to the special sorts of responsibilities they have in preparing for and responding to bioterror threats and attacks.

Mills and Werhane anticipate a shift in emphasis of the mission of the health care organization, as it must now be concerned with providing massive care to the entire community instead of providing care for a defined patient population. The threat of terrorism makes it imperative that all components of the health care system, both public and private organizations and agencies, take a systematic approach in agreeing on priorities and goals, as their interactions will determine successful delivery. The focus of organization ethics in health care moves from an examination of the appropriateness of stakeholder interactions with the individual organization in the context of the organization's mission, to examination of systemwide interactions and their effect on the system's priorities and goals.

In the last part Alan R. Fleischman and Emily Wood recommend standards for the conduct of research after tragic events. Although such research can provide important information to improve the health and well-being of present and future victims, specific ethical challenges must be addressed. Human-made disasters have profound effects on victims, rescue workers, their families, and others in the community that may impair their ability to reach voluntary and uncoerced decisions about research participation. Because such potential participants may be vulnerable and also subject to being overburdened with redundant research, they deserve special consideration. Fleischman and Wood propose specific recommendations to assist investigators, institutional review boards, public health officials, and political leaders to help serve the interests of these individuals.

We end where we began, with genes and national security, but this time with an eye to the future rather than to the past. Eric M. Meslin brings together a number of related topics, including research, public policy, and industry responsibilities. Science has added a new tool to the terrorist's toolkit—genetic technology to create bioweapons. Meslin observes that it is clear that action is necessary at many levels of science and public policy. But what action? What are the ethical responsibilities of the science community, government, and industry? What are the consequences of acting (or not acting)? And what, if anything, can bioethics offer? After briefly reviewing that state of knowledge and understanding of bioterrorism before October 2001, he discusses responses of scientists, government, and the private sector to threats posed by application of genetic knowledge to bioterrorism.

Each author has taken an otherwise familiar set of issues and analytical approaches and elaborated them from the standpoint of extreme circumstances not normally examined in contemporary bioethics. They conjoin civic obligations with bioethical discourse in ways that cast new light on both. Taken together, they respond to the question whether a field born under one set of social assumptions can sustain itself in a changed environment, and what lessons it may thereby teach and learn.

Notes

1. "Pentagon Plans to Proceed with Development of Anthrax Strain." 2001. Available at NYTimes.com (visited September 5).

2. Jonathan D. Moreno. 2001. *Undue Risk: Secret State Experiments on Humans.* New York: Routledge.

3. "Poll: Americans' Faith in Clinical Trials Shaken." 2002. Reuters Health, March 27.

4. Advisory Committee on Human Radiation Experiments. 1996. *The Human Radiation Experiments.* New York: Oxford University Press.

5. "Building Public Trust: Actions to Respond to the Report of the Advisory Committee on Human Radiation Experiments." 1997. United States Government, Human Radiation Interagency Working Group. Pittsburgh, PA: United States Government Printing Office.

Contributors

George J. Annas, JD, MPH
Professor of Health Law, Human
Rights, and Bioethics
Chair, Health Law Department
Boston University School of Public
Health

Ronald Bayer, PhD
Professor of Public Health
Mailman School of Public Health
Columbia University

James F. Childress, PhD
Hollingsworth Professor of Ethics
Director of the Institute for Practical
Ethics
University of Virginia

James Colgrove MPH, MA
Center for the History and Ethics of
Public Health
Mailman School of Public Health
Columbia University

Evan G. DeRenzo, PhD
Center for Ethics
Washington (DC) Hospital Center

Lisa A. Eckenwiler, PhD
Assistant Professor of Philosophy
Department of Philosophy
Old Dominion University

Alan R. Fleischman, MD
Senior Vice President
New York Academy of Medicine

Lawrence O. Gostin, JD, LLM
Professor of Law, Georgetown
University Law Center
Professor of Public Health, Johns
Hopkins Bloomberg School
of Public Health
Director, Center for Law and the
Public's Health

James G. Hodge, Jr., JD, LLM
Adjunct Professor of Law, George-
town University Law Center
Assistant Scientist, Johns Hopkins
Bloomberg School of Public Health
Project Director, Center for Law and
the Public's Health

Kenneth Kipnis, PhD
Professor of Philosophy
Department of Philosophy
University of Hawaii

Paul A. Lombardo, PhD, JD
Associate Professor of Medical
Education
Director of the Program in Law and
Medicine
Center for Biomedical Ethics
University of Virginia

Eric M. Meslin, PhD
Professor of Medicine, Medical and
Molecular Genetics,
and Philosophy
Director of the Center for Bioethics
Indiana University

Ann E. Mills, MBA
Assistant Professor of Medical
Education
Center for Biomedical Ethics
University of Virginia

Ford Rowan, JD
Rowan & Blewitt
Herndon, Virginia

Griffin Trotter, MD, PhD
Assistant Professor of Ethics
Assistant Professor of Surgery
Center for Health Care Ethics
St. Louis University

Patricia H. Werhane, PhD
Ruffin Professor of Business Ethics
Darden Business School
University of Virginia

Emily B. Wood
Program Officer
Center for Urban Bioethics
New York Academy of Medicine

Jonathan D. Moreno, PhD
Kornfeld Professor of Biomedical
Ethics
Director of the Center for Biomedical
Ethics
University of Virginia

The nineteenth and twentieth centuries have given us as much terror as we can take.

—Jean-Francois Lyotard

I

Public Health

1

"Of Utmost National Urgency": The Lynchburg Colony Hepatitis Study, 1942

Paul A. Lombardo

"Viewing wartime research through the lens of history approximately three months after the terrorist attack of September 11, 2002," a story written by a Washington, D.C., journalist,[1] raised a series of critical issues about the conduct of medical research. The story described the intentional inoculation of children and adults with a tainted vaccine in an experiment designed to determine why the vaccine had caused hepatitis in thousands of soldiers. The recipients lived in a facility for the mental disabled, and the experiment occurred on the heels of United States entry into World War II.

The story, perhaps of only historical interest in other times, became unexpectedly topical in the wake of events of September 11. It reminded us how fragile the balance is between the imperative of biomedical progress, always pursuing new avenues to conquer disease, and the protectionist ethic shielding vulnerable experimental subjects that has come to characterize modern regulation of biomedical research. How might that balance be tipped if secret research critical to the national defense was carried out during wartime? It is clear that existing legal protections would forbid similar projects today. But could the fear of terror and the fog of war tempt researchers to set aside usual ethical presumptions to conduct desperately needed studies on subjects hidden from public view in the secure and controlled environment of an institution?

Since the 1970s, government-funded research on human subjects in the United States has been bounded by extensive legal regulations. Those rules—for a long time honored more in the breach than the observance—have become the subject of heated debate in the research community. Do they actually protect subjects? Do they forestall or impede important medical developments? Does the cost of compliance outweigh the rare harms such rules prevent? No easy answers are available, and recent research scandals at major universities only fueled the controversy about public oversight of scientific enterprise.

To complicate matters, initiation of military hostilities in response to terrorist attacks has left little time to consider how our perceptions of ethical rules that govern clinical research might change when a metaphorical "war on disease" is waged alongside an actual war with bombs and bullets. Can ethical touchstones, such as the need for informed consent, or special protections to be accorded vulnerable populations, be put aside temporarily to allow research judged critical to the national interest? To answer those questions it is necessary to see how far we have come in the past century in our thinking about the need for scientific peer review, informed consent, and open disclosure concerning results of clinical research. In looking backward, we are reminded that controversies about experiments on vulnerable populations are not new.

At the turn of the century antivivisectionists focused on experiments that tested vaccines on children in orphanages to capture the attention of reformers. Although medical researchers took great offense at charges made against them, as the pace of biomedical research accelerated, many antivivisectionist prophecies eventually came true. Scandals after inoculation of children with new vaccines for polio in the 1930s renewed the antivivisectionist cause and other types of research on the institution-bound mentally disabled are part of the lore of the search for a polio vaccine (Lederer 1995, 107–108).

In the mid-1930s Dr. John Kolmer tested a live polio vaccine on himself, his two children, and twenty-two other youths. His work ran parallel to the work of Drs. Maurice Brodie and William H. Park, who developed a different type of vaccine against polio. By 1935 approximately 10,000 children had received the Park-Brodie vaccine; another 12,000 had been immunized with Kolmer's vaccine. Not until a U.S. Public Health Service physician reported that twelve people receiving one of the vaccines had developed polio and six of them died, did distribution of those agents cease (Leake 1935, 2152).

Although the Kolmer scandal involved no specific facility, other investigators found their subjects inside institutional walls. In 1952 Dr. Hilary Koprowski, another field officer in the war to eradicate polio, shocked the medical community by announcing he and his colleagues had fed twenty "non-immune human volunteers a suspension of cotton-rat brain and spinal cord" infected with an attenuated strain of polio virus mixed in chocolate milk (Koprowski, Jervis, and Norton 1952, 108). The author relegated to footnotes the comment that "for obvious reasons, the age, sex and physical status of each volunteer are not mentioned" (Koprowski et al. 1952, 111). The researchers repeated feedings for several "volunteers" six to seven months later using virus collected from stools passed after the first feedings, and were happy to report that "[i]n not a single instance were there any signs of illness noted"(Koprowski et al. 1952, 122, 125). This work was roundly criticized in the *Lancet*, which commented sarcastically on evolving meanings of the word "volunteer." The *Lancet* forecast that "[w]e may yet read in a scientific journal that an experiment was carried out with twenty volunteer mice, and that twenty other mice volunteered as controls" (Annotations 1952, 552).

The next year, Kroprowski et al. reported studies on 181 children described as "inmates of a State institution for mental defectives." Perhaps sensitized by earlier criticism, they disclosed that sixty-one of those children were given doses of live virus, but only after "permission of each child's parents had been legally obtained" (Koprowski et al. 1953, 271–280). Sources of "volunteers" for these studies were New York state's Letchworth Village and California's Sonoma State Hospital, institutions for the mentally ill and mentally retarded (Koprowski et al. 1956, 954).

Soon after the appearance of the group's 1952 article, Dr. Howard A. Howe of Johns Hopkins disclosed that after the 1950 epidemic of polio in Baltimore, he had experimented on eleven two- to five-year-old "inmates' of the Rosewood Training School in Maryland. His objective was to compare the "antibody response of the chimpanzee and the child" with polio antigens (Howe 1952, 265). Howe explained that the physical condition of the subjects did not impede his research, even though "[a]ll were low grade idiots or imbeciles with congenital hydrocephalus, microencephaly, or cerebral palsy." Sensitive to the need for proper consent, he noted that written permission of parents or guardians was obtained for each subject and that the Maryland Commissioner of Mental Hygiene, as well as doctors at Johns Hopkins and the Training School itself, had cooperated in the experiments (Howe 1952, 273).

Polio was only one disease that gave rise to experiments on residents of state mental health facilities. Perhaps the most notorious of all studies on a disabled population in a captive setting is the now infamous Willowbrook hepatitis study. Children at Willowbrook, a Staten Island, New York, institution for the mentally disabled, were intentionally infected with hepatitis virus as part of the search for a vaccine to prevent that disease (Grodin and Glantz 1994, 16–17). The scandal that resulted when the study was subjected to public scrutiny was a signal event in the movement for government regulation of biomedical research, particularly research on vulnerable populations (Rothman 1984). Nevertheless, it is a measure of our ambivalence regarding ethically questionable but successful research that Dr. Saul Krugman, architect of the study, later won an award for his development of a hepatitis vaccine as a consequence of his study at Willowbrook.

As one pediatrician recalled years later, the prevailing ethos for research on children in the 1950s did not require parental permission even in studies that carried no therapeutic benefit for the child-patient. Despite occasional criticisms, or misgivings of individual researchers[2] (Human Radiation Experiments 1996, 203), in that era, said the doctor, "everyone was a draftee" in a national war on disease (199). That perception was confirmed in Henry Beecher's celebrated expose of ethical lapses in clinical research, which included two examples showing questionable studies done in institutions for people with mental disabilities (Beecher 1966, 1354–1360). In a context where "nontherapeutic" research on children was accepted, and institutionalized children provided a ready cohort, investigators such as Koprowski and Howe did not hesitate to enlist young "volunteers" for science. Whatever criticisms did surface during the war on polio, they generally captured little public attention and were usually overshadowed by the very real fears of parents, terrorized by the prospect of epidemic disease such as polio.

A Battle on Two Fronts: War and Disease

But when disease and war broke out simultaneously, the niceties of parental consent and public disclosure were, if anything, even less relevant to research considered necessary to the national interest. The demand for a fighting force that was both battle ready and disease free

led to the Lynchburg Colony hepatitis study. In the wake of the December 8, 1941, attack on Pearl Harbor, millions of newly mobilized
soldiers prepared for war. Part of their training included physical
conditioning to enhance endurance and efficient performance in combat.
Medical screening and vaccination for infectious diseases also figured
into their preparation. One of the required vaccinations, developed by
the Rockefeller Institute, was designed to provide immunity to yellow
fever. More than a million Brazilians had received the vaccine before it
was determined that it was the likely source of "yellow jaundice," a
strain of hepatitis that affected many of the recipients. Nevertheless,
with America's entry into World War II a near certainty, the Rockefeller
Institute began producing yellow fever vaccine using human sera as a
stabilizer, and offered it free for military use. Despite warnings from
researchers about the "jaundice" side effect, the vaccine was distributed
(Chase 1982, 275).

As mobilization intensified during this time, 28,000 servicemen who
had been injected with the vaccine came down with hepatitis; 100 of
them died (Williams 1951, 226–228). Later figures suggested as many as
50,000 infections resulted from the tainted vaccine (Chase 1982, 275).
On April 15, 1942, the Surgeon General temporarily interrupted the
program and had existing stores of vaccine destroyed or recalled (Seef
et al. 1987, 965–970).

In June 1942, with military researchers still unsure about the causative
agent for the vaccine-related hepatitis, public health service officers in
San Juan, Puerto Rico, reported an outbreak of jaundice in the U.S.
Virgin Islands. Not coincidentally, many inhabitants of the Virgin Islands
had also recently been inoculated against yellow fever. Three doctors
were dispatched by the National Institute of Health (NIH) to investigate
the seeming epidemic: John W. Oliphant, Alexander G. Gilliam, and Carl
L. Larson. They discovered that Virgin Islanders had received the same
batch of vaccine that had led to illness in Army inductees[3] (Oliphant,
Gilliam, and Larson 1943, 1233–1242). The problem of infected vaccine
became a public matter after a press release by Secretary of War Henry
L. Stimson. The *Chicago Tribune* highlighted the release, announcing
that "28, 585 cases of jaundice had developed, apparently from the use
of yellow fever vaccine among army men between January 1 and July
4." The *Tribune* also focused on Stimson's report of sixty-two deaths

that occurred after vaccinations. Numbers of infections and fatalities attributable to vaccination were not released for the Navy or the Marine Corps, although the proportion of cases was not thought to be as high as that in the Army (Chicago Tribune 1942). In an editorial three days later, printed under the headline "A Grievous Error," the *Tribune* questioned seeming inconsistencies in the accounts of vaccine-related disease released by the War Department. The *Tribune* also challenged assurances repeated in the *Journal of the American Medical Association* (1942) suggesting that the thousands of cases of "jaundice" had no appreciable affect on the health of soldiers. "How did it happen that wholesale vaccinations were undertaken with a vaccine which quite obviously had not been thoroly [sic] tested in advance? Somebody was guilty of a grievous error of judgement." The *Tribune* called for an inquiry to explain how twenty times more servicemen could be casualties of vaccination than had thus far been wounded in combat (Editorial 1942).

In defense of the medical establishment, *JAMA* retaliated with its own editorial, charging that the *Tribune's* demand for an inquiry "presupposes a stupidity on the part of medical science which is wholly unjustified." The *Chicago Tribune* has done a disservice to American medicine. Certainly by the fears it may create among soldiers now being inducted into our armed forces it will injure morale and make more difficult the task of assembling the type of force that must be assembled to meet the challenge of our enemies" (*Journal of the American Medical Association* 1942, 1110). *JAMA* noted that the "best medical talent available in the United States" had taken up the vaccination question, with civilian consultants joining the Division of Medical Science of the National Research Council in the search for a solution.

Some of that talent was hard at work even as the battle of headlines in the civilian and medical presses raged. Returning to Washington, the three NIH doctors sent a memorandum to the chief of the Division of Infectious Diseases proposing a study to be undertaken at the Virginia State Colony. The Colony, located near Lynchburg Virginia, was by then one of the largest facilities in the country for the care of disabled patients. Chartered in 1910 as a special asylum to care for people in Virginia with epilepsy, by 1916 it had been expanded to accommodate people with mental retardation; its official name was the Virginia Colony for the Epileptic and Feebleminded.

The memorandum contained these assertions:

Yellow fever is of immediate importance to the armed forces of the United States serving in, or who may have to serve in, yellow fever foci. Hence a safe, reliable vaccine is of utmost national urgency. Vaccine as now produced provides a reasonably reliable preventive, but recent military experience has shown that unexpected serious consequences have followed its use. These consequences might have been disastrous had they occurred in certain combat units. Therefore, it is clear that a prompt solution to the problem of the etiology of jaundice following vaccination against yellow fever is a matter of extreme national urgency.

Because of the national importance of the problem, and because work done in England and South America has disclosed no satisfactory laboratory animal for use in jaundice studies, it is deemed by us to be justifiable and necessary to use human beings as experimental subjects. (Memorandum 1942)

The memorandum described a "tentative outline for proposed yellow fever vaccine at Lynchburg State Colony, Colony, Virginia." First, a group of Colony residents would undergo preliminary examination and laboratory study to select the experiment participants. These with senility, arteriosclerosis, and infectious diseases such as syphilis would be excluded. A small blood sample would be taken from potential subjects to evaluate their general health. After initial screenings, fifty subjects would be given a dose of the "Rockefeller vaccine" or another type of vaccine that had produced "jaundice" in an unusual number of earlier recipients. Physical examinations and laboratory follow-up would continue on a weekly basis for this group "until jaundice or some evidence of liver damage appears." In the event of such clinical findings, laboratory and clinical observations would be more frequent. No plans for palliation or withdrawal from the study in the event of serious health sequelae were mentioned.

A second group of patients would be observed after they were inoculated with "freshly drawn blood serum from jaundiced patients" in the first experimental group. Laboratory animals would also be injected with these sera. Another experiment was proposed that would involve inoculating groups of twenty to fifty patients with several other types of vaccines and sera, some of which had been heated enough to kill the yellow fever virus.

The memorandum was authorized for transmission up the chain of command through the Division of Infectious Diseases and was finally approved by NIH Director Dr. R. E. Dyer. Classified memoranda later passed between Dr. Oliphant and the War Department Medical Corps concerning the number of subjects and the specific inoculum they received (Oliphant 1943). Dyer submitted articles describing the Colony experiments to the War Department for vetting before publication[4] (Dyer 1943), but none described the study location or affected population.

Barely a year after the Oliphant memorandum, the first professional article appeared describing the study's results. In it Oliphant recalled the history of the military outbreak of hepatitis, noting that "[h]uman volunteers were available for experimental work" (Oliphant, Gilliam, and Larson 1943, 1235). The "volunteers" had been located in "an institution of about 1700" of both genders, and "ranging in age from 15–57." Of a total of almost 190 subjects, 30 developed hepatitis. Their symptoms included nausea and vomiting, low-grade fever, and anorexia, and lasted as long as seven weeks in the worst cases. In general, the course of the disease was described as "quite mild"[5] (Oliphant et al. 1943, 1239–1240).

Oliphant apparently returned to the Colony to repeat inoculation experiments on thirty residents, at least ten of whom had contracted "experimental jaundice" in the 1942 study. Although the group who originally "volunteered" apparently had become immune to hepatitis, four additional cases of infection occurred among the twenty new subjects. Oliphant confirmed that the clinical and pathological courses of serum hepatitis after vaccination and naturally occurring infectious hepatitis were "indistinguishable" (Oliphant 1944a, 1614–1616). The general difference between the forms of disease was most obvious in the incubation period. According to a doctor who monitored the experiments, liver damage from the two forms was identical, with minor damage in some cases and "terrifically damaged livers" in others. Similarly, the length of illness varied from very light to more extensive, including "nerve degeneration, brain damage, and all sorts of prolonged illness" (Stanhope-Bayne Oral History 19, 692–693).

Dr. Oliphant also recounted the experiment in the prestigious Harvey lecture series of the New York Academy of Research in 1944 (Oliphant 1944b), and the next year he was recommended for meritorious promotion for his successful demonstration that the cause of hepatitis in soldiers receiving the yellow fever vaccine was the serum component of the vaccine. His superiors described his contribution as "the most outstanding work done on this subject" (Memorandum 1945).

On January 10, 1952, Dr. John Oliphant died. His obituary included details of continuing work on hepatitis that occurred in servicemen after blood transfusions. In a paragraph that highlighted the difference between the rules of research in that earlier era and proscriptions that apply today, the obituary also described Oliphant's work on "jaundice" undertaken on volunteers from three federal prisons (*Washington Post* 1952; *Washington Times Herald* 1952; *Evening Star* 1952).

The Dangers of Retrospective Assessment

What are we to make of the Lynchburg Colony hepatitis study today? It clearly would not be acceptable under current regulations. It could provide no medical benefit for the subjects, and despite the relatively "mild" symptoms of hepatitis infection described by the researchers, the subjects had been put at risk of serious illness and even death. Calling subjects "volunteers" underscores the problematic nature of whatever "consent" they may have given. This population consisted of some people with very real mental disabilities. Others, if not cognitively impaired, were relegated to the institution because they were allegedly incapable of functioning in society at large. It would be the height of irony to have deemed them capable of what today might be covered under the rubric of informed consent. In this like the polio studies earlier, "volunteers" were hardly voluntary participants in dangerous medical research.

Realizing that the Lynchburg study took place between 1942 and 1944, it is impossible to avoid a comparison with the simultaneous Nazi death camp experiments that were eventually condemned in the Nuremberg doctors' trials. But torture and killing were not merely by-products of Nazi "research," and its gruesome scope, duration, and cruelty set it apart from any other medical study we can cite. Thus at one level, comparison between Lynchburg and the death camps seems strained. On another level, however, some parallels are obvious. The Nazis intentionally infected some subjects with typhus in an attempt to discover new modes of treatment. Their motives, recited in their defense at Nuremberg, were exactly the same as those of the Lynchburg Colony investigators. They were concerned that soldiers might be caught up in an epidemic for which there was no cure (Lifton 1986, 169). Other experiments that sought medical solutions to battlefield hazards were justified similarly, with reference to the ultimate trump card of wartime exigency. Like the Germans, American doctors no doubt believed that some sacrifices were required from all citizens in wartime in order to preserve the nation. They found it "justifiable and necessary to use human beings as experimental subjects" so that they might perfect a yellow fever vaccine that would protect American soldiers. Both in the medical war and the shooting war, anyone could be drafted.

But even if we assume "utmost national urgency," what would justify using an institutionalized population to the exclusion of others? As is always the case, a closed facility allows much more efficient control of a clinical experiment. The subjects may not leave, and researchers can monitor their symptoms or evaluate therapies systematically without the comings and goings of an outpatient study. In wartime, with the added desire for secrecy, a rural facility out of the public view would provide an ideal research setting. But institutions for the disabled are hardly the only locations where those conditions exist. A military school or army base would also be both controlled and secure. Available records do not suggest whether such alternative sources for subjects were considered.

Fifteen years after the Lynchburg Colony hepatitis study, Dr. Saul Krugman was seriously criticized for intentional infection of Willowbrook patients with hepatitis in a setting where, he insisted, they were almost certain to contract the disease eventually. No such conditions were present for Lynchburg Colony residents, who were no more likely to encounter hepatitis than any civilians. Nor were they in a population that would benefit from an improved yellow fever vaccine, since most would never have occasion to be vaccinated. If moral judgments are relative and if our ethical yardstick is applied to both Lynchburg and Willowbrook, Willowbrook wins.

We are left only with uncomfortable conclusions about the Lynchburg study. Its location was no doubt chosen for convenience and efficiency and out of the belief that disabled residents owed a debt to society and had little to lose, while the health of the nation purportedly hung in the balance. This should be a reminder that research shielded from the public eye by institutional walls and further overshadowed by a cloud of war may give rise to events we are loath to discuss later in the public light. Official secrecy, vulnerable populations, and the terrors of both disease and war make for a perilous combination. The Lynchburg Colony hepatitis study is yet another example of how such a mixture can easily yield ethically problematic results.

Notes

1. Building on earlier reporting (see Cynthia T. Pegram, "Army experimented at the Colony during WWII," the *News & Advance*, Lynchburg, VA, Feb. 18, 2001, and Cynthia T. Pegram, "Training center residents used in WWII experiment," the *News & Advance*, Lynchburg, VA, April 25, 1995), Peter Hardin, Washington bureau chief of the *Richmond Times Dispatch*, broke the story under this headline: "State patients once used as guinea pigs," *Richmond Times Dispatch*, November 25, 2001, A1.

2. At a national meeting in the 1960s, one researcher admitted that he had "sinned" in performing lumbar punctures in "normal infants" without parental permission.

3. The study was described in a number of subsequent publications, see W.A. Sawyer et al., "Jaundice in Army Personnel in the Western Region of the United States and its Relation to Vaccination against Yellow Fever" [two part article], *American Journal of Hygiene*, vol. 39, 1944, pp. 437–431; vol. 40, 1944, pp. 35–105; Douglass W. Walker, "Some Epidemiological Aspects of Infectious Hepatitis in the United States Army." *American Journal of Tropical Medicine*, vol. 25, 1945, pp. 75–82.; John W. Oliphant, "Homologous Serum Jaundice: Experimental Inactivation of Etiologic Agent in Serum by Ultraviolet Irradiation," *Public Health Reports*, vol. 61, April 1946, pp. 598–602. Details of the Lynchburg study were also described in a 1987 article that reported long-term consequences of epidemiological follow-up of servicemen who endured viral hepatitis in 1942. See Seef, L.B. et al., "A Serologic Follow-up of the 1942 Epidemic of Post-Vaccination Hepatitis in the United States Army," *New England Journal of Medicine*, vol. 316 (April 16, 1987), pp. 965–970.

4. "I should appreciate it very much if you will let me know if there is anything in this article which should not be published." Handwritten note: "I told Dr. Dyer I saw no reason why it should not be published."

5. Oliphant's later Harvey lectures article claimed the youngest subject was 13 (see p. 261). He also showed 37 infected subjects out of a total of 273 subjects (p. 263).

References

Annotations. 1952. *Lancet*. Cclxii (March 15).

Beecher, Henry K. 1966. "Ethics and Clinical Research." *New England Journal of Medicine*. 274 (June 16): 1354–1360.

Chase, Allan. 1982. *Magic Shots*. New York: William Morrow.

Chicago Tribune. 1942. "Jaundice Cases Reach 28,585 in Army; 62 die." July 25.

Dyer, R.E. to Colonel Stanhope Bayne-Jones. August 4, 1943.

Editorial. 1942. "A Grevious Error." *Chicago Tribune.* July 27.

Evening Star. 1952. "Dr. John W. Oliphant, Authority on Viruses, Found Dead in Garage." January 11.

Grodin, Michael A. and Leonard H. Glantz, eds. 1994. *Children as Research Subjects: Science, Ethics and the Law.* New York and Oxford: Oxford University Press.

Hardin, Peter. 2001. "State Patients Once Used as Guinea Pigs." *Richmond Times Dispatch.* November 25, A1.

Howe, Howard E. 1952. "Antibody Response of Chimpanzees and Human Beings to Formal-Inactivated Trivalent Poliomyelitis Vaccine." *American Journal of Hygiene.* 56 (November): 265–286.

Journal of the American Medical Association. 1942. "Jaundice following Yellow Fever Vaccination." 119 (August 1): 1110.

Koprowski, H., G.A. Jervis, and T.W. Norton. 1952. "Immune Response in Human Volunteers upon Oral Administration of a Rodent Adapted Strain of Poliomyletis Virus." *American Journal of Hygiene.* 55 (January): 108–126.

Koprowski, Hilary et al. 1953. "Further Studies on Oral Administration of Living Poliomyelitis Virus to Human Subjects." *Proceedings of the Society for Experimental Biology and Medicine.* 82 (February): 277–280.

Koprowski, Hilary et al. 1956. "Clinical Investigations of Attenuated Strains of Poliomyletis Virus: Use as a Method of Immunization of Children with Living Virus." *Journal of the American Medical Association.* 160 (March 17): 954–966.

Leake, J.P. 1935. "Poliomyelitis following Vaccination Against that Disease." *Journal of the American Medical Association.* (October 5). Cited in: Chase, Allan. 1982. *Magic Shots,* 283–284. New York: William Morrow.

Lederer, Susan. 1995. *Subjected to Science: Human Experimentation in America before the Second World War.* Baltimore: Johns Hopkins University Press.

Lifton, Robert Jay. 1986. *The Nazi Doctors.* New York: Basic Books.

Memorandum. 1942. Doctors Oliphant, Gilliam, and Larson to L.F. Badger, Acting Chief, Division of Infectious Diseases. (August 4). "Tentative Outline for Proposed Yellow Fever Vaccine Study at Lynchburg State Colony, Colony Virginia." National Archives.

Memorandum: Surgeon John W. Oliphant. March 9, 1945. National Archives II, College Park record group 112 and record group 90 PHS.

Oliphant, John W. to Colonel Stanhope Bayne-Jones. July 6, 1943.

Oliphant, John W. 1944a. "Infectious Hepatitis: Experimental Study of Immunity." *Public Health Reports.* December 15: 1614–1616.

Oliphant, John W. 1944b. "Jaundice following Administration of Human Serum." *Harvey Lectures.* Lancaster, PA: Science Press (lecture delivered March 16, 1944).

Oliphant, John W., Alexander G. Gilliam, and Carl L. Larson. 1943. "Jaundice following Administration of Human Serum." *Public Health Reports*. 58 (August 13): 1233–1242.

Rothman, David. 1984. *The Willowbrook Wars*. New York: Harper & Row.

Seef, L.B. et al. 1987. "A Serologic Follow-up of the 1942 Epidemic Post-Vaccinaion Hepatitis in the United States Army." *New England Journal of Medicine*. 316 (April 16): 965–970.

Stanhope-Bayne Oral History. 1966. OH 19, History of Medicine Division, National Library of Medicine.

The Human Radiation Experiments: Final Report of the President's Advisory Committee. 1996. New York and Oxford: Oxford University Press.

Washington Post. 1952. "PHS Expert on Blood Plasm Found Dead in His Garage." January 11.

Washington Times Herald. 1952. "Dr. Oliphant Was Director at Bethesda." January 11.

Williams, Ralph Chester. 1951. *United States Public Health Service—1798–1950*. Washington, DC: Commissioned Officers Association of the United States Public Health Service.

2

Protecting the Public's Health in an Era of Bioterrorism: The Model State Emergency Health Powers Act

James G. Hodge, Jr. and Lawrence O. Gostin

Perhaps no duty is more fundamental to American government than protecting the public's health (Gostin 2000, 16). Beginning on September 11, 2001, the state's obligation to safeguard public safety took on new urgency. Attacks resulted in a staggering loss of lives, estimated from 2,600 to 2,900 (Lipton 2001) and exposed the country's vulnerability to catastrophic acts of war. In the ensuing weeks of fall 2001, public health and law enforcement officials discovered that some person or group had intentionally contaminated letters with potentially deadly anthrax spores. These letters were mailed to individuals in government and the media in several states and the District of Columbia. Thousands of persons were tested for exposure and hundreds were treated; five persons died. The persons responsible for disseminating anthrax through the mail have not been identified. Government officials predict the potential for additional bioterrorism attacks as the war on terrorism continues in Afghanistan and surrounding territories.

The anthrax exposures confirmed weaknesses in the nation's public health system that has, as a central purpose, protection of the population from infectious diseases. Training exercises demonstrated that preventing mass causalities or infections resulting from bioterrorism is difficult (Ingelsby, Grossman, and O'Toole 2000). Public health authorities and the private sector (e.g., health care workers and primary care institutions) lack the infrastructure, resources, knowledge, coordination, and tools to respond effectively to intentional and possibly mass exposure to infectious disease. For many of the most serious agents of bioterrorism, technology is inadequate to detect, test, vaccinate, and treat the general public

Before September 11, federal and state public health authorities had allocated limited resources and engaged in limited planning for a major bioterrorism event (Fialka et al. 2001). Congress authorized the spending of over $500 million early in 2001 for bioterrorism preparedness through the Public Health Threats and Emergencies Act. Most agree that additional commitments to improve surveillance of unusual diseases or clusters, train health care workers, increase existing vaccination and treatment supplies, and collaborate across state boundaries are necessary to improve the public health infrastructure (Shalala 1999).

For state and local public health agencies that may find themselves on the front line of defense to a bioterrorism event, prevention through preparation is essential. Many state health departments do not address bioterrorism in their emergency response plans. The Centers for Disease Control and Prevention (CDC) requested that all states seeking nearly a billion dollars of new federal funds for bioterrorism prevention prepare systematic response plans. Advance planning is key, but it presupposes that public health authorities are legally empowered to respond to potential or actual threats. Some states have relatively recent laws or regulations (e.g., Colorado) to address response; however, in many states existing legal standards are absent, antiquated, fragmented, or insufficient.

During this tumultuous time, public health law scholars at the Center for Law and the Public's Health at Georgetown and Johns Hopkins Universities were asked by the CDC and a series of national partners (National Governors' Association, National Conference of State Legislatures, Association of State and Territorial Health Officials, National Association of City and County Health Officers, National Association of Attorneys General, and Turning Point Public Health Statute Modernization National Collaborative) to develop the Model State Emergency Health Powers Act (MSEHPA).

The challenge was to create a comprehensive law that provides public health authorities with a series of powers they may require to respond to catastrophic public health emergencies (including bioterrorism events) while also respecting individual and group rights. This is the quintessential challenge posed by the exercise of coercive powers (quarantine laws, mental health confinement, vaccination requirements): protecting the public's health while respecting personal rights. It reflects the ethical interplay between inherent rights of individuals and communal interests.

Many legal and ethical scholars view the crux of this challenge as the extent to which individual rights should yield to safeguard the health and needs of persons in the community. In recent years, bioethicists sometimes seemed to suggest that respecting individual civil liberties was an overriding good. They tended to deemphasize the historical, legal, and frankly utilitarian perspective that centers on the obligation of each individual to contribute to the larger good of the community. In our view, individuals are not entitled to be free from every infringement of their freedoms, only those infringements that are without justification (Gostin 2002). The rights of individuals may be balanced with societal interests provided the balance does not support restraints that are excessive, arbitrary, or egregious (e.g., based on racial or ethnic grounds). Particularly during times of emergency, additional restraints of civil liberties may be justified by the compelling need to protect public health.

The MSEHPA answers this challenge by empowering public health authorities with broad powers and simultaneously limiting the exercise of those powers to the least restrictive means necessary to accomplish the communal goal of abating serious threats to the public's health. The Act vests state and local public health authorities with powers to track, prevent, and control disease threats resulting from bioterrorism or other public health emergencies. These powers include measures (testing, treatment, and vaccination programs; isolation or quarantine powers; travel restrictions) that may infringe individual civil liberties (rights to due process, speech, assembly, travel, and privacy); however, their exercise is restricted in time, duration, and scope. Coercive powers, particularly isolation and quarantine, are exercised on a temporary basis, only as long as is reasonably necessary, and only among persons who justifiably may pose a risk to others because of their contagious conditions. In addition, the dignity of individuals is respected. Their rights to contest coercive use of these powers, even during an emergency, are secure.

Certainly, balancing communal interests and individual rights during a public health emergency is precarious. The MSEHPA is built on the traditional and historical precept that protecting the public health during an emergency is an essential goal of government. An early draft of the Act was criticized by some for its failure to accommodate civil liberties. A subsequent and final draft as of December 21, 2001, responded to these concerns (available at www.publichealthlaw.net). As over half of the states have introduced legislative bills based on the Act, the debate between protecting public health and individual rights has shifted to state and local political arenas.

Bioterrorism: Past and Present

Bioterrorism involves intentional use of an infectious agent—microorganism, virus, infectious substance, or biological product—to cause death or disease in humans or other organisms in order to influence negatively the conduct of government or intimidate a population (MSEHPA 2001a, 1–104). The intentional spread of anthrax through the U.S. mail is an example of current bioterrorism activity in the United States. Numerous attempts and actual bioterrorist acts, with various degrees of success and impact, are documented in American and world history. In the United States, British and French troops exchanged dry goods intentionally contaminated with smallpox with Native American populations (Root-Bernstein 1991). In 1972 several persons were arrested for possessing kilograms of typhoid bacteria intended to contaminate the water supply of several Midwestern cities (Alexander 2000). In 1984 members of the Rajneeshee cult contaminated restaurant salad bars in Oregon with a form of *Salmonella*, resulting in over 700 cases of nonfatal food poisoning (Tucker 1999). The Chemical and Biological Weapons Nonproliferation Project of the Monterrey Institute's Center for Nonproliferation Studies catalogued over 400 incidents of known bioterrorist activity worldwide between 1900 and 1999. In each of the past several years, the Federal Bureau of Investigation (FBI) has investigated hundreds of claims of bioterrorism threats.

Public health and other authorities conducted numerous hypothetical and table-top exercises in the past decade to prepare for such an event. The subject of many of these exercises became reality in fall of 2001. On October 4, 2001, the media reported that an individual in a Florida office building was exposed to anthrax, a biological agent that can be deadly when inhaled and the infection it causes is untreated. Public health authorities in Connecticut, Florida, New York, Maryland, Nevada, New Jersey, and Washington, D.C., tracked numerous additional cases of exposure and infection. Law enforcement and public health officials determined that most exposures resulted from intentional efforts to spread the pathogen in contaminated letters delivered through the U.S. Postal Service. Authorities quickly began warning the public through broadcasts and printed sources to be cautious about suspicious packages or powdery substances in the mail, although government warnings were mixed in their accuracy and tone (Miller and Stolberg 2001). Media coverage was dominated by images of people lining up for testing and health officials clad in plastic biodefense suits collecting samples of anthrax from mailrooms, elevators, and trucks. Mail service in some places was suspended or significantly delayed. Countless false reports of exposure to anthrax or unidentified substances emerged.

These attacks fueled apprehension among government officials and the public about future bioterrorism attacks (Parker, Watson, and Johnson 2001). Seventy percent of the public believes a biological or chemical attack on the United States will occur in 2002 (Snapshot 2001). Fears of bioterrorism and emerging infectious diseases are justifiable. A broad range of groups or individuals may have access to and use biological agents as weapons to inflict harm throughout the population. Many infectious agents, including genetically enhanced ones, may be used. Diseases such as smallpox, tularemia (rabbit fever), plague, and viral hemorrhagic fever may present far more serious dangers to the public health than the noncontagious and largely treatable anthrax.

Bioterrorists may infect individuals through several routes: intentional spread of contagious diseases through individual contact; air-borne dissemination; or contamination of transportation systems, buildings, and other public places, as well as water, food, controlled substances, and other widely distributed products. Equipment necessary to manufacture biological weapons is easy to obtain and conceal. Concentrations of people in large urban centers, as well as modern rapid-transit systems, facilitate the spread of infectious diseases. Public doubts about the possibility for an individual or group intentionally to unleash harmful agents on innocent civilians have been negated (Hodge 2002).

Public Health Law Reform

Law has long been considered an essential tool for improving public health outcomes, especially among state governments that have traditionally and structurally been the repositories of public health powers

(Gostin 2001). Statutory laws and administrative rules generally guide the activities of public health authorities, assign and limit their functions, authorize spending, and specify how authorities may exercise their delegated authority (Gostin 2000). The obsolescence, inconsistency, and inadequacy in existing state public health laws expose flaws and can render these laws ineffective or even counterproductive (Gostin, Burris, and Lazzarini 1999).

State statutes frequently are constructed in layers over time as lawmakers responded to various disease threats (e.g., tuberculosis, polio, malaria, HIV-AIDS). Consequently, existing laws may not reflect contemporary scientific understanding of disease such as surveillance, prevention, and response, or legal norms for protection of individual rights. Administrative regulations may supplement existing statutes with more up-to-date public health approaches, but may also be limited by original grants of delegated rule-making authority.

Existing public health laws may predate vast changes in constitutional (equal protection, due process) and statutory (disability discrimination, privacy, civil rights) law that have changed social and legal conceptions of individual rights. Authorities acting pursuant to these provisions may be vulnerable to legal or ethical challenges on grounds that their actions are unconstitutional or preempted by current federal or state laws.

The independent evolution of health codes across states, tribal authorities, and territories led to variations in the structure, substance, complexity, and procedures for detecting, controlling, and preventing disease. Without a coordinated, national public health system, disease detection and reporting systems, response capabilities, and training capacity differ extensively among jurisdictions. These differences could hamper coordination and efficient responses in a multistate public health emergency (likely with modern bioterrorism threats). Confusion and complexity among inconsistent state laws may create ambiguities that also prevent public health authorities from acting rapidly and decisively. These authorities may be unsure of the extent of their legal authority, the chain of command during an emergency, or the proper exercise of existing legal powers.

Reforming current state public health laws is particularly important concerning key variables for preparedness.

Planning, Coordination, and Communication

Most state statutes do not require public health emergency planning or establish response strategies. Essential to the planning process is the expression of clear channels for communication among responsible government officials (public health, law enforcement, emergency management) and the private sector (health care workers and institutions, pharmaceutical industry, nongovernment organizations). Coordination among federal, tribal, state, and local levels and legislative, executive, and judicial branches of government is also critical. State public health laws can implement systematic planning processes that involve numerous stakeholders. However, many not only fail to facilitate communication, but may actually proscribe exchange of vital information among principal agencies due to privacy concerns. Some even prohibit sharing data with public health officials in adjoining states (Gostin et al. 1996). Laws that complicate or hinder data communication among states and responsible agencies could impede a thorough investigation and response to public health emergencies.

Surveillance

Continuing, effective, and timely surveillance is an essential component of public health preparedness (Horton et al. 2002). For example, the dispersal of pathogens may not be evident, and early detection could save many lives by triggering an effective containment strategy that includes testing, vaccination, treatment, and, if necessary, isolation or quarantine. Existing state laws may thwart effective surveillance. Many states do not require reporting for the most dangerous agents of bioterrorism such as viral hemorrhagic fevers and smallpox, or timely reporting for other dangerous agents such as tularemia. Virtually no state requires immediate reporting for all the critical agents identified by the CDC. At the same time, states do not require, and may actually prohibit, public health agencies from monitoring data collected through the health care system. Private information that might lead to early detection (e.g., unusual clusters of fevers or gastrointestinal symptoms) held by hospitals, managed care organizations, and pharmacies may be unavailable because of insufficient reporting mechanisms or privacy concerns.

Managing Property and Protecting Persons

Authorizations for use of coercive powers are the most controversial aspects of public health laws. Nevertheless, they may be necessary to manage property or protect persons in an emergency. Numerous circumstances might require management of property, such as decontamination of facilities; acquisition of vaccines, medicines, or hospital beds; or use of private facilities for isolation, quarantine, or disposal of human remains. In the recent anthrax attacks, public health authorities had to close some public and private facilities for decontamination. Consistent with legal fair safeguards, including compensation for taking private property used for public purposes, laws are required to manage property to contain a serious health threat.

It may also be necessary to exercise powers over individuals to avert significant threats to the public's health. Vaccination, testing, physical examination, treatment, isolation, and quarantine each may help contain the spread of infectious diseases. Although most people will comply with these programs during emergencies for the same reason they comply during nonemergencies, because it is in their own interests and/or desirable for the common welfare, compulsory powers may be required for those who will not comply and whose conduct poses risks to others or the public. These people may be required to yield some of their autonomy or liberty to protect the health and security of the community.

The Model State Emergency Health Powers Act

The MSEHPA presents a synthesis of public health law for controlling infectious diseases during emergencies that balances the needs of public health with the rights and dignity of individuals. Although developed quickly in the aftermath of the events of September 11, the Act's provisions and structure are based on existing federal and state laws and public health practice. The Act does not create new powers for public health authorities; each of its provisions is based on existing theories of public health law. Rather, it organizes and modernizes these legal powers to facilitate a coordinated approach to public health emergency response. The index for the MSEHPA was derived from a consultation of experts in law, public health, emergency management, and national security

(Cantigny Conference 2001). An early draft of the Act was vetted through national partners and critiqued through hundreds of comments received from heads of government agencies, national organizations, legislators, public health officials, legal practitioners, scholars, and members of the general public. Over half of the states introduced legislative bills in the 2001–2002 legislative session based on the Act. Virtually all state legislatures, governors' offices, and many state and local public health agencies used the Act as a guide for considering reforms of their existing legal protections.

The MSEHPA addresses each of the key variables for public health preparedness discussed above. Among its central purposes, it requires development of a comprehensive public health emergency response plan that includes coordination of services, procurement of necessary materials and supplies, housing, feeding, and caring for affected populations, and administration of vaccines and treatment; authorizes collection of data and records and access to communications; facilitates early detection of a health emergency; grants state and local public health officials the authority to use and appropriate property to care for patients and destroy dangerous or contaminated materials; authorizes officials to care and treat ill or exposed persons and to separate affected individuals from the population at large to prevent further transmission; and ensures that the rights and needs of infected or exposed persons are respected (Hodge and Eber 2002).

Public Health Emergencies

Most powers granted to state and local public health authorities through the Act are triggered by the governor's declaration of a public health emergency in response to dire and severe circumstances. A declared state of emergency terminates as soon as the health threat is eliminated, or automatically after 30 days, unless reinstated by the governor or annulled through legislative or court action. A public health emergency is defined as (1) the occurrence or imminent threat of an illness or health condition, caused by bioterrorism or a highly fatal biological toxin or novel or infectious agent (that was previously controlled or eradicated) that (2) poses a high probability of a significant number of human fatalities or incidents of serious, permanent, or long-term disability in the affected population.

Bioterrorism events involving intentional efforts to spread infectious diseases may call for a declaration of emergency. Emergencies can also arise through unintentional spread of infectious organisms. The inclusiveness of this definition of public health emergency may be important during a potential or actual bioterrorism event. After initial individual diagnoses are made, it may be some time before public health officials can determine whether the infections were intentional. Several diseases that might be used by bioterrorists are endemic to the United States, such as plague, anthrax, and tularemia (Chin 2000), and careful epidemiologic investigation may be required before the source can be identified (Pavlin 1999). Empowering authorities to act *before* a determination of bioterrorism is made appropriately allows for immediate control measures and public health interventions. Thus, under the definition, it is inconsequential how an emerging infectious condition arose in the population. The potential that the condition may have a severe impact on the morbidity and mortality of populations within a prescribed period of time is central to the declaration of an emergency (Hodge and Eber 2002).

Civil libertarians and other concerned citizens voiced objections to the Act's emergency declaration. They may view the declaration of a state of emergency as authorization for public health authorities to do virtually anything to abate the existing threat. This includes infringing or individual rights in the interests of protecting public health. Indubitably, during an emergency, certain civil liberties may have to be restricted compared with the exercise of these rights in nonemergencies. Yet, the Act specifically protects individual interests from authoritarian actions by government. The governor of a state may be empowered to declare a state of public health emergency, but the legislature, by majority vote, may discontinue the declaration at any time. Similarly, courts have the power to review whether a governor's actions fail to comply with the standards and procedures in the MSEHPA. Thus, each branch of state government has a role in sustaining an emergency declaration consistent with constitutional principles of checks and balances.

Furthermore, provisions of the MSEHPA protect individuals better than most existing state laws. The Act sees a public health emergency as a distinct event that requires a distinct government responses. It sets a very high threshold for the declaration of a public health emergency through a series of definitions and structural protections. It further conditions the use of a defined and limited set of powers on the declaration and continuation of the emergency status. In many states, however, no definitive statutory criteria exist for the declaration of a public health emergency. Rather, emergency management laws may be used to address public health emergencies broadly. Declaring a general state of emergency in response to a bioterrorism event may allow government to act in indeterminable ways to address the threat. Lacking effective statutory guidance, public health authorities may have to rely on existing, antiquated statutory laws, or regulations that are hastily created in specific response to potential or unknown threats. Thus, the MSEHPA provides a refined set of powers that respects individual rights in balance with public health. Existing state emergency laws may allow authorities to restrict individual freedoms more severely to control the impact of a societal emergency.

Information Sharing and Surveillance Measures

The MSEHPA enhances existing state surveillance and reporting practices to facilitate the prompt detection of a potential or actual threat by requiring:

• Health care providers to report cases of bioterrorist-related or epidemic diseases that may be caused by any of thirty-five infectious agents listed in federal regulations (Federal Regulations 2001) or other nonlisted agents;
• Coroners and medical examiners to report deaths that may have resulted from an emerging or epidemic infectious disease or from a suspected agent of bioterrorism;
• Pharmacists to report unusual trends in prescriptions for antibiotics and other drugs used to treat infectious diseases in addition to substantial increases in the sale of various over-the-counter remedies; and
• Veterinarians or veterinary laboratories to report animals having or suspected of having diseases that may be potential causes of a public health emergency.

Reports are to be made within twenty-four hours to the appropriate health authority, and should contain identifying information about the reporter and subject of the report. On receiving a report, officials can use the information to ameliorate possible public health risks. They may contact and interview individuals mentioned in the report and obtain names and addresses of others who may have been in contact or exposed to the individual. The Act encourages sharing of these data among public safety and emergency management authorities at federal, state, local, and tribal levels to prevent, treat, control, or investigate a public health emergency. Officials are restricted from sharing any more information than necessary to control or investigate the threat. Stricter regulations in the Act govern access to medical records and charts of individuals under quarantine or isolation where individual privacy interests may be heightened.

Managing Property   Once a public health emergency is declared, the MSEHPA allows authorities the power to seize private property for public use that is reasonable and necessary to respond to the emergency. This includes the ability to use and take temporary control of certain private sector businesses and activities that are of critical importance to epidemic control measures. To eliminate safely infectious waste such as bodily fluids, biopsy materials, sharps, and other materials that may contain pathogens or otherwise pose a public health risk, authorities may take control of landfills and other disposal facilities. To ensure safe handling of human remains, officials may control and use mortuary facilities and services. They are also authorized to take possession and dispose of all human remains. Health care facilities and supplies may be procured or controlled to treat and care for patients and the general public. In all of these circumstances, the Act requires the state to pay just compensation to the owner of facilities or materials temporarily or permanently procured for public use. As in nonemergencies, public health agencies may condemn and destroy private property that poses a danger to the public without compensating the owners.

Other permissible property-control measures include restricting certain commercial transactions and practices (price gouging) to address problems arising from the scarcity of resources that often accompanies public emergencies (Kirsch 1993). The MSEHPA allows public health officials to ration or otherwise regulate distribution of scarce health care supplies and to control the price of critical items. They also may compel health care providers to perform medical examination and testing services.

The restrictions and uses of private property during a public health emergency may interfere with individual property rights, but the provisions of the MSEHPA do not violate constitutional or ethical precepts. Property rights have always been conditioned on the right of government to take property (subject to compensation) for public uses, or to limit an owner from using or holding a property that constitutes a nuisance, or harm, to others. Even during nonemergencies, the rights of property owners are subject to these limitations.

Control of Persons   Public health authorities must use every available means to prevent transmission of infectious disease and to ensure that all cases of such disease are subject to proper control and treatment. During a declared public health emergency, authorities may ask any person to be vaccinated or submit to a physical examination and/or medical tests without due process. Thus, no hearing or other procedural safeguard is available to persons who may oppose vaccination, examination, and testing. Lack of due process is sustained by the fact that individuals are not compelled to participate in these programs but are free to choose to do so. However, those who choose not to participate may be subject to isolation or quarantine measures.

The Act's quarantine and isolation provisions may be used to limit the freedom of individuals exposed to or infected with a contagious disease, respectively, to interact with the general public. Quarantine and isolation are classic public health powers. During nonemergencies, their practice is typically limited to controlling the transgressions of a very small number of persons whose behavior may lead to infecting others with a serious contagious disease or other potential harms. During a public health emergency, where potentially thousands of persons are exposed or infected with a contagious disease, use of quarantine or isolation powers may be widespread to protect community populations. Still the MSEHPA attempts to balance the welfare and dignity of individuals with communal interests. Accordingly, when implementing isolation or quarantine measures, public health authorities must use "the least restrictive means necessary to prevent the spread of a contagious or possibly contagious disease to others"; arbitrary or discriminatory quarantines will not satisfy this standard; maintain safe, hygienic conditions for persons in isolation or quarantine that minimize the risk of further disease transmission; provide adequate food, clothing, drugs, health care, means of communication, and other necessities; and adhere to strong due process protections for affected individuals.

Except where failure to quarantine or isolate persons immediately may significantly jeopardize the health of others, public health officials must obtain a court order before implementing these measures. The court must approve isolation and quarantine only if the public health authority can show the measures are reasonably necessary to prevent or limit transmission of a contagious or possibly contagious disease to others. Persons or groups subject to quarantine or isolation must receive written copies of orders accompanied by an explanation of their rights. They are entitled to be represented by counsel at individual or collective hearings to challenge the order generally or the conditions, terms, and treatment of their confinement. Even in cases of immediate quarantine or isolation, a court order must be sought promptly.

These procedural safeguards protect individuals from arbitrary or unjust detention. Even with such protections in place, the psychological toll on society occasioned by isolation and quarantine should not be underestimated. The MSEHPA recognizes the need for mental health support, and requires that public health authorities provide information about and referrals to mental health personnel to address psychological problems arising from the emergency.

Private sector health care workers are encouraged to assist in vaccination, testing, examination, treatment, quarantine, and isolation programs. The Act allows public health authorities to condition future licensing status of in-state workers on their providing assistance (where possible), and to waive licensing requirements for out-of-state personnel who are willing to help. Thus, the Act does not compel private health care workers to participate in public health measures during an emergency. It does provide some strong incentives to encourage participation because of the critical role of these individuals in such an event.

Conclusion

Preparing for existing and future bioterrorism events in the United States requires federal, state, and local public health authorities to collaborate with law enforcement and emergency management personnel to strengthen the national public health infrastructure. Working to improve public health detection, prevention, and response capabilities requires effective training, additional resources, use of existing and new technologies, and public health law reform. Inadequacies in existing state laws fail to authorize, or may even thwart, effective action. Law reform is necessary to improve planning, detection, and response capabilities.

The MSEHPA is a statutory framework of public health powers that allows authorities to plan, detect, manage, and control public health emergencies. These provisions are balanced against the need to safeguard individual rights and property interests. Maintaining this balance, however, is not easy. There continue to be sharp debates about the extent to which the state should restrict individual rights to safeguard the public's health and safety. Ultimately, these disagreements should be resolved through the legislative process as states consider bills based in whole or part on the Act. Legal reform may not be a panacea for the unforeseeable conflicts between individual and community interests that may arise during an emergency, but it presents an opportunity for resolving some of the difficult legal and ethical issues that history and experience suggest we will face.

References

Alexander, Y. 2000. "Terrorism in the Twenty-First Century: Threats and Responses." *DePaul Business Law Journal*. 12: 59–81.

Cantigny Conference on State Emergency Health Powers and the Bioterrorism Threat. April 26–27, 2001. Sponsored by the Centers for Disease Control and Prevention, American Bar Association Standing Committee on Law and National Security, and National Strategy Forum.

Center for Law and the Public's Health at Georgetown and Jones Hozkines Universities. The Model State Emergency Health Powers Act. Washington, D.C., 2001a and 2001b. Available at: www. publichealthlaw. net.

Chin, J. ed. 2000. *Control of Communicable Diseases Manual*. Washington, D.C.: American Public Health Association.

Code of Federal Regulations 42 C.F.R. § 72, app. A (2001).

Fialka, J. et al. 2001. "Are We Prepared for the Unthinkable?" *Wall Street Journal*. September 18, B1.

Gostin, Lawrence O. 2000. *Public Health Law: Power, Duty, Restraint*. Berkeley: University of California Press and Milbank Memorial Fund.

Gostin, Lawrence O. 2001. "Public Health Law Reform." *American Journal of Public Health*. 91: 1365–1368.

Gostin, Lawrence O., ed. 2002. *Public Health Law and Ethics: A Reader*. Berkeley: University of California Press and Milbank Memorial Fund.

Gostin, Lawrence O., Scott Burris, and Zita Lazzarini. 1999. "The Law and the Public's Health: A Study of Infectious Disease Law in the United States." *Columbia Law Review*. 99: 59–128.

Gostin, Lawrence O. et al. 1996. "The Public Health Information Infrastructure: A National Review of the Law on Health Information Privacy." *Journal of the American Medical Association*. 275: 1921–1927.

Hodge, James G. 2002. "Bioterrorism Law and Policy: Critical Choices in Public Health." *Journal of Law, Medicine and Ethics*. 30: 254–261.

Hodge, James G. and Gabriel B. Eber. 2002. "Legal Aspects of Bioterrorism and Infectious Disease Outbreaks." In *Planning for Bioterrorism: Individual and Community Response*, edited by Robert J. Ursano, Carol S. Fullerton, and Ann E. Norwood. London: Cambridge University Press.

Horton, Heather et al. 2002. "Disease Reporting as a Tool for Bioterrorism Preparedness." *Journal of Law, Medicine and Ethics*. 30: 262–266.

Inglesby, Tom, R. Grossman, and Tara O'Toole. 2000. "A Plague on Your City: Observations from TOPOFF." *Biodefense Quarterly*. 2: 1–10.

Kirsch, George R. 1993. "Hurricanes and Windfalls: Takings and *Price Controls* in Emergencies." *Viginia Law Review*. 79: 1235–1270.

Lipton, Eric. 2001. "Hard to Figure: A Difference in the Numbers." *New York Times*. October 25, B1.

Miller, Judith and Sheryl G. Stolberg. 2001. "Wider Anthrax Monitoring; U.S. Officials Acknowledge Underestimating Mail Risks," *New York Times*. October 25, A1.

Parker, L., T. Watson, and K. Johnson. 2001. "Anthrax Incidents Create Growing Sense of Anxiety." *USA Today*. October 15, A1.

Pavlin, J.A. 1999. "Epidemiology of Bioterrorism." *Emerging Infectious Diseases*. 5: 528–530.

Root–Bernstein, R.S. 1991. "Infectious Terrorism." *Atlantic Monthly*. 267: 44–50.

Shalala, Donna E. 1999. "Bioterrorism: How Prepared Are We?" *Emerging Infectious Diseases*. 5: 492–493.

Snapshot. 2001. *USA Today*, October 25, 1A.

Tucker, J.B. 1999. "Historical Trends Related to Bioterrorism: An Empirical Analysis." *Emerging Infectious Diseases*. 5: 498–503.

3

Terrorism and Human Rights

George J. Annas

It is increasingly difficult to distinguish fact from fiction, reality from fantasy, and truth from lies. Secrecy and fear, of course, infinitely compound this problem, and invite us to lose whatever perspective we have and simply support "our side" in the war on terrorism. To the question, "How will the war on terrorism affect bioethics?", reasonable responses include "Who cares?," "That's the least of our worries," and "How self-absorbed can bioethicists be that their first worry is about how terror affects their field?"

I have sympathy for all these views, but nonetheless agreed to write this chapter. I do so not because I think that if I didn't "the terrorists win," but rather because I am hopeful that even though the short-term effect of 9/11 was to curtail and compromise human rights and basic bioethics principles, its long-term effect has at least some reasonable probability of enhancing both worldwide. The movement toward a synthesis of bioethics and human rights tentatively begun well before 9/11, takes on more urgency in its wake. Far from hampering efforts to enhance public health and safety, taking human rights and bioethics seriously makes public health and safety measures more effective, at least in democracies, where public trust in government is essential to its success.

Choosing Fantasy

It is a commonplace in science fiction that what cannot be understood is often seen as magic or miracle, and arouses both fear and wonder. This is certainly true of much novel human experimentation. There is, nonetheless, a tendency to treat medical research and its claims as if they are all true, rather than to submit them to skepticism of the scientific method, which requires proof, not just claims. At the other extreme, some people are willing to accept even the most sinister conspiracy theories and bizarre accounts of present-day research. For example, in my most recent book, *Some Choice: Law, Medicine and the Market*, I included an updated version of three of my dark, fictional pieces combined into one chapter, chapter 13. Entitled "Our Most Important Product," in this incarnation it is an imagined transcript of a 1994 meeting of what I describe as a "top secret federal interagency group known as Perfect People 2002" (Annas 1998b). The minutes include discussions not only of research projects to construct the perfect human (replacing the perfect soldier project) but also of implanting nonremovable monitoring and behavior-modification devices in newborns, using comatose women as surrogate mothers for genetic experiments, providing additional funding to create humans with gills (projects to create people with wings and artificial wheels were temporarily suspended), and supporting an effort to capture twenty-five males and females from each of the world's "vanishing tribes" and relocate them to an island sanctuary for genetic variation research.

Even though the section on the human genome diversity project had been rejected by *Nature* (the editor wrote me that two of the four associate editors he asked to read it thought it was a serious scientific proposal), I did not anticipate that readers would take chapter 13 as fact (at least not for very long). Nonetheless, two reviewers of the book called me to ask about this chapter particularly, and another summarized the contents of every chapter except this one in his review. And for the last three years I have continued to receive at least one e-mail a month from readers who are convinced that chapter 13 is fact, not fiction. Some want to make sure I am still alive and in good health after divulging the existence of this secret group, but most want to know if I can help them get access to more minutes of the group, or if I can tell them what it has been up to recently. With the March 2002 revelation by the Bush administration that since 9/11 a "shadow government" has been operating in secret bunkers outside Washington I expect more e-mails, and I would not even be too surprised to learn that a Perfect People 2020-type committee actually exists.

Two of the most popular movies since 9/11 also illustrate contemporary inability to distinguish (or want to distinguish) fantasy from reality:

Black Hawk Down and *The Fellowship of the Ring*. Both movies were based on books, one about a factual event, the other pure fantasy. Nonetheless, they have similarities that help explain their post-9/11 popularity.

Black Hawk Down is the story of the fifteen-hour battle of Mogadishu, Somalia, in which American Rangers and Delta Force members fought off an overwhelmingly larger Somali forces after two of their Black Hawk helicopters had been shot down. Eighteen American soldiers died in the battle. Two observations stand out for me, one from the finely reported book, the other from the deftly crafted movie. Mark Bowden, who interviewed most of the Americans involved in the battle, notes in a new afterword in the paperback edition:

> Their experience of battle, unlike that of any other generation of American soldiers, was colored by a lifetime of watching the vivid gore of Hollywood action movies. In my interviews with those who were in the thick of the battle, they remarked again and again how much they felt like they were *in a movie*, and had to remind themselves that this horror, the blood, the death, was real. They describe feeling weirdly out of place, as though *they did not belong here*, fighting feelings of disbelief, anger, and ill-defined betrayal. *This cannot be real.* (Bowden 2000, 345–346; emphasis in original)

This description will, of course, resonate with most Americans who watched the second plane hit the World Trade Center, or who watched (and rewatched) the replays. Who hasn't thought, "this cannot be real." The primary lesson of the movie was drawn by *Wall Street Journal* movie reviewer Joe Morgenstern, who reviewed *We Were Soldiers* together with *Black Hawk Down*. He maintained that the message of both films is best articulated by the narrator at the end of *Soldiers*: "In the end they fought not for their country or their flag, they fought for each other." Morgenstern concluded his review, "Those who think such films will strengthen Americans' resolve in the war on terrorism, or any other, aren't watching the big picture on the screen" (Morgenstern 2002, W4).

The most popular and critically acclaimed movie since 9/11 is based on J.R.R. Tolkien's *The Fellowship of the Ring*. The movie (which, like *Black Hawk Down*, closely follows the book) involves the quest of a fantasy character, the hobbit Frodo, who is chosen to attempt to destroy the ring of power before it can be used by an evil wizard to rule the world. Frodo, who is fearful of the task, laments in words that bring 9/11 to mind (and for this reason were used by the studio to promote the movie), "I wish it need not have happened in my time." Frodo's friend, the good wizard Gandalf, replies, "So do I and so do all who live to see such times. But that is not for them to decide. All we have to decide is what to do with the time that is given us" (Tolkein 1954, 82). There are many reasons for this movie's popularity after 9/11, but the most likely explanation is that, like *Black Hawk Down*, it provides moviegoers with a good-versus-evil drama at a time when we really want to believe that we are the good guys, fighting evil in the real world.

Good versus Evil

Terrorism is evil; human rights (and bioethics) are good. In a time of terror, when many Americans fear for their personal safety and that of their families, it seems reasonable to do what we can to protect ourselves, and to permit (and even require) our government to do what it can to protect us. One prominent bioethicist, for example, reacted to 9/11 by saying, "we are all soldiers now" (Caplan 2001). This implies the necessity for the type of solidarity exhibited by soldiers in battle as portrayed in *Black Hawk Down* and *We Were Soldiers*. A well-known health lawyer responded by proposing that states enact new bioterrorism-quarantine laws that, among other things, would require American citizens to submit to examination and treatment by physicians or public health officials, and require physicians and hospitals to do whatever public health officials told them to do (including forced treatment) or face criminal prosecution or internment (Gostin et al. 2001a). This is a classic good-versus-evil view of the world, but fantastically treats only public health officials as the good, and Americans and their physicians (instead of terrorists) as the evil enemy. In this fantasy, public health officials are to wear the ring of power themselves in times of emergency.

Is it true that we must trade our human rights for safety to fight terrorism effectively? Must we, for example, dispense with the core value of modern bioethics—autonomy—in the face of a bioterrorist attack? I think the answer to both of these questions is no, and that trading human rights for safety will leave us with neither. Far from having to compromise human rights and bioethical principles in time of terror, honoring these principles is our best defense against future terrorist attacks. Most specifically, taking the human right to health seriously in the United

States instills trust in government officials and makes the public much more likely to follow reasonable government advice in an emergency. Globally, promoting human rights, including the right to health, is also likely to be the most effective action health care professionals can take to deter terror.

Three bioethics examples help illustrate how taking human rights seriously, even in times of national emergency, can be both the right policy and the most effective policy. They also illustrate the overlap, and thus potential merger, of bioethics and human rights, at least as related to health. Two of the examples attempt to displace human rights for expediency, the other illustrates an attempt, albeit a clumsy one, to respect human rights and bioethics. The examples are the Bush-Rumsfeld decision to ignore the Geneva Conventions for Al Qaeda and Taliban prisoners held at Guantanamo, the Center for Disease and Prevention (CDC)-financed proposal that states force medical treatment on Americans in the event of a bioterrorist attack, and the CDC-Food and Drug Administration offer of an investigational anthrax vaccine to those potentially exposed in the anthrax attacks.

Prisoners of War

Treatment of prisoners of war is the subject of the third of four Geneva Conventions, most recently revised in 1949 after World War II. The Conventions are the core of international humanitarian law, and also cover care of the wounded and sick, as well as treatment of civilian populations. The United States has historically insisted that other countries follow its provisions. Nonetheless, after transferring more than 100 Al Qaeda and Taliban prisoners from Afghanistan to its military base at Guantanamo, Cuba, the United States took the position that the Geneva Conventions do not apply because the suspected terrorist "detainees" are not prisoners of war. On January 18, 2002, for example, President Bush decided both that the prisoners at Guantanamo would not be given P.O.W. status, and that the United States would not abide by Geneva Convention III in their treatment (Seelye 2002). Both decisions were wrong as a matter of human rights law and a matter of effective policy.

The treatment of prisoners is, of course, a major human rights and bioethics concern. Physicians have often been called on by prison officials to help maintain order by dispensing drugs, and to help in torture by determining whether it is safe to continue torture or interrogation, making them agents of the state in the treatment of prisoners. All medical codes of ethics prohibit physicians from participating in torture in any way. And Article 13 of the Geneva Convention III states explicitly:

Prisoners of war must at all times be humanely treated. Any unlawful act or omission by the Detaining Power causing death or seriously endangering the health of a prisoner of war in its custody is prohibited, and will be regarded as a serious breach of the present Convention. In particular, no prisoner of war may be subjected to physical mutilation or to medical or scientific experiments of any kind which are not justified by the medical, dental or hospital treatment of the prisoner concerned and carried out in his interest. Likewise, prisoners of war must at all times be protected, particularly against acts of violence or intimidation and against insults and public curiosity.

The United States was correct to state that under the Geneva Convention not everyone in military custody must be granted P.O.W. status. But the decision of who is and who is not a P.O.W. cannot be made arbitrarily. Instead, the Convention requires that all military prisoners have P.O.W. status until a "competent tribunal" determines they are not in a category of persons protected by the Convention (Article 5). Members of militias and organized resistance movements, for example, qualify for P.O.W. status if they are under command, have a distinctive sign recognizable at a distance, carry arms openly, and conduct their operations in accordance with the laws and customs of war (Article 4A). Since the United States brought the prisoners to Guantanamo for questioning, the provision of the Convention that prohibits trying to force P.O.W.s to divulge more than their name, rank, and serial number is probably the one the government sought to avoid most.

The United States endured a firestorm of international protests about conditions of the prison camp at Guantanamo, transportation of prisoners to it (at least one was drugged for the long plane trip, and all were shackled and blindfolded), and their housing in open cages (Sennott and Bender 2002). Ultimately, it took a former military leader, Secretary of State Colin Powell, to impress upon President Bush how important the Geneva Conventions were to U.S. soldiers who are, of course, subject to capture themselves, and whom the U.S. military very much wants protected by the Conventions (Seelye and Sanger 2002).

Americans themselves, however, did not seem to mind too much how the prisoners were treated. David Letterman probably captured the mood of the country when he listed his top ten complaints made by prisoners at Camp X-ray. Complaint number 10, "Three meals a day and none of them are goat," and number 4, "Achmed totally stole my skit idea for camp talent shows." Bush ultimately at least partly changed his mind. He decided that the Geneva Conventions did apply; although he continued to insist that no prisoner would be given P.O.W. status. This decision, of course, is itself a violation of Article 5 of Geneva III, and makes one wonder what the president meant by saying the Convention applied to the prisoners.

In the end the United States was left looking like an unprincipled bully, a superpower that chose to ignore international law and human rights when it suited its purposes, even regarding treaties it has ratified. These actions severely undermined the country's credibility in supporting human rights worldwide, and unnecessarily put our armed forces at much higher risk of not having the Geneva Conventions applied to them when captured by another country. As of March 2002, the Defense Department has not publicly disclosed any useful information it has obtained by unlawfully interrogating the Guantanamo prisoners, and has had to seek congressional approval to do DNA "fingerprinting" on the prisoners in an attempt to identify them. Before the Guantanamo prisoner debacle the United States had the unquestioned support of most of the world in its fight against terror. Belittling the Geneva Conventions, however, has cost the country international support and severely undermined what had until then been a sense of moral superiority over its enemies. Good versus evil has become much more complicated.

Taking human rights seriously in this context would have better sustained international support for our fight against terrorism. Moreover, following a Convention-mandated screening process, the United States could have lawfully questioned those prisoners (likely a majority) who did not qualify for P.O.W. status under the Conventions. In short, nothing useful was gained, and much was lost, in the administration's attempt to trash the Geneva Conventions.

Military physicians have performed much better, and have honored both medical ethics and the human rights provisions of Geneva I that cover wounded prisoners. After the fiercest battle in Afghanistan (part of Operation Anaconda), for example, the surgeon in command of the U.S. Army field hospital at Bagram Air Base, Lt. Col. Ronald Smith, told reporters who asked him that Taliban and Qaeda wounded were being treated side by side with American wounded, noting that "the ethics of combat surgery" require it (Burns 2002).

Preparing for Bioterrorism

About six weeks after 9/11, the Johns Hopkins–Georgetown Center for Law and the Public's Health announced that its lawyers had drafted a "model" state emergency-bioterrorism law that if enacted by individual states would permit the governor to put sweeping powers in the hands of public health officials in a public health emergency such as a bioterrorist attack (Gostin et al. 2001a). Among its provisions, all drawn from existing laws of a variety of states in a cut-and-paste exercise, the act makes it a crime for members of the public to refuse to obey the orders of a public health official, including orders to be tested and to be vaccinated or treated. Physicians are also subject to criminal penalties for not following the orders of public health officials to test or treat, and these orders are "immediately enforceable by any peace officer." Individuals who refuse to be tested or treated can immediately be put in isolation or quarantine. Public health officials are immune from civil action against them, even if they negligently cause death or serious personal injury.

These provisions, of course, are contrary to constitutional law, which, for example, gives individuals a right to refuse any treatment, as well as contrary to basic principles of medical ethics, which would not permit physicians to treat patients against their will, or to treat patients in a manner the physician believed would be injurious to them, even under threat of criminal prosecution. What could prompt lawyers at prominent academic institutions to react to 9/11 in a way that is blatantly anti-American and, if anything, echoes the old Soviet system in which public officials were given arbitrary and unaccountable power over citizens? The most likely answer is a combination of fantasy and fear. Both were combined in role playing terrorism games such as "Topoff" (a hypothetical plague attack) and Dark Winter (a hypothetical small pox attack). The fear factor was multiplied on 9/11.

As Karl von Clausewitz noted in his famous treatise *On War* (1950), at the outset of a war most information will be misinformation, "and the timidity of men gives fresh force to lies and untruths. As a general rule, everyone is more inclined to believe the bad than the good. Everyone is inclined to magnify the bad in some measure . . ." (51). This certainly seems to be the case here, and the authors of the October 23 "model" bill very soon retreated from their initial proposal.

The cover page of the October 23 version states that it was prepared "for" the CDC and "in collaboration with" the National Governors' Association (NGA), National Conference of State Legislatures (NCSL), Association of State and Territorial Health Officials (ASTHO), National Association of City and County Health Officers (NACCHO), and National Association of Attorneys General (NAAG). In addition, chief drafter Larry Gostin told *USA Today* that his proposal was "strongly endorsed" by Health and Human Services Secretary Tommy Thompson (Copeland 2001, 3A). Gostin also told the *Johns Hopkins Public Health Magazine* that the act was "polished and strong because we had a brain trust of the best public health minds at Hopkins and the best legal minds at Georgetown, thus ensuring the best dividends for the nation" (Darraj 2001).

This may have been wishful thinking. Faced with public criticisms, the authors retreated to revise their "polished product." A revised version of the "model" act was made available on December 21, labeled "a draft for discussion" and prepared not "in collaboration with" but rather simply "to assist" the groups previously listed. No one any longer, implicitly or explicitly, endorsed the act, even the authors themselves. Most telling, the cover page now contains an explicit disclaimer:

The language and content of this draft Model State Emergency Powers Act do not represent the official policy, endorsement, or views of the Center for Law and the Public's Health, the CDC, NGA, NCSL, ASTHO, NACCHO, or NAAG, or other governmental or private agencies, department, institutions, or organizations which have provided funding or guidance to the Center for Law and the Public's Health. This draft is prepared to facilitate and encourage communication among the various interested parties and stakeholders about the complex issues pertaining to the use of state emergency health powers. (Gostin et al. 2001b)

To underline the point that the act was not endorsed by anyone, including its financial sponsor, director of the CDC, Jeffrey Koplan, responded to a letter written to Secretary Thompson by the New England Coalition for Law and Public Health (a group of health law academics, including me, from Boston University, Northeastern University, Tufts University, M.I.T., Brandeis, and Harvard) criticizing the act, in a letter to me dated December 28, 2001. In his words, "The draft model act does not represent any official or unofficial CDC position" (Koplan 2001).

Even though representing no one's views, and contrary to most law professors' views that it should not be taken seriously, the draft nonetheless took on a life of its own, and has required considerable work on the part of members of the New England Coalition and other patient-consumer advocacy groups to explain why its draconian provisions are not only unnecessary but also counterproductive (Mariner 2001). The authors themselves have been helpful in this regard. Co-drafter Steve Teret, for example, explained that he had just finished reading Jose Saramago's *Blindness* when asked to help on this draft. He told an interviewer that the horrific quarantine described in this fictional epidemic of blindness was something he could not get out of his mind. In his words, "It was the most disturbing book I've ever read" (Darraj 2001). Of course fiction often is more informative than nonfiction, especially in leading us to think about the future. Nonetheless the drafters ignored the most important public health message in the book, "Ah, yes, the quarantine, it didn't do any good" (Saramago 1997, 222).

Or maybe they did understand the limitations of large-scale quarantine, but just didn't have time to think it through in the post-9/11 panic atmosphere. Lead drafter Larry Gostin, for example, turned out to be the group's most articulate critic of quarantine. He told the *Boston Globe* in early November, for example, "Not only have quarantines not been effective, they have been the grounds for ignoble responses" (Mishra and Daley 2001, B1). And with colleagues at Hopkins, Gostin acknowledged in an article published in the *Journal of the American Medical Association* (*JAMA*) in December that quarantines can create more problems than they solve, and "in most infectious disease outbreak scenarios, there are alternatives to large-scale quarantine that may be more medically defensible, more likely to effectively contain the spread of disease, less challenging to implement, and less likely to generate unintended adverse consequences" (Barbera et al. 2001, 2714).

Given this, it is remarkable that quarantine would be made the centerpiece of public health emergency legislation, even cut-and-paste legislation, proposed for the twenty-first century. As the *JAMA* authors also correctly note, public trust is the key to effective public health action. Almost twenty-five years ago I wrote an editorial entitled "Where Are the Health Lawyers when We Need Them?" arguing that lawyers who work in the medical area "must understand the health care system and how it affects individual patients" if they are to do more good than harm (Annas 1978). Today the same message could be brought to lawyers who want to work in the public health and bioterrorism arenas. For all our sakes, it is critical that public health lawyers not overreact out of fear and endorse measures that not only violate basic bioethics and human rights principles, but also are likely to be counterproductive.

Since proposals such as the so-called model act can serve only to erode public confidence, it seems to me that its authors have an ethical and professional responsibility to withdraw this fatally flawed proposal from the public arena before it does actual damage. In retrospect, it was simply a mistake, perhaps understandably made without careful thought in the immediate aftermath of 9/11. On reflection, I would hope even assemblers of this draft can see that it is not necessary to trade civil or human rights for safety in this area. Rather, a public that believes that its officials will respect their basic human rights is much more likely to follow reasonable actions recommended by public officials in times of emergency. In this regard, treating our fellow citizens as the enemy and using police tactics to force treatment and isolate them is much more likely to cost lives than it is to save them (Annas 2002).

Anthrax Vaccine for Civilians

The use of force in public health emergencies is not only unnecessary, it is also most likely to be directed at minorities and the poor, as were quarantines in the past (Barbera et al. 2001). The lesson from the only actual bioterrorist attack experienced by Americans, the three letters containing anthrax that were sent through the mails in the wake of 9/11, support both this observation as well as the proposition that Americans require accurate information, not intimidation, to follow public health advice. In these attacks, for example, Americans almost uniformly rushed toward physicians and hospitals, not away from them, and demanded to be screening and treated, rather than resisting such care. Thankfully, even though the original official government response was antiscientific (Tommy Thompson opining that the first attack was not bioterrorism, but that the individual diagnosed with anthrax probably got it drinking from a stream), public health follow-up was much better, and ultimately only twenty-two people developed anthrax, five of whom died (Gerberding et al. 2002).

More than 10,000 people were advised to take antibiotics on the presumption that they were at risk to contract inhalation anthrax. In late December the FDA, Department of Defense, and CDC together released anthrax vaccine that had previously been available only to military personnel for use by those who were exposed. Of the 10,000 people eligible to take the vaccine, only 152 actually did (Connolly 2002). What is the lesson from this experience? Does it, for example, show that it is better to force people to be treated than to leave the decision to individuals?

I think the answer is that although the offer of the anthrax vaccine was extraordinarily clumsy, the CDC and FDA were right to insist that informed consent (the most important doctrine of modern medical ethics) be required and that no one be pressured to take the vaccine. On the other hand, I think they were wrong to make the vaccine available under these highly charged circumstances without making a recommendation to those eligible to receive it. If the agencies did not believe that the vaccine was useful as a postexposure treatment, they should not have made it available. If they did believe it was useful, they should have recommended it and informed those eligible for it of the basis for this recommendation.

To make the vaccine available without a recommendation seems like an incredibly cynical political move, designed by the FDA and CDC much more to cover their respective asses in case additional people developed anthrax, rather than to help protect those exposed. How else can these two bold-printed lines in the consent form be read?: "DHHS is *not* making any recommendation whether you should or should not take this vaccine. DHHS is making the vaccine available to you to allow you to decide whether or not you wish to use the vaccine."

On what basis (since there are no data from humans) could individuals make this decision if those with the most experience with the vaccine refused even to advise them about what was medically reasonable? In the context of a government offer to participate in an experiment on a vaccine the government did not recommend, it is easy to understand why at least some black postal workers said they were reminded of Tuskegee, and were not about to be made experimental subjects (Connolly 2001, A1). The legacy of Tuskegee is, of course, one of mistrust in the government, especially in the Public Health Service, and trust once lost is extraordinarily difficult to regain.

The flawed process of making the anthrax vaccine available to potentially exposed civilians also raises a generic issue that demands more attention than it has received to date: what should FDA testing rules be for efficacy of drugs and vaccines designed to counteract biological weapons? The FDA correctly determined that it would be unethical (a violation, for example, of the Nuremberg Code) to conduct human trials of efficacy of these drugs and vaccines by exposing subjects to potentially lethal agents. But what is the alternative? In 1999 the FDA issued proposed new regulations for comment that suggested that animal testing could substitute for human testing regarding efficacy, and both the U.S. Senate and House of Representatives endorsed the proposed rules in the wake of 9/11 (FDA 1999a). This seems reasonable. Nonetheless, the fact that these agents, even after they are approved, will not have been used on humans should mean both that their labeling be restricted for military or emergency use only (no unapproved uses), and that even in emergencies they be given only when qualified scientists believe it is the best available alternative, and only with informed consent of individuals— soldiers or civilians—involved.

This is one of the lessons from the Gulf War in which investigational drugs and vaccines were forced on soldiers under the ruse that informed consent was "not feasible." It took an act of Congress to undo the FDA's emergency wartime waiver of informed consent, and we should not make the same mistake again in the war on terror (Annas 1998a; FDA 1999b).

Conclusion

The 9/11 attacks were almost unimaginable, but not totally. Tom Clancy in fact imagined an attack by a highjacked 747 passenger jet on the U.S. Capitol Building in his 1994 novel, *Debt of Honor* (although after 9/11 even Clancy said he could never have imagined four such planes attacking simultaneously). In Clancy's 1996 sequel to the *Debt of Honor*, *Executive Orders*, he imagines the president declaring a national state of emergency in response to a terrorist attack using a strain of Ebola virus that is transmissible through the air. No expert on law, human rights, or bioethics, Clancy nonetheless makes a point that has escaped many more learned commentators: acts of bioterrorism cannot and will not be dealt with at the state level under the old state police powers doctrine; rather they are attacks on the United States and will be the responsibility of the federal government under national security powers (Annas 2002). Some things have changed irrevocably since 9/11, and one of these things is that public health is now (as it should be) a federal issue. This makes adherence to human rights principles in public health emergencies even more important, because federal power is so much stronger than the power of individual states.

In times of war and terror all kinds of overreactions that ignore human rights, including not only consent waivers, but also proposals for secret trials, unlawful detention, torture, and even misguided "model acts," are predictable. In times of crisis we have to be reminded over and over again that human rights, especially liberty and democracy, and the U.S. Constitution (not secrecy and unaccountability) are our foundational values. Human rights are not only our allies in war and terror, they are our best defense against aggressors. As Richard Horton, editor of the *Lancet*, put it so eloquently less than a month after 9/11:

Principles of harm reduction are more realistic and practicable than false notions of a war on terrorism. Attacking hunger, disease, poverty, and social exclusion might do more good than air marshals, asylum restrictions, and identity cards. Global security will be achieved only by building stable and strong societies. Health is a an undervalued measure of our global security. (Horton 2001)

We will survive only as long as we uphold human rights; and the more we undermine human rights and democracy, the less reason we will have to fight for our survival, and the less we will deserve to survive. In this fight it is critical to recognize that freedom is not just an end of economic development and social justice, it is a means as well (Sen 1999). And the importance of human rights (and bioethics) is that they are universal and apply to all humans on the simply basis that we are all members of the same species. It is this recognition, and actions founded on it, that will ultimately preserve both our lives and our liberty. As John F. Kennedy put it so well in the wake of the Cuban Missile Crisis that came as close as we have ever come to world-destroying nuclear war, in words that were also used by Hollywood to conclude the movie *Thirteen Days*, "no government or social system is so evil that its people must be considered as lacking in virtue." Kennedy continued in reference to the Soviet Union:

Let us not be blind to our differences—but let us also direct attention to our common interests . . . for in the final analysis, our most common link is that we all inhabit this small planet. We all breathe the same air. We all cherish our children's future. And we are all mortal. (Kennedy 1963)

The chief prosecutor at Nuremberg, U.S. Supreme Court Justice Robert Jackson, was, of course, correct to say (in a dissenting opinion) that "the Constitution is not a suicide pact" (Terminiello v. Chicago 1949). But he was more eloquent at Nuremberg when he argued to the judges there that unless we afford all people, even Nazi defendants, with basic human rights, history will rightfully judge us harshly. In his words, "To pass these defendants a poisoned chalice is to put it to our lips as well" (Opening Speeches 1946, 5).

References

Annas, George J. 1978. "Where Are the Health Lawyers when We Need Them?" *Medicolegal News*. 6.2: 3, 25.

Annas, George J. 1998a. "Protecting Soldiers from Friendly Fire: The Consent Requirement for Using Investigational Drugs and Vaccines in Combat." *American Journal of Law and Medicine*. 24.2: 245–259.

Annas, George J. 1998b. "Our Most Important Product." In *Some Choice: Law, Medicine and the Market*, 140–152. New York: Oxford University Press.

Annas, George J. 2002. "Bioterrorism, Public Health, and Civil Liberties." *New England Journal of Medicine* 346: 1337–1342.

Barbera, Joseph et al. 2001. "Large-Scale Quarantine following Biological Terrorism in the United States: Scientific Examination, Logistic and Legal Limits, and Possible Consequences." *Journal of the American Medical Association*. 286: 2711–2717.

Bowden, Mark. 2000. *Black Hawk Down*. New York: Penguin Books.

Burns, John F. 2002. "After Battle, Injured Foes Are Treated with Allies." *New York Times*. March 10, 18.

Caplan, Arthur. 2001. "New World Calls for New Health Care." Available at www.msnbc.com/news/635352.asp?0si (visited September 28, 2001).

Connolly, Charles. 2001. "Vaccine Plan Revives Doubts on Anthrax Policy." *Washington Post*. December 24, A1.

Connolly, Charles. 2002. "Workers Exposed to Anthrax Shun Vaccine: Law Participation Is Blamed on Confusing Signals from U.S. Health Authorities." *Washington Post.* January 8, A6.

Copeland, Larry. 2001. "CDC Proposes Bioterrorism Laws." *USA Today.* November 8, 3A.

Darraj, Susan M. 2001. "Model Legislation: Balancing Civil Rights and Public Health." *Johns Hopkins Public Health Magazine.* Fall. Available at www.jhsph.edu/magazine/model.htm.

Food and Drug Administration. 1999a. "New Drug and Biological Products: Evidence Needed to Demonstrate Efficacy of New Drugs for Use Against Lethal or Permanently Disabling Toxic Substances when Efficacy Studies in Humans Cannot Be Conducted." *Federal Register.* 64: 53,960 et seq.

Food and Drug Administration. 1999b. "Supplementary Information on Interim Final Rule: Human Drugs and Biologics, Determination that Informed Consent Is NOT Feasible or Is Contrary to the Interests of Recipients—Revocation of 1990 Interim Final Rule and Establishment of New Interim Final Rule." *Federal Register.* 64: 54, 180 et seq.

Gerberding J. et al. 2002. "Bioterrorism Preparedness and Response: Clinicians and Public Health Agencies as Essential Partners." *Journal of the American Medical Association.* 287: 898–900.

Gostin, Lawrence et al. 2001a. "Model State Emergency Health Powers Act." *CNN.* Available at www.cnn.com/2001/HEALTH/10/31cdc.bioterrorism.ap/index/html.

Gostin, Lawrence et al. 2001b. December, "Model State Emergency Health Powers Act." *Public Health Law.* Available at www.publichealthlaw.net.

Horton, Richard. 2001. "Public Health: A Neglected Counterterrorist Measure." *Lancet.* 358: 1112–1113.

Kennedy, John F. 1963. "Commencement Address, American University, June 10." *University of Massachusetts Boston John Fitzgerald Kennedy Library.* Available at www.cs.umb.edu/jfklibrary/j061063.htm.

Koplan, Jeffrey P. 2001. Letter to George J. Annas dated December 28 (available from the author).

Mariner, Wendy. 2001. "Bioterrorism Act: The Wrong Response." *National Law Journal.* December 17.

Mishra, Raja and Daley, Beth. 2001. "New Bill Targets Disease." *Boston Globe.* November 11, B1, B7.

Morgenstern, Joe. 2002. "War Is Hell, Effect Sell: 'We Were Soldiers' Loses Message in the Shelling." *Wall Street Journal.* March 1, W1, W4.

Opening Speeches of the Chief Prosecutors. 1946. *The Trial of German Major War Criminals,* vol. 1. London: His Majesty's Stationery Office, 5.

Saramago, Jose. 1997. *Blindness.* New York: Harcourt (Giovanni Pontiero, tr.)

Seelye, Katharine Q. 2002. "A P.O.W. Tangle: What the Law Says." *New York Times.* January 29, A14.

Seelye, Katherine and David Sanger. 2002. "Bush Reconsiders His Stand on Status of the Detainees." *New York Times*. January 29, A1, A14.

Sen, Amartya, 1999. *Development as Freedom*. New York: Knopf.

Sennott, Charles and Bryon Bender. 2002. "US Handling of War Captives Draws Fire." *Boston Globe*. January 23, A1, A10.

Terminiello v. Chicago, 337 U.S. 1 (1949) (Jackson, dissenting).

Tolkien, J.R.R. 1954. *The Lord of the Rings*. New York: Ballantine Books.

von Clausewitz, Karl. 1950. *On War*. Washington, DC: Infantry Journal Press.

4

Rights and Dangers: Bioterrorism and the Ideologies of Public Health

Ronald Bayer and James Colgrove

The history of American public health is punctuated by controversies over the extent to which the state may legitimately impose restrictions on liberty in the name of the common good, and over the extent to which protection of the public's welfare has served as a pretext for erosion of fundamental rights. Such conflicts were animated by deep-rooted mistrust of overreaching, by concerns about arbitrary exercises of power, and by the antiauthoritarian ethos that is such a prominent feature of American politics and civic culture. Periods of divisive controversy alternated with times of consensus during which dissident ideologies and underlying tensions largely disappeared from view. Extraordinary events, however, forced into the open assumptions underlying the dominant views of public health and revealed the existence of unresolved tensions, kindling anew debates over matters long thought to be settled. The shattering of the illusion of American continental impregnability by the events of September 11, 2001, and by the subsequent anthrax scare provided the occasion for a debate over the ideologies of public health. A controversy was sparked by proposals to enact a model emergency health powers act that would radically enhance the power of the state to respond to threats to the public health.

Looking Backward

In the nineteenth and early twentieth centuries public health officials who sought to institute mandatory vaccination programs, quarantines, and surveillance repeatedly faced resistance. Control of smallpox through government authority to compel vaccination and isolation of the infected served as a rallying point for groups and individuals motivated not only by antigovernment ideology but by concrete fears of physical harms that sometimes resulted from the procedure. Many state laws during this period were repealed or modified in response to pressure from opponents, especially in the second half of the nineteenth century when antivaccination societies gained strength (Kaufman 1967). In Milwaukee, for example, forceful application of the state's mandatory vaccination law sparked riots among the city's large German immigrant population in the 1890s (Leavitt 1982). Health officers who went into neighborhoods seeking to vaccinate residents and remove sick individuals to quarantine hospitals were greeted by angry mobs throwing rocks. In Massachusetts, a smallpox epidemic in 1901–1902 was the occasion for a court challenge to the state's compulsory vaccination law that ultimately led to a landmark Supreme Court ruling establishing the right of the government to use its "police powers" to control epidemic disease (Albert, Ostheimer, and Breman 2001). In its seven to two decision the Court affirmed the right of the people, through their elected representatives, to enact "health laws of every description to protect the common good" (Jacobson v. Commonwealth of Massachusetts 1905).

The history of efforts to impose quarantines on those viewed as threats to public health involved the exercise of authority that from the perspective of less threatening moments looks excessive and profoundly unfair (Fox 1988). On occasion the association of diseases with disfavored minority groups led to harsh measures supported by large segments of the population. In New York City, for example, arriving immigrants in 1892 could be isolated under squalid conditions to prevent the spread of cholera and typhus. At a moment of massive immigration and concomitant nativist sentiment, health officials encountered little popular opposition to their efforts (Markel 1997).

Finally, popular as well as professional opposition characterized early efforts to initiate case reporting by name to public health registries for purposes of disease control. Physicians opposed such requirements as an intrusion on their autonomy and as a violation of the confidentiality of the doctor-patient relationship (Fox 1988). Reflecting on controversies that greeted his efforts to mandate the reporting of tuberculosis cases as he moved forward to begin surveillance of sexually transmitted diseases, Herman Biggs, Commissioner of Health in New York, remarked early in the twentieth century, "The ten year long opposition to the reporting of tuberculosis will doubtless appear a mild breeze compared with the stormy protest against the sanitary surveillance of the venereal diseases" (Winslow 1929). Despite the existence of such opposition, reporting of cases by name to local and state health departments and to special confidential registries ultimately became part of the tradition and practice of public health (Thacker and Berkleman 1988). The same was true for mandatory vaccination.

The courts almost always deferred to public health authorities who deprived individuals of their liberty in the name of public health. Thus one state high court declared at the beginning of the twentieth century, "It is unquestionable that the legislature can confer police powers upon public officers for the protection of the public health. The maxim *Salus populi supreme lex* is the law of all courts in all countries. The individual right sinks in the necessity to provide for the public good" (Parmet 1985, 61). Perhaps most remarkable, such a plenary grant of authority could still be found to be constitutional in the seventh decade of the twentieth century. In upholding the detention of a person with tuberculosis pursuant to statute that provided virtually no procedural protections, a California appellate court in 1966 declared, "Health regulations enacted by the state under its police power and providing even drastic measures for the elimination of disease . . . in a general way are not affected by constitutional provisions, either of the state or national government" (In re Halko 1966).

The breadth of public health powers that were virtually unchallenged through most of the twentieth century increasingly became subject to scrutiny in the century's last decades. And when that occurred, the roles of mandatory screening and examination, reporting names those who were sick or infected to public health registries, and imposition of quarantine once again became the subject of dispute. Development of a robust jurisprudence of privacy (Karst 1980), and the "due process revolution" that extended rights to prisoners, mental patients, and others under the authority of the state (Tribe 1978) ultimately brought into question assumptions that protected public health from searching constitutional scrutiny. But whereas the groundwork was prepared in the transformations of American politics, law, and culture in the 1960s and 1970s, it was the AIDS epidemic that forced a fundamental rethinking of the dominant ideology of public health.

The controversies that raged during the 1980s, when the HIV epidemic emerged in the United States, reveal the profound effects that political and historical context have had on the enforcement of health. In the epidemic's early years a broad coalition of gay rights activists and civil libertarians were largely successful in their efforts to place the protection of privacy and individual rights at the forefront of the public health agenda (Bayer 1988). Fierce battles occurred when proposals were made to mandate reporting of people with HIV infection, and it was not until many years later that such reporting became possible. Intense controversy also surrounded efforts to preserve the right of individuals to determine whether they would be tested for the infection. Policies were adopted requiring exacting and specific informed consent for testing, and only in the 1990s did significant public support emerge for relaxing these standards. Finally, every attempt to use the power of quarantine to control those whose behavior placed their sexual partners at risk provoked extensive debate about the counterproductive impact of recourse to coercion.

Paralleling the development of a rights-based perspective on public health, and drawing on some of the same broad cultural changes, was the emergence of visible antivaccination movement in United States. During the late 1970s and 1980s heterogeneous collections of groups and individuals representing various goals, ideologies, and strategies came together to question the safety and efficacy of vaccines and the ethics of compulsory policies. A common thread of the movement is the argument that public health officials have willfully denied the dangers of immunization, which render any attempt to compel the procedure ethically unjustifiable (Freed, Katz, and Clark 1996). An antistatist, antiauthoritarian outlook characterizes many of the groups in the movement. The libertarian Association of American Physicians and Surgeons (2002) thus declared in a position paper, "It's obscene to threaten to seize a child just because his parents refuse medical treatment that is obviously unnecessary and perhaps even dangerous. [We believe] that parents with the advice of their doctors should make decisions about their children's medical care—not government bureaucrats."

Bioterrorism

In the late 1990s the threat of bioterrorism surfaced as a concern of a few public health officials and experts. Alarmed by reports that Iraq had invested in a bioweapons program, the lethal gas attack by a Japanese cult, and information regarding activities of the former Soviet Union, advocates sought to jar America into coming to grips with the danger of and its utter lack of preparedness for a potential attack. That the efforts were spearheaded by D.A. Henderson, who had gained worldwide recognition for his work in the global smallpox-eradication campaign, lent credibility to these efforts (Bor 1999). For him, the prospect of the use of biological weapons was "more likely than ever before" (Henderson 2001, 1918). In early 1999 President Clinton announced that he was allocating $158 million to the Department of Health and Human Services for research into and preparation for bioterrorism. Additional sums would be requested for the next year (Garrett 1999).

The mounting concern had its antagonists, especially among those identified with the public health left. Victor Sidel and his colleagues thus wrote in the *American Journal of Public Health*, "Should we be guided by a perspective that focuses on a hypothetical bioterrorism as a main concern while relegating to the background the monumental issues of infectious disease, food borne illness, and chemical accidents, not to mention the daily problems that are inadequately attended? The road to bioterrorism preparedness may be paved with good intentions [but] traveling down that road may be a disastrous course for public health"(Sidel, Cohen, and Gould 2001, 717). But such opposition could not stem the growing sense of concern.

On April 26–27, 2001, a meeting to address the public health threat posed by bioterrorism was convened by the Centers for Disease Control and Prevention (CDC), the American Bar Association's Standing Committee on Law and National Security, and the National Strategy Forum. Held outside Chicago, the Cantigny Conference brought together federal, state, and local public health and law enforcement officials, representatives of the Departments of Defense and Justice, as well as university-based researchers. The goal of the meeting, which strikingly did not include representatives of civil rights and liberties organizations, was to consider the extent to which states had the legal capacity to invoke emergency powers in the face of an act of bioterrorism, and whether current public health law would be adequate to the challenge posed by such an event. A premise of the meeting was that law was a central component of the public health infrastructure, that there could be no preparedness that did not include the statutory authority that would govern efforts of officials faced with a terrorist-created emergency.

From the outset officials at the CDC underscored the necessity of a legal framework that would govern access to medical and other records, permit the control over private property, allow procurement and rationing of medicines and vaccines, and provide for control over individuals who were thought to pose a risk. Such control would include the possibility of mandatory examinations and implementation of quarantines when deemed necessary to prevent spread of disease. Whereas conference participants appeared to acknowledge that in the face of a bioterrorist attack public health authorities would be able to count on voluntary cooperation of the population, they noted that "statutory mechanisms needed to be in place for dealing with uncooperative people." Although public health officials had experience in the exercise of compulsory powers, the extent to which coercion might be called upon in a bioterrorist event would be much greater.

It was the specific dimensions posed by the threat of bioterrorism that suggested the need to confront the adequacy of public health laws, many of which were enacted in the early twentieth century and had not been updated in decades. Conference participants expressed concern about ways in which some recent modifications in the law were designed to impose due process limits on the exercise of public health powers, and that some privacy protections might serve as impediments to action in the face of an emergency. Thomas Gillespie of the Johns Hopkins Center for Civilian Biodefense Studies, directed by D.A. Henderson, thus noted that it might be necessary to change the health care system, "which currently treats the individual patient with the highest regard and is less concerned with the public good." Most important, given the leadership role he ultimately assumed in drafting the model public health act, Larry Gostin noted that the rights-centered transformation of recent decades had created a situation in which "laws that protect individual rights appear to have superseded those preserving the common good." It was, of course, no small irony that Gostin, director of the Georgetown–Johns Hopkins Center for Law and the Public's Health, had himself been a forceful advocate for civil liberties during the 1980s and 1990s and as such had been instrumental in the very transformation he now viewed with some concern.

Emerging from the Cantigny Conference was a consensus on the powers that would be required by public health officials faced with a bioterrorist event. They mirrored the conventional strategies of infectious disease control that emerged at the end of the nineteenth century and in the first decades of the twentieth century: reporting of cases by medical personnel; mandatory medical examinations; contact investigation; and imposition of isolation and quarantine. In addition, the importance of having authority to seize, confiscate, and make use of private property, including hospitals, was noted.

The Cantigny Conference participants were committed to drafting a model act that would help states clarify and strengthen their existing public health laws. But the time frame for such an undertaking remained unspecified. In part, this was so because an ambitious effort, funded by the Robert Wood Johnson Foundation, to redraft public health laws was already very far along. It took the assaults of September 11 to create the context within which a sense of urgency would take hold.

Ideology, Politics, and the Model State Emergency Health Powers Act

Soon after the events of September 11, Gene Matthews, legal advisor to the CDC, called on Larry Gostin quickly to prepare a model public health emergency act. "It wasn't," said Matthews, "in anyone's interest to have 50 states running off in different directions on this" (Matthews 2002). On October 30, a model act that had been speedily drafted was released to the public. In every way the proposed statute bore the marks of an initiative with powerful and broad-based official backing. A press release by Secretary of Health and Human Services Tommy Thompson noted that the Act was the outgrowth of a "CDC-led process" (U.S. Department of Health and Human Services 2001). The CDC's director Jeffrey Koplan commented that adoption of the emergency act would facilitate his agency's efforts. "Many of the current laws don't make sense anymore . . . This will update the public health laws to fit the world we live in" (McKenna 2001). An official at the National Governors' Association said that the Act "goes a long way to helping governors improve their public health infrastructure to respond to today's health emergencies" (Center for Law and the Public's Health 2001b). It is thus not surprising that press reports saw in the proposed act a government initiative.

The *Atlanta Constitution* headlined "CDC Pushes Bill Boosting State's Powers" (McKenna 2001). For Gostin and his colleagues the draft, while open to refinement, was "polished and strong" (Darraj 2001), nearly ready for consideration by state legislatures (Center for Law and the Public's Health 2001b).

Those who drafted the Act were haunted by the specter of a catastrophic threat to the public health, and although the impetus for the proposed legislation was the prospect of bioterrorism, concern extended much more broadly (Center for Law and the Public's Health 2001a). Indeed the Act referred to dangers associated with "emergent and resurgent infectious diseases" as well as "epidemics and pandemic threats." In the face of challenges that posed a "substantial risk of a significant number of human fatalities or incidents of permanent or long term disability," the governor was to be given authority to declare a public health emergency. If the situation warranted, and when prompt action was necessary, such a declaration could be issued without consultation with public health officials. It would also allow the governor to mobilize the state's militia and initiate a range of extraordinary measures that would last for thirty days, at which point it could be renewed. The legislature could intervene to override the executive decision only after sixty days and only by a two-thirds vote of both chambers.

Although its preamble noted the importance of balancing the "common good with individual liberties" and asserted that it was designed to grant authority to prevent and manage emergency health threats without unduly interfering with civil rights and liberties, the Act allowed for coercive interventions bearing on privacy, bodily integrity, and liberty backed by the threat of criminal sanction. Health care providers and medical examiners would be required to report to public health authorities within twenty-four hours the name, date of birth, gender, race, and current address of individuals with conditions that could be related to bioterrorism or other highly fatal or dangerous infectious agents. In a marked departure from convention, pharmacists were to be included among those required to report unusual increases in prescriptions for conditions that could be linked to public health emergencies. Based on such reports, public health officials were to engage in the time-tested process of contact investigation designed to trace the origin and track the potential spread of disease.

Far more striking were the powers enumerated under Article 13 dealing with "control of persons" and the extent to which those powers were to be enforced through the threat of criminal sanction and potential deprivation of liberty. The public health authority was granted the right to "compel" individuals to undergo medical examination and medical testing, and those who refused would be liable for misdemeanors. When authorities were uncertain if individuals who refused to undergo examination or testing had been exposed to an infectious agent or otherwise posed a threat to public health, they could impose isolation or quarantine. When it was determined that public health required either treatment of those who were sick or vaccination of those who were at risk for infection, such interventions could be mandated under threat of a misdemeanor charge. Furthermore, "if by reason of refusal of vaccination or treatment" the individual was thought to pose a danger to public health, he or she might be subject isolation or quarantine. Health care providers who refused to be party to such interventions would be subject to criminal prosecution.

Recognizing that much had occurred since quarantine laws of an earlier era were enacted, the model legislation sought to balance due process considerations with exigencies imposed by public health emergencies. In general, quarantines and isolation were to be imposed only after courts had issued a written *ex parte* order, based on a showing that probable cause existed that such measures were necessitated by a threat to public health. When urgency dictated immediate action, however, deprivation of liberty could occur without a court order being obtained first. Those quarantined or isolated could request a court hearing and representation by counsel. Such hearings were to be held within seventy-two hours of the request. The court's determination regarding both initial and continued isolation or quarantine was to be based on presentation of clear and convincing evidence.

In all, the Act was a stark expression of the view that grave threats to public health might necessitate abrogation of privacy rights, imposition of medical interventions, and deprivation of freedom itself.

Release of the Act was the occasion of considerable media attention, much of which was subtly supportive of the drafters' analyses of public health infrastructural inadequacies and limits of the prevailing legal regime (Copeland 2001). An editorial in the *New Republic*, for example, concluded, "Here's hoping we won't have to experience a real outbreak before we realize that when it comes to public health, temporarily sacrificing liberty may be the price of staying alive" (Brownlee 2001).

That was the perspective shared by sympathetic public health officials and by legislators who moved swiftly in a number of states to introduce legislation that largely mirrored the model act. "In tough times you have to make tough decisions," said an assistant commissioner of public health in Massachusetts (Lasalandra 2001). In Minnesota, Thomas Huntley, a Democratic Farm Labor Party representative, announced plans to introduce his public health emergency legislation in January 2002. Noting the existence of quarantine laws the state had relied on in the 1950s, he declared that in the earlier period "the minuscule trade-off in individual liberties was clearly understood in light of the consequences of letting these diseases run rampant. We must be prepared and empowered to take the same course of action if necessary to prevent similar epidemics, particularly since bioterrorists have engaged our country in this kind of warfare" (deFiebre 2001). In California, Republican Assemblyman Keith Richman acknowledged that his proposed legislation, which was virtually identical to the model act, would raise questions about civil liberties. But given the risks of smallpox, from which one-third of the infected could die, "we should have a public health law in place that could minimize the situation as much as possible" (Tansey 2001). Finally, in New York, Democratic Assemblyman Robin Schimminger also asserted that civil liberties concerns paled by comparison to what would be necessary in "extraordinary circumstances." "We're dealing with a bona fide public health emergency declared by the governor and confirmed by the legislature in which the hazard to the public is contagious and insidious" (Ernst 2001).

In striking contrast to those who endorsed the model act's provisions, many policy makers and health advocates viewed the proposal as a grave threat rather than as a necessary tool in the struggle against bioterrorism. These critics came from the left as well as the right, and shared deep suspicion of the state's authority, even when exercised in the name of public health. Where architects of the Act and their allies believed it was possible to delegate extensive authority to officials faced with emergencies, opponents saw only prospects of the abuse of power. Whereas the nightmare that informed the world view of the Act's advocates involved tens of thousands of imperiled individuals, the true threat, according to opponents, was arrogation of unlimited executive authority to confront dangers that could instead be managed by measures that were respectful of privacy and individual rights.

Among the broadest challenges was an open letter to the Secretary of Health and Human Services by the New England Coalition for Law and Public Health, an ad hoc group of law professors and others concerned with public health policy led by Boston University's George Annas. The coalition asserted that it was not necessary to enhance public health emergency powers. Indeed, what modification was required would entail imposition of constitutional limits on older public health statutes. Whereas the Act forcefully asserted the need to engage coercive authority of the state during emergencies, the coalition saw such "undue reliance" on power as a diversion from the central problem: failure adequately to fund public health departments and hospital emergency services, or to provide preventive care and treatment to those in need. Recourse to threats and coercion treated the people as if they, rather than pathogens, posed a problem. "In other words this statute limits individual rights without providing individuals with any substantial assurance of protection against bioterrorist attacks or other more ordinary threats to public health."

Finally, the coalition denounced the breadth of statutory language that would permit declaration of a state of emergency when less drastic efforts might suffice. "Individual civil liberties and property rights may be disregarded even when more benign measures might achieve a comparable results" (New England Coalition for Law and Public Health 2001, 2). The Act was described as a replica of statutes from the early twentieth century, an era of therapeutic limits, "when officials had to rely on quarantining sick people because they have little else at hand" (Parmet and Mariner 2001). Annas (2001) described it as "the old Soviet model of public health (lots of power and no standards for applying it), hardly a 'new' American model."

Like the New England Coalition, groups with special concern about privacy expressed alarm at the way in which the model act treated medical information. The Health Privacy Project at Georgetown University's Law Center noted that the "breathtakingly expansive scope of the definition" of public health emergencies could open the way to name-based reporting of cases of HIV and hepatitis, "a controversial proposition indeed" (Health Privacy Project 2001, 1–2). Furthermore, the Act was denounced for the inadequacy of protections afforded medical information on identifiable individuals. Crafted to highlight problematic features of the Act's specific provisions, the Project's challenge was embedded in a perspective radically distinct from that which animated the work of the drafters. Giving voice to an understanding that had taken hold in the first years of the AIDS epidemic, the critique concluded by asserting that gaps in public health capacity to respond to emergencies could be resolved by "fully" respecting civil liberties and privacy rights. "These ends are not mutually exclusive; rather they are integrally linked" (Health Privacy Project 2001, 5).

To the Lambda Legal Defense and Education Fund—a gay and lesbian civil rights organization that had been involved for more than a decade in combating policies such as reporting names of HIV-infected individuals—the Act was anathema. With its recourse to compulsory measures, threats of quarantine and criminalization, and reliance on collaboration between public health and law enforcement agencies, it represented a regressive step that could have dire effects on those the AIDS advocacy group had so fiercely sought to protect (Lambda Legal Defense and Education Fund 2001).

But from whatever vantage point they challenged the Act, informing the liberal opposition's position was the unmistakable sense that, wittingly or not, the drafters permitted themselves to bring forth the public health equivalent of policies emanating from John Ashcroft's Justice Department. As the threat of war and terrorism provided a warrant for cabining civil liberties, the danger of bioterrorism provided justification for yet one more perilous threat to fundamental rights.

But broad and thoroughgoing challenges came not only from those who embraced liberal political values and a progressive social agenda. Conservative libertarians also saw in the Act exemplification of an appalling philosophical outlook. It represented "an unprecedented assault on the constitutional rights of the American people [and] on our fundamental principles of limited government and separation of powers" (Schlafly 2001). Like critics on the left, groups such as the Association of American Physicians and Surgeons denounced intrusions on privacy that would occur as the result of disease-reporting requirements, imposition of medical interventions and vaccinations, and criminalization of refusals to undergo such treatment. Invocation of a broad power to quarantine was viewed as especially egregious. In short, said the physicians' group, the model act "turns governors into dictators," permitting them to "create a police state by fiat" (Association of American Physicians and Surgeons 2001).

Ironically, as liberal civil libertarians responded with dismay to what they took to be Larry Gostin's betrayal of his libertarian past, conservative opponents characterized Gostin as the embodiment of left-wing values. Jennifer King, an official with the American Legislative Exchange Council, portrayed Gostin as a "very strong public health, police state type." Nothing more tellingly revealed his commitments than the work he had done as one of more than 500 consultants assisting the Clintons during the ill-fated effort at health care reform (Betsch 2001).

Finally, with its authorization of mandatory vaccinations on penalty of criminalization and quarantine, and with its invocation of a much-hated century-old Supreme Court decision upholding imposed immunization, it was inevitable that the Act would draw the ire of anti-vaccination advocates. These groups typically, although not always, shared the antistatist perspectives of the broader conservative libertarian movement. In one such on-line denunciation (Richardson 2002), which was especially harsh in its reference to Gostin because of his "long history of trying to brainwash people into sacrificing individuals' rights for society," the Act was described as "horrifying." It would impose immunizations on adults and children and would enhance the "powers of public health bureaucrats." The legislation offered the false promise of security in exchange for the freedom to make one's own medical decisions. This was all too predictable given the history of coercive childhood vaccinations. It was time for the "extortion" to stop.

Denunciations from groups that believed that the exercise state authority, even the name of public health, had to be carefully circumscribed, and from those who had a visceral antagonism to state authority, were not unexpected. Perhaps more striking was the response of constituencies that, according to first reports, had enthusiastically participated in the legislative initiative. Indeed, in the weeks after the late-October public release of the Act, the very organizations that had been listed as collaborators in its development sought to distance themselves from it.

The same official at the National Governors' Association (NGA) who at first described the Act as "extremely useful" later was compelled to acknowledge that the NGA had not taken a full position on the Act, that a number of states had indicated "we don't need this," and "governors don't like models, they like options" (Thomasian 2002). The Association of State and Territorial Health Officials (ASTHO) noted that "at the request of the CDC" it circulated the document for review and comment, and many respondents expressed discomfort with overreliance on criminalization, recourse to mandatory treatment and vaccination, and reliance on quarantines. Most significant, ASTHO noted that the model act would best serve as a "tool" for states as they considered the necessity of new or amended authority; in no way was it to be viewed as a template for a radical revision of extant public health laws. States should "retain the flexibility to adopt all or part of the model act as they deem appropriate for their jurisdictions" (Association of State and Territorial Health Officials 2001). A similar stance was adopted by the National Association of County and City Health Officials (Brown 2002). Although the National Association of Local Boards of Health did not immediately take a position on the Act, its director for governmental relations cautioned about the dangers of thoroughgoing legislative reform. "It has been my experience that the more comprehensive legislation becomes, the greater the effect of the law of unintended consequences. State and legislating jurisdictions within them should be encouraged to adopt as little new law as possible and to focus on amendments of existing statutes only as much as necessary" (Pratt 2001). Finally, the National Council of State Legislatures (NCSL) indicated that it did not typically indorse model acts. An observer sympathetic to the project of reform recounted that the NCSL had "gone ballistic" on being listed as a collaborator on the draft (Fox 2002). One account of meetings convened by the Council suggested that most attendees saw the model as "bad" legislation. At least two legislators underscored the extent to which it appeared like a "governmental takeover" (Guiden 2001). In lieu of wholesale reform, many groups suggested using the Act as a checklist for thinking about the adequacy of extant legislative provisions.

This then was the context in which those who crafted the model act were compelled to undertake the redrafting. It was a process that would seek to preserve core elements of the Act while modifying aspects—language and substance—that provoked criticism from those alarmed by the breadth of the statutory formulations and the impact they could have on the rights of those who might become subjects of the Act's compulsory dimensions. In undertaking the refinement, drafters could not ignore the fact that even among many who thought legislative reform to meet the challenge of bioterrorism was necessary, there appeared to be no great enthusiasm for the grand recodification foreseen when the Act was first released. Thus whatever was done would have to be understood as providing states with a checklist of matters with which they would have to deal. Thus said Maryland's Health Secretary Georges Benjamin, "States should look at [the Act] as a menu . . . I think the most important thing is that people not take any model act and simply try to push it through Willy Nilly" (Gillis 2001).

Nevertheless, in light of the fact that the CDC was to be distributing approximately $1 billion to states for emergency preparedness, and that in making its determination the CDC would look for evidence that efforts had been made to provide the legal infrastructure for confronting public health threats, it was inevitable that action at the state level would be forthcoming. Whether CDC funding was viewed as an inducement or a bludgeon depended very much on how one saw the effort to craft a legislative bulwark against bioterrorism.

At the end of December 2001 a new draft was made public. Changes, both cosmetic and substantive, were evident (Center for Law and the Public's Health 2001c). The amended Act reflected the political lessons of the previous six weeks. Perhaps most striking was the characterization of the relationship between the legislative proposal and constituencies that had been portrayed as "collaborators" in crafting the earlier effort. Now the Act was described as serving to "assist" those very organizations. Indeed the National Association of Attorneys General was simply listed as having provided "input and suggestions." To dispel the illusion that the Act represented CDC-endorsed legislation, a disclaimer asserted that the emergency measure did not "represent the official policy, endorsement or views" of the federal agency. Oddly, the disclaimer was extended to the CDC-funded Center for Law and the Public's Health that had itself drafted the model act! In all, a distinct effort was made to avoid the suggestion that states had before them a legislative measure that had the full backing of powerful national public health and law enforcement bodies.

The new draft also underwent significant linguistic transformation. Whereas the earlier version unabashedly employed terms that reflected the necessity of coercive measures, the new draft sought to soften the harsh tone. Thus, for example, the subsection dealing with property— which evoked such concern on the part of those who viewed it as an invitation to unwarranted seizures—was now denominated "management" rather than "control" of property. The subsection dealing with compulsory powers over individuals, which drew the ire of those committed to civil liberties, was no longer termed "control of persons"; now it was called "protection of persons." Finally, the new draft subtly acknowledged that the original version had, by emphasizing the importance of coercive measures, inadequately underscored the centrality of a well-financed and organized public health system. The preamble now declared, "although modernizing public health is an important part of protecting the population during public health emergencies, the public health system itself needs improvement."

More important were substantive changes, all of which sought to prevent exercise of authority from becoming an occasion for abuse of power. First, responding to the alarm evoked by the very breadth of the definition of threats that could occasion the declaration of an emergency, the new draft eliminated references to "epidemic and pandemic diseases" (critics asserted that the flu and AIDS could trigger a declaration). In so doing the drafters sought to demonstrate that their understanding of what constituted an emergency was similar to that of their antagonists, who asserted that there were, of course, situations that might require the exercise of extraordinary public health powers. What had been the sweeping authority of the governor to impose a state of emergency with very limited legislative oversight was now to be subject to the possibility of an override by a simple majority of both legislative houses. Concerns that the October version would have permitted gross violations of privacy was similarly given credence. Mandatory reporting by name remained a central element of the Act, but steps were taken to ensure that the data would be protected from unwarranted disclosure and misuse. Criminalization of refusals to undergo treatment and vaccinations by those deemed a potential threat to public health were gone, although those who declined such interventions would still be subject to isolation and quarantine. Gone too were criminal sanctions for physicians and other health care providers who refused to impose treatment or vaccination, although their licensure could be endangered. The capacity to move swiftly to impose isolation and quarantine, so central to the original Act, remained untouched. The revised legislative proposal did, however, provide a much more extensive elaboration of due process procedures that would surround such deprivations of liberty.

Some of those who expressed fierce opposition to the October draft acknowledged that the proposed substantive changes had improved the legislation. Core concerns remained, however, revealing a deep philosophical divide. Thus, for example, the Health Privacy Project noted improvements represented by the narrower definition of public health emergencies but continued to voice objections to the way in which the Act would violate the privacy of medical information. Bluntly it said, "The necessary changes . . . have not been made" (Health Privacy Project 2002). George Annas revealed the gulf that separated those who saw limitations on liberty as central to the response to public health threats and those who were profoundly skeptical of this assumption. "We do not have to trade off civil liberties for public health to effectively respond to a bioterrorist attack" (Annas 2002). Indeed, he viewed the constitutional premise on which the act was predicated—the 1905 Jacobson v. Massachusetts decision—as part of a bygone era. Invoking the lessons of the AIDS epidemic he concluded, "The promotion of human rights can be essential to deal effectively with an epidemic" (Annas 2002).

The New York Civil Liberties Union (2002), in testimony before a state legislative committee, gave voice to the fundamental opposition that no cosmetic changes or limited adjustments could address. The Act was an "anachronism" and failed to "fully anticipate the ways in which [it] would empower the state to violate fundamental rights and liberties." Giving credence to the need to respond to real incidents of bioterrorism, it believed it crucial to recognize the history of abuse by the state. "Government acting in the name of public safety, has demonstrated bad judgment and worse using state police powers in a discriminatory manner to suspend freedoms based upon race or national origin." Given such a perspective it is not surprising that the group challenged even the revised version of the Act in every detail: the definition of public health emergency was still too broad; the requirement that names be used for reporting purposes ignored the principle that without demonstration of an overriding interest such a privacy-violating measure was unacceptable; the "protection of persons" clauses presumptively overrode the individual's right to refuse medical treatment; the Act failed to incorporate procedural protections already available in some states, including New York. Finally, the limited scope of judicial review on matters of treatment, testing, isolation and quarantine "constituted a fundamental and "fatal" flaw in the act (New York Civil Liberties Union 2002).

The arguments of the libertarian right were not very different, although they were informed by a characteristic stridency. The Association of American Physicians and Surgeons denounced the new draft as a "disingenuous effort to mute criticism." Limitations on liberty for ordinary citizens were less severe, but the draft still imperiled clinicians and those who owned medical facilities. "Their property can be commandeered and their skills usurped to perform duties that might well violate their oath to serve patients to the best of their own judgment and ability." In short, the revision was "still a prescription for tyranny" (Association of American Physicians and Surgeons 2002). The American Legislative Exchange Council (2002) also acknowledged that changes had been made in the October draft but asserted that "the release of a revised draft [did] not mask the original intent of the authors." Finally, Georgia Republican congressional representative Bob Barr described the act as a "fearsome power grab" by the CDC and the nation's governors. Barr drew a parallel between the proposed legislation and the Clinton administration's effort at health care reform. The earlier attempt was a "federal takeover" of the health care industry. Now there was an effort "to hijack not only the health care industry, but also the constitutional freedoms of [Americans]." The entire enterprise was "unprecedented," at least in "non-dictatorial regimes" (Barr 2002).

Although some antivaccine advocates found in the modification an acceptable compromise—quarantine for refusal to undergo immunization rather than criminalization (Reiss 2002)—the most redoubtable voice of the movement continued to denounce the proposal. Terming the CDC-funded drafting effort as one that "Treats us like runaway slaves in need of subjugation," Barbara Loe Fisher, head of the National Vaccine Advisory Center, attacked the Act's continued use of compulsion as a choice between freedom and vaccination. Linking her struggle to a broad liberty-preserving agenda she declared, "I've said many times during the past decade that if the state can tag, track down and force citizens to be injected with biologicals of unknown toxicity, then there will be no limit on what individual freedoms the state can take away in the name of the greater good tomorrow. Now tomorrow is here" (Fisher 2002).

It was against a backdrop of such fervid attacks and more sober critiques that the work of state legislatures took place. Some states considered legislation based on the revised version, whereas others moved to adopt even more scaled-back versions that would be acceptable to those concerned about overreaching. Thus, for example, in Wisconsin adaptations from the Act were characterized as "pretty minor" by a state senator (Rosenzweig 2002). In Ohio the health department cautiously reconsidered its options given the need to face a legislature "very leery of big government" (Govern 2002). The California state health department remained skeptical of the need for wholesale legislative action even though a bill closely following the October version of the model act was introduced into the legislature (Reilly 2002). In Minnesota, the need to accommodate those opposed to the Act resulted in a legislative proposal that was "barely adequate," according to the state's epidemiologist, who had been among the proponents of a more expansive version (Hull 2002).

But despite such resistance it was clear by March 2002, five months after the model act was first proposed, that significant legislative activity was inspired by the proposal to create a legal infrastructure responsive to the threat of bioterrorism. Indicative of the state of affairs was the enthusiastic involvement of Richard Gottfried, chair of the New York State Assembly's health committee (Gottfried 2002). Long an advocate of both public health and privacy rights, an architect of the state's extensive AIDS confidentiality act, Gottfried assisted the Milbank Memorial Fund in convening two meetings in early 2002 for state legislators and their staff members. At those sessions the concept of creating a legal infrastructure for responding to bioterrorism received an enthusiastic response. As of April 2002 the Center for Law and the Public's Health reported that legislation had been introduced in thirty-two states based wholly or in part on the model act (Hodge 2002). In many states, bills were being sponsored by legislators with considerable political influence, in contrast to the first round of bills in the fall of 2001, some of which were introduced by less well-connected lawmakers. Nevertheless, despite such extensive activity, only two states, Utah and South Dakota, had by the spring of 2002 enacted emergency health powers legislation. Only in the case of the former did the model act serve as a template.

Conclusion

Whatever the ultimate legislative outcome, the debate inspired by the MEHPA illuminated the enduring ideological tensions that inform the world of public health. In the 1980s the AIDS epidemic provided the occasion for articulation of a new paradigm of public health. Given biological, epidemiological, and political factors that shaped the public policy discussion, it became possible to assert that no tension existed between public health and civil liberties, that policies that protected the latter would foster the former, and that policies that intruded on rights would subvert the public health. And what was true AIDS was true for public health more generally. Indeed, the experience of AIDS provided the opportunity to rethink the very foundations of public health with its legacy of compulsory state powers. Even when some elements of the privacy- and rights-based approaches to AIDS were subject to modification in the 1990s as the epidemic was "normalized," the core values that had taken hold remained largely undisturbed.

The effort to articulate a new public health ideology masked a conflict that, however dormant, remained prime for exacerbation under appropriate conditions. At one pole were those who, like health and human rights activist Jonathan Mann, had come to believe that "it may be useful to adopt the maxim that health policies and programs should be considered discriminatory and burdensome on human rights until proven otherwise" (Mann, Gostin, and Gruskin 1994, 16). Very different was the view that respect for individual rights, however important, could and should be subordinated to the common good when threats to public health emerged. From this perspective the compulsory vaccination decision of the Supreme Court in 1905 rested on sound moral as well as constitutional assumptions.

It was possible, given the nature of HIV as a behaviorally transmitted virus, to avoid confronting tensions between these ideologies of public health because of the strategic importance of engaging those most at risk in the work of prevention. But with a threat that involved virulent communicable viral or bacteriological agents, such strategic constraints would not inform the discussion. It was inevitable, then, that in the shadow of September 11 the conflict over rights and dangers would resurface, shattering for the time being the illusion of a single guiding vision for public health.

References

Albert, Michael R., Kristen G. Ostheimer, and Joel G. Bremen. 2001. "The Last Smallpox Epidemic in Boston and the Vaccination Controversy, 1901–1903." *New England Journal of Medicine.* 344(5): 375–379.

American Legislative Exchange Council. 2002. "ALEC Opposes the Model State Emergency Health Powers Act." American Legislative Exchange Council web site. Available at www.alec.org/viewpage.cfm?phname=5.103 (visited March 4, 2002).

Annas, George. 2001. Letter to James Hodge. November 1.

Annas, George. 2002. "Bioterrorism, Public Health, and Civil Liberties." *New England Journal of Medicine.* 346: 1337–1342.

Association of American Physicians and Surgeons. 2001. "Model Emergency Health Powers Act (MSEHPA) Turns Governors into Dictators." Association of American Physicians and Surgeons web site. Available at www.aapsonline.org/testimony/emerpower.htm (visited February 4, 2002).

Association of American Physicians and Surgeons. 2002. "Revised Draft of Model State Emergency Health powers Act (Dec. 21) Still a Prescription for Tyranny." Association of American Physicians and Surgeons web site. Available at www.aapsonline.org/testimony/emerpower2.htm (visited February 4, 2002).

Association of State and Territorial Health Officials. 2001. Summary of Comments on October 23, 2001, Draft of Model State Emergency Health Powers Act, November 5. Washington, DC: Association of State and Territorial Health Officials.

Barr, Bob. 2002. "A Fearsome Power Grab by the CDC and State Governors." Congressman Bob Barr web site. Available at hillsource.house.gov/barr/newsdescr.asp?N=20020215170247 (visited March 13, 2002).

Bayer, Ronald. 1988. *Private Acts, Social Consequences: AIDS and the Politics of Public Health.* New York: Basic Books.

Betsch, Michael. 2001. "Bio-terror Response Plan Would Invade Civil Liberties." CNSNews web site. Available at www.cnsnews.com/Nation/Archive/200112/NAT20011211a.html (visited April 15, 2002).

Brown, Donna. 2002. Personal communication to James Colgrove. January 29.

Brownlee, Shannon. 2001. "Why America Isn't Ready for Bioterrorism." The New Republic Online. Available at www.thenewrepublic.com/102901/brownlee102901.html (visited January 23, 2002).

Bor, Jonathan. 1999. "Spreading the Word About Bioterrorism." The Baltimore Sun. December 27, A1.

Center for Law and the Public's Health. 2001a. *The Model State Emergency Health Powers Act (Draft as of October 23, 2001)*. Washington, DC: Center for Law and the Public's Health.

Center for Law and the Public's Health. 2001b. "Model Emergency Health Powers Act in Repsonse to Bioterrorism Written for the CDC and Governors." News release. October 30.

Center for Law and the Public's Health. 2001c. *The Model State Emergency Health Powers Act (Draft as of December 21, 2001)*. Washington, DC: Center for Law and the Public's Health.

Copeland, Larry. 2001. "CDC Proposes Bioterrorism Laws." *USA Today*. November 8, A3.

Durraji Susan Muaddi. 2001. "Model Legislation: Balancing Civil Rights and Public Health." *Johns Hogkins Public Health Magazine*, Special Edition, late Fall 2001. Available at www.jhsph.edu/magazine/model.htm (accessed February 5, 2002).

deFiebre, Conrad. 2001. "More Power Sought to Fight Bioterror." *Star Tribune* (Minneapolis). November 6, B1.

Ernst, Tom. 2001. "Bill Proposes Quarantine Powers During Crisis." *Buffalo News*. November 21, B3.

Fisher, Barbara Loe. 2002. "Editorial: Vaccinating America at Gunpoint." National Vaccine Information Center Web site. Available at www.909shot.com/smallpoxspecialrpt.htm (visited March 13, 2002).

Fox, Daniel. 1988. "From TB to AIDS: Value Conflicts in Reporting Disease." *Hastings Center Report*. 16 (December): 11–17.

Fox, Daniel. 2002. Interview with Ronald Bayer. March 7.

Freed, G.L., S.L. Katz, and S.J. Clark. 1996. "Safety of Vaccinations. Miss America, the Media, and Public Health." *Journal of the American Medical Association*. 276(23): 1869–1872.

Garrett, Laurie. 1999. "Wake-Up Call on Germ Warfare." *Newsday*. February 21, A4.

Gillis, Justin. 2001. "States Weighing Laws to Fight Bioterrorism." *Washington Post*. November 19, A1.

Gottfried, Richard. 2002. Interview with Ronald Bayer. March 14.

Govern, Jodi. 2002. Interview with James Colgrove. March 18.

Guiden, Mary. 2001. "Lawmakers Not Keen on 'Model' Public Health Law." Available at www1.stateline.org/print_story.do;jsessionid=gi6uwx9ld1?storyId=212079 (visited March 4, 2001).

Health Privacy Project, Institute for Health Care Research and Policy, Georgetown University. 2001. Letter to Lawrence O. Gostin. November 7.

Health Privacy Project, Institute for Health Care Research and Policy, Georgetown University. 2002. "Health Privacy Project Comments on Model State Emergency Health Powers Act, January 18, 2002." Washington, DC: Institute for Health Care Research and Policy.

Henderson, D.A. 2001. "Biopreparedness and Public Health." *American Journal of Public Health*. 91(12): 1917–1918.

Hodge, James. 2002. Personal communication to Ronald Bayer.

Hull, Henry. 2002. Interview with Ronald Bayer. March 7.

In re Halko. 1966. 54 Cal. Report. 661.

Jacobson v. Commonwealth of Massachusetts. 1905. 197 U.S. 11.

Karst, K.L. 1980. "The Freedom of Intimate Association." *Yale Law Journal*. 99: 624–692.

Kaufman, Martin. 1967. "The American Anti-Vaccinationists and Their Arguments." *Bulletin of the History of Medicine*. 41.5: 463–478.

Lambda Legal Defense and Education Fund. 2001. Letter to Lawrence O. Gostin. December 20.

Lasalandra, Michael. 2001. "Smallpox Attack Preparedness Plan Would Give Officials Sweeping Powers." *Boston Herald*. November 8, 16.

Leavitt, Judith Walzer. 1982. *The Healthiest City: Milwaukee and the Politics of Health Reform*. Princeton, NJ: Princeton University Press.

Mann, Jonathan M., Lawrence Gostin, and Sofia Gruskin. 1994. "Health and Human Rights." *Health and Human Rights*. 1: 7–23.

Markel, Howard. 1997. *Quarantine! East European Jewish Immigrants and the New York City Epidemics of 1892*. Baltimore: Johns Hopkins University Press.

Matthews, Gene. 2002. Interview with Ronald Bayer. March 6.

McKenna, M.A.J. 2001. "CDC Pushes Bill Boosting States' Powers." *Atlanta Journal and Constitution*. October 30, A8.

New England Coalition for Law and Public Health. 2001. Letter to Health and Human Services Secretary Tommy Thompson. November 13.

New York Civil Liberties Union. 2002. Testimony of Robert Perry on behalf of the New York Civil Liberties Union before the Assembly Standing Committee on Health and the Assembly Standing Committee on Codes Concerning the Model State Emergency Health Powers Act. March 14.

Parmet, Wendy. 1985. "AIDS and Quarantine: The Revival of an Archaic Doctrine." *Hofstra Law Review*. 14: 53–90.

Parmet, Wendy E. and Wendy K. Mariner. 2001. "A Health Act that Jeopardizes Public Health." *Boston Globe*. December 1, A15.

Pratt, Ted. 2001. Memorandum to Lawrence Gostin, James Hodge, and Richard Goodman. November 8.

Reilly, Kevin. 2002. Interview with James Colgrove. March 6.

Reiss, Lisa. 2002. Testimony on behalf of Connecticut Vaccine Information Alliance before Public Health Committee of Connecticut State Assembly. February 19.

Richardson, Dawn. 2002. Posting to groups.yahoo.com/group/i-v-y/message/5971 (visited March 18, 2002).

Rosenzweig, Peggy. 2002. Interview with James Colgrove. March 15.

Schlafly, Phyllis. 2001. "Where Do Politicians Go in Their Afterlife?" *Toogood Reports*. December 20. www.toogoodreports.com/column/general/schlafly/122001.htm (visited March 4, 2002).

Sidel, Victor W., Hillel W. Cohen, and Robert M. Gould. 2001. "Good Intentions and the Road to Bioterrorism Preparedness." *American Journal of Public Health*. 91.5: 716–718.

Tansey, Bernadette. 2001. "Health Bill Endangers Civil Rights." *San Francisco Chronicle*. November 25, A1.

Thacker, S.B. and R.L. Berkleman. 1988. "Public Health Surveillance in the United States." *Epidemiologic Reviews*. 10: 164–190.

Thomasian, John. 2002. Interview with James Colgrove. March 8.

Tribe, Lawrence. 1978. *American Constitutional Law*. Mineola: New York Foundation Press.

U.S. Department of Health and Human Services. 2001. "Statement by HHS Secretary Tommy G. Thompson regarding the Model Emergency Health Powers Act." News release. October 30.

Winslow, C.-E.A. 1929. *The Life of Hermann Biggs*. Philadelphia: Lea & Febiger.

II
Resource Allocation

5

Triage in Response to a Bioterrorist Attack

James F. Childress

Bioterrorism and Triage

In a letter dated August 30, 2001, and read before the U.S. Senate Committee on Foreign Relations on September 5, 2001, Joshua Lederberg (2001b, 6), a Nobel laureate, focused on the threat of biological warfare; that is, "use of agents of disease for hostile purposes." Noting that up to a dozen countries have developed such a capability, he further observed:

Considerable harm could be done (on the scale of, say, a thousand casualties) by rank amateurs. Terrorist groups, privately or state-sponsored, with funds up to $1 million, could mount massive attacks of 10 or 100 times that scale. Important to keep in mind: if the ultimate casualty roster is 1,000, there will have been 100,000 or 1,000,000 at risk in the target zone, legitimately demanding prophylactic attention, and in turn a draconian triage. Several exercises have given dramatic testimony to how difficult would be governmental management of such incidents, and the stresses on civil order that would follow from inevitable inequities in that management.[1]

Among numerous difficult issues that such bioterrorist attacks raise are several ethical ones, particularly those surrounding draconian triage in light of the limited surge capacity of the health care system, including public health and medical care. One question is whether inevitable inequalities in access to medical resources in any system of triage, rationing, or allocation in response to a bioterrorist attack are necessarily, as Lederberg suggested, inevitable in the sense of injustice and unfairness. Justice in its formal sense requires that we treat equals equally and similar cases similarly, and fairness at a minimum requires impartial treatment. Unless triage, rationing, and allocation are always unjust and unfair, a claim that is implausible, the critical ethical question concerns which material criteria of justice are defensible. If formal justice requires treating similar persons in a similar way, it is essential to determine which similarities (and dissimilarities) are morally relevant, and this is the function of material criteria. Different theories of justice in general and in relation to specific problems, such as rationing health care, identify different properties or characteristics as relevant and allocation that befits those properties or characteristics (Beauchamp and Childress 2001).[2]

Two policy analysts note:

Earlier, policymakers spoke of the general problem of allocating scarce medical resources, a formulation that implied hard but generally manageable choices of a largely pragmatic nature. Now the discussion increasingly is of rationing scarce medical resources, a harsher term that connotes emergency—even war-time—circumstances requiring some societal triage mechanism. (Rettig and Lohr 1981)

This comment focuses on problems of distributing health care in the society at large, but it applies with particular force to distributing various kinds of health care, for example, vaccines, prophylactic measures, therapy, and supportive care, after a bioterrorist attack. Rationing and triage do seem harsher than allocation in ordinary discourse. But even a rigorous distributional system, which may seem harsh and even draconian, may not be unjust and unjustified by utilitarian or egalitarian approaches. Some ethicists favor the "more neutral and descriptive language of patient selection" (Kilner 1990, xi). However, I focus here on the model of triage, because it is commonly used, widely discussed, and perhaps the most instructive, but I also use the language of rationing, allocation, distribution, and selection, as appropriate.

"Triage," a French word meaning sorting, picking, grading, or selecting according to quality, was first applied in English (as early as 1717) to separation of wool by quality and later to separation of coffee beans into three classes: best quality, middling, and triage. The last class, consisting of bad or broken beans, was the lowest grade. The French under Napoleon developed a system of sorting casualties in war, but did not call it triage until later. Triage in war implied giving the worst-off, rather than the best-off, priority (within limits). In the U.S. Civil War, treatment was usually provided in turn without regard to wounded soldiers' specific conditions. However, in World War I, the U.S. Army adopted the idea of a sorting station from the French and the British armies as well as the term triage, which, by World War II, was not as widespread as the term sorting. One statement of U.S. military policy is that triage-sorting

implies the evaluation and classification of casualties for purposes of treatment and evacuation. *It is based on the principle of accomplishing the greatest good for the greatest number of wounded and injured men in the special circumstances of warfare at a particular time.* The decision which must be made concerns the need for resuscitation, the need for emergency surgery and the futility of surgery because of the intrinsic lethality of the wound. Sorting also involves the establishment of priorities for treatment and evacuation (emphasis added; Rund and Rausch 1980, 9).

Similar formal policies have been adopted for civilian disasters, such as a nuclear disaster and earthquakes. As a result of the great increase in use of emergency rooms, hospitals established triage systems in the early 1960s to facilitate treatment of emergency patients. In such systems, a triage officer quickly assesses patients' needs as immediate (posing a threat of death or serious physical impairment if not treated immediately), urgent (requiring prompt but not immediate treatment), and nonurgent, or in a more complex five-category system as life-threatening, urgent, semiurgent, nonurgent, and no need for care.[3]

Thus triage largely refers to particular systems of allocation or rationing but is not equivalent to allocation, rationing, or distribution in general. As a specific system, triage sorts or grades persons according to their needs and probable outcomes of interventions. In its more formal developments, it classifies persons according to set categories. Furthermore, medical triage is a form of allocation or rationing under critical or emergency circumstances, where decisions must be made immediately about particular patients because some of them probably have life-threatening conditions and not all of them can be treated at once.

Utilitarian and Egalitarian Approaches to Triage

Medical and Social Utility

Triage is one way to ration health care when caregivers cannot meet everyone's needs at the same time and to the same degree. Systems of triage, whether informal or formal, all have an implicit or explicit utilitarian rationale—they were designed to produce the greatest good for the greatest number by meeting human needs most effectively and efficiently under conditions of scarcity. They are designed to satisfy the formal criterion of justice—to treat similar cases similarly and equals equally—and their material criteria for distribution, at a minimum, focus on patients' needs and/or probability of successful treatment.

Those who deny that triage has a utilitarian rationale fail to distinguish *medical utility* from *social utility*. And those who recognize but reject utilitarian triage often ignore this distinction too (see, for example, Baker and Strosberg 1992). In addition, critics may fail to see that utility is one important principle alongside several others, that it merits serious consideration at every point, and that, in certain forms, it is compatible with egalitarian approaches. Indeed, there is a prima facie moral duty, although not an absolute one, to produce the greatest good for the greatest number, subject to other moral limits and constraints.

In its simplest formulation, the principle of utility requires that we assess actions, practices, and policies according to whether or not they fulfill this duty. In medical utility the relevant population includes only those who currently have medical needs or are at risk for such needs. Allocation decisions that seek to maximize the welfare of that population compare respective needs and probabilities of benefit of different parties in order to do the greatest good for the greatest number.

If triage is understood as the classification of persons in need or at risk in order to satisfy medical utility, assigning priority to the best off or the worst off or some mix should depend less on principle than on the particular context, including such factors as available personnel and technologies, and when, if ever, additional resources can be expected. For instance, what can and should be done for persons who have been exposed to or are at risk of exposure to different biological agents will vary from context to context.

Pesik, Keim, and Iserson (2001, 644) identified several factors that they believe should and should not be considered in rationing scarce resources in response to a terrorist attack. All of the criteria they proposed involve medical utility, but one also involves (narrow) social utility, whereas the criteria they oppose mainly involve (broad) social utility. Their list is generally sound, but it neglects some important social functions or special responsibilities that may merit attention and priority in the event of a bioterrorist attack.

Should Consider	Should Not Consider
Likelihood of benefit	Age, ethnicity, or gender
Effect on improving quality of life	Talents, abilities, disabilities, or deformities
Duration of benefit	Socioeconomic status, social worth, or political position
Urgency of the patient's condition	Coexistent conditions that do not affect short-term prognosis
Direct multiplier effect among emergency caregivers	Drug or alcohol abuse
Amount of resources required for successful treatment	Antisocial or aggressive behaviors

Degree of need and probability of success, particularly the latter, have been featured in triage systems based on medical utility. The relevant and morally justifiable material criteria in the context of a terrorist attack include likelihood of benefit, effect on quality of life, duration of benefit, and urgency of need (Pesik et al. 2001). Another criterion focuses on the amount of resources required; this is what others sometimes call the principle of conservation (Winslow 1982, 73–76, 142–143). "The likelihood of benefit using minimal resources takes precedence to maximize the efficient use of scarce medical supplies" (Pesik et al. 2001, 644). In short, "practitioners must prioritize intervention to those who will benefit most from the fewest resources" (Pesik et al. 2001, 644). Their criteria and their concentration on probable benefit with the fewest resources are justifiable within a framework of medical utility in response to a bioterrorist attack.

More problematic, however, is their claim that this formulation "widens the scope of patients for whom medical intervention is deemed futile" (Pesik et al. 2001, 644). It is a mistake to use the language of futility to characterize a judgment made on the basis of medical utility. Medical interventions should be deemed futile only when they cannot be performed because of the patient's condition, would not produce a physiological effect, or would not produce benefit (Beauchamp and Childress 2001, 133–35, 161–62). When medical interventions are denied to particular individuals in order to provide them to others who have a higher probability of benefit with use of fewer resources, that is a matter of utility, not futility. Those interventions would not necessarily be futile for individuals who do not receive them; rather they are unjustifiable in the system of utilitarian triage as long as resources are limited. Describing such a triage system as widening the scope of futility ignores the harsh reality and invites self-deception.

Another criterion that Pesik and colleagues propose is "direct multiplier effect among emergency caregivers." Even though it seeks to maximize medical utility, it is also a criterion of (narrow) social utility, because it assigns priority on the basis of a specific social function. It is important not only to distinguish medical utility and social utility, while recognizing that they may overlap at points, but also to distinguish two types of social utilitarian judgments: narrow and broad social utility.

Triage has often included social utility, as well as medical utility, in military and civilian disasters. It seeks to salvage those in need, and salvageability may reflect both medical and social judgments. For instance, according to a major text on surgical triage in the military, "traditionally, the military value of surgery lies in the salvage of battle casualties. This is not merely a matter of saving life; it is primarily one of returning the wounded to duty, and the earlier the better" (Winslow 1982, 11). A similar expansion of salvageability in triage occurs in civilian disasters, such as plans in San Francisco to cope with a devastating earthquake or national plans to cope with nuclear destruction (Winslow 1982). In the debate about triage after nuclear destruction, Thomas O'Donnell (1960, 70), a moral theologian, maintained that "those casualties whose immediate therapy offers most hope for the conservation of the common good should receive first priority." Furthermore, "unless the individual is considered as very important to the common good, and is salvable, it would seem unreasonable for the medical personnel to expend their efficiency on a few when it could be conserved for the greater number in more remediable need." This proposal, he noted, was in accord with national policy regarding a nuclear disaster (O'Donnell 1960, 70). Even though the language of "conservation of the common good" appears to be unduly broad and vague, triage that reflects such conceptions generally operates with a narrow formulation of social utility limited to specific functions and roles within a circumscribed context.

Even the strongest opponents of social utilitarian frameworks of rationing may recognize exceptions to a more egalitarian approach, such as a lottery or queuing. For instance, Paul Ramsey (1970) generally called for random allocation of scarce life-saving medical resources once judgments of medical utility had been made and scarcity remained. His egalitarian reasoning focused on the equal worth of human lives (Ramsey 1970, 255). In addition, he stressed the difficulty, if not impossibility, of securing agreement about relevant social values in an unfocused, pluralistic society such as ours. Generally, a "society is largely an unfocused meshing of human pursuits" (Ramsey 1970, 275). Nevertheless, Ramsey accepted limited social utilitarian exceptions to an egalitarian framework in certain circumscribed or focused contexts; for instance, he justified assigning priority to persons at risk when they can discharge specific functions highly valued by the community in a crisis or emergency such as an earthquake. These functions would be similar to those performed by sailors on a lifeboat after shipwreck (Ramsey 1970).

In the lifeboat analogy, a pluralistic community, with a variety of values and goals, becomes focused in some disasters as a result of a substantial threat to its survival. Its survival becomes an overriding goal, in part because it is a condition for realizing other goals. Ramsey sometimes suggested that a community could justifiably become focused on goals other than survival and use those goals to identify exceptional social functions for which people should be saved. At any rate, he rejected exceptions based on individuals' broad social worth (their overall social value) in a pluralistic society. He only admitted exceptions based on specific and urgent instrumental social value, judged according to essential social functions, in limited and focused circumstances: "Triage decisions are all a function of the narrowly defined, exceptional purposes to which a community of men may have been reduced. In these terms, comparative social worthiness can be measured" (Ramsey 1970, 258). A society, or parts of a society, under bioterrorist attack would become such a focused community, with its very survival possibly at stake. Hence, judgments of narrow social utility could be justified in such a setting.

In the case of natural or man-made disasters, victims most in need of help—on whom normally we would lavish resources—must simply be set aside, and nothing be done for them. First priority must be given to victims who can quickly be restored to functioning. They are needed to bury the dead to prevent epidemic. They can serve as amateur medics or nurses with a little instruction—as the triage officer directs the community's remaining medical resources to a middle group of the seriously but not-so-seriously injured majority. Even among these, I suppose a physician should first be treated. (Ramsey 1970, 258)

Most of the criteria that Pesik and colleagues excluded, as I suggested, pertain to broad social utility or social value. Nevertheless, in concentrating on medical utility and one criterion that combines medical utility with narrow social utility (the direct multiplier effect among emergency caregivers), they failed to see that a bioterrorist attack may threaten the social system as well as the health care system, and that some social functions other than those related to health care may be essential to prevent major social disruption. Hence, in some contexts, political position, which they excluded, could be essential to communal survival. Later I return to how we might determine essential specific social functions and roles.

Egalitarian Perspectives

How do these different conceptions of utility in triage systems fit with egalitarian concerns? It is important to stress that they are not all equally problematic from an egalitarian standpoint. First, in contrast to what some egalitarian critics claim, medical utility does not infringe the principle of equal regard for individual persons and their lives. My claim presupposes that counting numbers of lives is compatible with a principle of equal regard for human lives, but this presupposition has been challenged. For example, John Taurek (1977) contended that numbers should not count in deciding whether to distribute a lifesaving drug to save five persons or to save one person when it is not possible to do both. Let's suppose that a drug could save either the five or the one, but not all, because of their respective medical conditions. Taurek (1977, 303) proposed the following in response to such an example:

Here are six human beings. I can empathize with each of them. I would not like to see any of them die. But I cannot save everyone. Why not give each person an equal chance to survive? Perhaps I would flip a coin. Heads, I give my drug to these five. Tails, I give it to this one. In this way I give each of the six persons a fifty-fifty chance of surviving. Where such an option is open to me it would seem to best express my equal concern and respect for each person.

By contrast, I maintain that numbers should count and that they can count without infringing equal concern or respect for each person. Without considering all of Taurek's positions, I contend that it is implausible for him to suggest, as he does (1977, 315–316), that saving the many over the one is like saving the rich over the poor. Instead, as Derek Parfit (1978, 301) held in criticizing "innumerate ethics," "if we give the rich priority, we do not give equal weight to saving each. Why do we save the larger number? Because we *do* give equal weight to saving each. Each counts for one. That is why more counts for more."

Making such a judgment of medical utility may even be morally required in some cases. Even when an owner of a drug has to decide how to use it, we can argue that he or she has an obligation to attempt to save more people, if possible, over the one person, absent more stringent, special moral relations such as contracts. In the context of a bioterrorist attack, citizens would believe that they have as much right to medical care as any others. Taurek would explain this moral intuition by a sense of prior social agreement about the use of a resource, perhaps involving social contributions through taxation.

Although medical utility does not infringe the principle of equal regard for individual lives, social utility does. But judgments of social utility are themselves variable, as I have stressed in distinguishing broad and narrow social utility. Either one infringes the principle of equal regard or respect. Judgments of broad social utility recognize the different social value of people's lives taken as a whole, including their various functions and roles. By contrast, judgments of narrow social utility recognize the different values of specific social functions and roles and assign priority to individuals discharging certain functions and performing certain roles.

Judgments of broad social utility infringe on equal regard, and it is not justifiable to use them as a basis for rationing in general or in an emergency, such as a bioterrorist attack. Nevertheless, it is possible to justify triage based on narrow social utility, at least when focused on specific and urgent functions and essential services in some crises and emergencies.

Even if a narrow social utilitarian framework is adopted together with medical utility, reasons may exist to include other egalitarian considerations and approaches. Egalitarians often favor approaches, at least within the limits of medical utility, that express transcendence of persons over their social roles and provide rough equality of opportunity. Hence, some prefer a mechanism, such as a lottery or queuing, that embodies these values.

One possibility that merits public deliberation is a weighted lottery (Elster 1989, 47–48, 113–115; Elster 1992, 110). From a social utilitarian standpoint, it is crucial to ensure that enough individuals survive who can discharge essential social functions, but it may not be necessary to save all individuals who hold such roles. Indeed, it may be fair and just to put essential workers and their families at some risk through a weighted lottery, in which these individuals would receive additional weights to ensure that enough of them will be saved to meet defined social needs, including but not limited to the provision of health care. In this system, some persons in essential social roles would not receive treatment. One position holds that using a lottery or queuing in rationing, rather than social utilitarian allocation, would probably have the result that those in social power who are at risk would take steps to increase the supply of resources in order to reduce their risk of exclusion.

Several considerations support a possible role for a lottery, even if it is heavily weighted, in the context of tragic choices in response to a bioterrorist attack. As Barbara Goodwin (1992, 178) observed, "Quite unphilosophical human beings have resorted to the lottery to make tragic choices in the context of natural or man-made disasters for a long time. When a group of people must distribute some unavoidable evil between themselves, they will almost instinctively choose a lottery as the method even if in the early stages of the discussion each is concerned to assert why she herself should not receive the evil allocation." In addition, the optimal context for the lottery, if it is to be just and viewed as just, is a "consensual group," particularly one with a common purpose.

As we have seen, however, when a group has a common purpose, when it becomes a focused community, it may be possible to make some allocative decisions on the basis of (limited) social utilitarian criteria; for example, who is necessary for the community's survival? Nevertheless, if the only common purpose is that each individual in the group wants to survive, for example, patients awaiting an organ transplant or those in the intensive care unit, a lottery or first-come, first-served, which Ramsey calls "an ongoing lottery," may embody equal respect, impartial treatment, and fairness in the competition, if medical utility does not determine the outcome. Thus, a lottery would express and symbolize some fundamental values, and it would be a way around the lack of consensus in an unfocused, pluralistic society about social utilitarian allocation criteria. In some circumstances of tragic choice, people rightly view the lottery as an acceptable way to allocate goods and burdens because of the limits of mindful choice, the blindness or impartiality of the lottery, and "the moral judgment that people should be treated as absolutely equal where basic life chances (chances of life or survival) are involved" (Goodwin 1992, 178).

In the 1990s lotteries were used several times to distribute new drugs that were available in only limited supply. Sometimes candidates for these agents, such as protease inhibitors to treat AIDS, either proposed or agreed to a lottery within certain limits set by medical utility. For instance, when Hoffman-LaRoche decided to offer Inviarase to patients with advanced AIDS outside current clinical trials, Dr. Alberto Avendano of the National Association of People with AIDS proposed a lottery, and both the drug manufacturer and the Food and Drug Administration agreed. Sixty percent of the first 2,000 slots were set aside for patients with CD4 counts less than $50\,mm^3$. According to Dr. Avendano, "The lottery seemed the closest to the most fair way." (Naughton 1995, 14–15) Although some held that patients with AIDS who had participated in clinical trials should have priority, others stressed the symbolic value of the lotteries. As Evan DeRenzo put it, "Lotteries say that after you meet medical criteria, all persons should have an equal shot at the good of society. Lotteries celebrate an understanding that all humans are endowed with equal dignity" (Naughton 1995, 14–15).

Perhaps the closest society can come to a community of consent is to ensure transparency and public participation in setting procedures and material criteria for triage in response to a possible bioterrorist attack, and it should do so.

Public Justification: Transparency, Participation, and Cooperation

My points presuppose a context of public justification. Even when criteria for rationing or triage are set primarily or exclusively by physicians, they operate in a public context. Secrecy is often impossible, as well as ethically problematic, in part because of the public nature of much health care, especially in hospitals. Because a health care team is involved, criteria must be justifiable to all participants. Even triage decisions in intensive care units are "public." They are made "in the presence of and with the involvement of a wide variety of interested spectators, other physicians and nurses, along with family members and friends" (Knaus 1989). One might even add administrators, insurers, and regulators. Thus, "public accountability" is necessary to ensure adequate representation of our pluralistic society. In addition to these general reasons for transparency and public accountability in setting triage criteria, specific reasons apply in the preparation for a possible bioterrorist attack.

Triage that may be required in response to such an attack may look very different from conventional triage in the emergency room and other civilian contexts, in part because of immediate uncertainty and diagnostic challenges. Emergency physicians Pesik, Keim, and Iserson (2001) propose that "to address these issues [raised by weapons of mass-destruction-terrorism—WMD-T] to the maximum benefit of our patients, we must first develop collective forethought and a broad-based consensus that these decisions must reach beyond the hospital emergency department." They continue: "Critical decisions like these should not be made on an individual case-by-case basis. Physicians should never be placed in a position of individually deciding to deny treatment to patients without the guidance of a policy or protocol" (Pesik et al. 2001, 642). Physicians, together with "emergency care providers, personnel, hospital administrators, religious leaders, and medical ethics committees need to engage in bioethical decisionmaking before an acute bioterrorist attack" (Pesik et al. 2001, 642).

This recommendation is too restricted; it has to be extended to ensure both transparency and public participation, in a context of public justification.[4] Public trust will be essential in a bioterrorist crisis. Hence, the public must have confidence in the procedures and standards of triage. Some people, perhaps many, will not receive vaccination, prophylaxis, or treatment. As a result, criteria must be publicly articulated and defended in advance.

Beyond public articulation and defense, procedures and standards of triage have to be developed with public participation, and here I go beyond the list of participants identified by Pesik and colleagues to include the general public. Public participation rests on several foundations. It is a matter of justice—the right to participate in decisions, especially government decisions, that may have a fundamental impact on life chances—and a matter of symbolic values, particularly the equal value of all, as well as a matter of building and maintaining public trust.

Organ allocation in the United States is instructive. Criteria for selecting recipients for organs from the waiting list are public and they were developed and modified with public participation, in part because the public's role is so crucial; it is they who provide the organs, and their trust is essential to their willingness to donate (Childress 1997). In response to a bioterrorist attack, maintaining the social order as well as the system of health care will depend on public cooperation, while some, perhaps many, individuals suffer and die. For voluntary cooperation, the public must perceive the triage as necessary and the procedures and standards as fair.

Public officials may be reluctant to disclose information to and invite the participation of the public in preparing for a possible bioterrorist attack because they view members of the public as nonparticipants in and perhaps even as obstacles to effective responses. In contrast, others hold that the public should be viewed as a capable partner and a capable ally; that a "generally effective and adaptive collective action" is possible, and that "failure to involve the public as a key partner in the medical and public-health response could hamper effective management of an epidemic and increase the likelihood of social disruption" (Glass and Schoch-Spana 2002). These authors propose five useful guidelines for integrating the public into planning responses to bioterrorism: "(1) treat the public as a capable ally in the response to an epidemic, (2) enlist civic organizations in practical public health activities, (3) anticipate the need for home-based patient care and infection control, (4) invest in public outreach and communication strategies, and (5) ensure planning that reflects the values and priorities of affected populations" (Glass and Schoch-Spana 2002, 217). Whether their proposal of a network of public responders is excessively optimistic, at minimum, there must be basic public confidence, trust, and cooperation; otherwise social disruption will be a high risk.

Public justification will be all the more difficult, but all the more indispensable, if criteria of triage are partially social utilitarian, even in the narrow sense. Determining which social functions are essential requires broad societal participation in order to reflect "the values and priorities of affected populations" (Baker and Strosberg 1992). Social utilitarian systems of allocation are inherently unstable and require either nondisclosure and deception or coercion for their maintenance. Instead individuals in need or at risk in contexts of limited medical resources will consent only to egalitarian criteria (Baker and Strosberg 1992). Certainly, a strongly egalitarian approach, such as a lottery or queuing, has widespread and justifiable appeal. However, in asserting their broad claim, Baker and Strosberg failed to distinguish medical utility from social utility and narrow from broad social utility. As a result, they failed to establish that triage based on medical utility, together with narrow social utility in an emergency created, for instance, by a bioterrorist attack, would not be publicly justifiable and stable, especially if the public has participated in the process of setting the criteria.

Another important issue that requires public attention concerns the families of essential social personnel. The status of families may be particularly important if a bioterrorist attack converts the initial victims into secondary agents, that is, individuals who can infect others. Even though this is not true for anthrax, it is true for several other possible biological agents including smallpox and plague. For instance, in May 20–23, 2000, Denver, Colorado, conducted a bioterrorism exercise called Operation Topoff. As this simulated attack unfolded, participants learned that plague aerosol had been covertly released three days earlier at the city's center for the performing arts, with over 2,000 cases of pneumonic plague, many deaths, and hundreds of secondary cases. Richard Hoffman and Jane Norton (2000), both of Colorado Department of Public Health and Environment, noted that

As more cases were identified, an anticipated issue emerged: who should receive antimicrobial prophylaxis? The governor's committee debated whether to limit prophylaxis to close contacts of infectious cases or offer it more widely (e.g., to all health-care workers, first responders, and public safety workers *and their families*) to gain the support and participation of key workers. The committee decided on the latter approach, but not unanimously (emphasis added).

The rationale in providing antimicrobial prophylaxis to families of key workers, as well as workers themselves, focused on the need to secure their voluntary cooperation, which would be critically important. The public's trust walled also be critically important, and it would be contingent in part on the public's perception that triage is necessary and fair.

This point also emerges from an analysis of the 2001 exercise Dark Winter, in which decision makers were presented with a fictional bioterrorist attack involving smallpox and had "to react to the facts and

context of the scenario, establish strategies, and make policy decisions."
According to one summary of the lessons of the exercise,

Dark Winter participants worried that it would not be possible to forcibly impose vaccination or travel restrictions on large groups of the population without their general cooperation. To gain that cooperation, the President and other leaders in Dark Winter recognized the importance of persuading their constituents that there was fairness in the distribution of vaccine and other scarce resources, that the disease-containment measures were for the general good of society, that all possible measures were being taken to prevent the further spread of the disease, and that the government remained firmly in control despite the expanding epidemic. (O'Toole, Mair, and Ingelsby 2002, 982)

Engendering and maintaining the public's trust will be more likely if the public has participated in setting procedures and material criteria and hence in determining what to emphasize in medical utility, which functions and roles are essential in judgments of narrow social utility, whether to include families as well as individuals whose functions and roles are essential, whether to provide prophylaxis and other treatments to all individuals in certain roles or to have a weighted lottery, and so forth. Such determinations are not clear cut, as the Denver experience indicated ("The committee decided but not unanimously"), and the public should participate in making them. As noted, the issues become even more difficult when, to contain infectious diseases, quarantine becomes necessary. The observation is sound that "The public will not take the pill if it does not trust the doctor."

When societies confront tragic choices, where fundamental social-cultural values are at stake, they must "attempt to make allocations in ways that preserve the moral foundations of social collaboration" (Calabresi and Bobbitt 1979, 18).

Notes

1. Although this letter (Lederberg 2001b) is very similar to a statement that Lederberg presented to the same committee on August 24, 2002, some of the language differs. Instead of "draconian triage," Lederberg referred to "massive triage." And, instead of "the stresses on civil order that would follow from inevitable inequities in that management," he noted "the stresses that control of such incidents would impose on civil order" (Lederberg 2001a). These different statements reflect a difference in tone if not in substance.

2. I have drawn some ideas about and formulations of these ethical issues, including a few paragraphs, from Childress, *Practical Reasoning in Bioethics* (1997).

3. Much of the previous two paragraphs derives from Childress (1997, 195–196). For this history, see Winslow (1982) and Rund and Rausch (1980), among others.

4. We also have to ensure that physicians, public health professionals, and other health care professionals are at the table when government officials formulate policies for possible bioterrorist attacks. One lesson from the Dark Winter exercise is that, "After a bioterrorist attack, leaders' decisions would depend on data and expertise from the medical and public health sectors"; another is that, "To end a disease outbreak after a bioterrorist attack, decision makers will require ongoing expert advice from senior public health and medical leaders" (O'Toole et al. 2002, 981–82). But prospective policies should also reflect those data, expertise, and advice.

References

Baker, Robert and Martin Strosberg. 1992. "Triage and Equality: An Historical Reassessment of Utilitarian Analyses of Triage." *Kennedy Institute of Ethics Journal.* 2 (June): 103–123.

Beauchamp, Tom L. and James F. Childress. 2001. *Principles of Biomedical Ethics,* 5th ed. New York: Oxford University Press.

Calabresi, Guido and Philip Bobbitt. 1978. *Tragic Choices.* New York: W.W. Norton & Company.

Childress, James F. 1997. *Practical Reasoning in Bioethics.* Bloomington: Indiana University Press.

Elster, Jon. 1989. *Solomonic Judgements.* Cambridge: Cambridge University Press.

Elster, Jon. 1992. *Local Justice: How Institutions Allocate Scarce Goods and Necessary Burdens.* New York: Russell Sage Foundation.

Glass, Thomas A. and Monica Schoch-Spana. 2002. "Bioterrorism and the People: How to Vaccinate a City against Panic." *Clinical Infectious Diseases.* 34: 217–223.

Goodwin, Barbara. 1992. *Justice by Lottery.* Chicago: University of Chicago Press.

Hoffman, Richard E. and Jane E. Norton. 2000. "Lessons Learned from a Full-Scale Bioterrorism Exercise." *Emerging Infectious Diseases.* 6.6: 652–653.

Kilner, John. 1990. *Who Lives? Who Dies: Ethical Criteria in Patient Selection.* New Haven, CT: Yale University Press.

Knaus, William. 1989. "Criteria for Admission to Intensive Care Units." In *Rationing of Medical Care for the Critically Ill,* 44–51. Washington, DC: Brookings Institution.

Lederberg, Joshua. 2001a. Testimony before the Committee on Foreign Relations, U.S. Senate, One Hundred Seventh Congress. August 24.

Lederberg, Joshua, 2001b. Letter to Hon. Joseph R. Biden, Jr., August 30, 2001, in *The Threat of Bioterrorism and the Spread of Infectious Diseases*. Hearing before the Committee on Foreign Relations, U.S. Senate, One Hundred Seventh Congress, First Session. September 5, 5–8. Washington, DC: U.S. Government Printing Office.

Naughton, Diane. 1995. "Drug Lotteries Raise Questions: Some Experts Say System of Distribution May Be Unfair." *Washington Post Health*, September 26, 14–15.

O'Donnell, Thomas. 1960. "The Morality of Triage." *Georgetown Medical Bulletin*. 14 (August).

O'Toole, Tara, Michael Mair, and Thomas V. Ingelsby. 2002. "Shining Light on 'Dark Winter'." *Clinical Infectious Diseases*. 34 (April 1): 972–983.

Parfit, Derek. 1978. "Innumerate Ethics." *Philosophy and Public Affairs*. 7 (Summer): 285–301.

Pesik, Nikki, Mark E. Keim, and Kenneth V. Iserson. 2001. "Terrorism and the Ethics of Emergency Medical Care." *Annals of Emergency Medicine*. 37.6: 642–646.

Ramsey, Paul. 1970. *Patient as Person*. New Haven, CT: Yale University Press.

Rettig, Richard and Kathleen Lohr. 1981. "Ethical Dimensions of Allocating Scarce Resources in Medicine: A Cross-National Study of End-Stage Renal Disease." Unpublished manuscript.

Rund, Douglas A. and Tondra S. Rausch. 1980. *Triage*. St. Louis: C.V. Mosby.

Taurek, John M. 1977. "Should the Numbers Count?" *Philosophy and Public Affairs*. 6 (Summer): 293–316.

Winslow, Gerald R. 1982. *Triage and Justice: The Ethics of Rationing Life-Saving Medical Resources*. Berkeley: University of California Press.

6

Overwhelming Casualties: Medical Ethics in a Time of Terror

Kenneth Kipnis

The events of September 11, 2001, have a peculiar significance for me. Like many, I was astounded by the damage that could be done by a few men armed with box cutters. And like millions who identify as New Yorkers, I was outraged by the insult to lower Manhattan: to its architectural integrity, its infrastructure, its people, to the very idea of New York. As I write, crowds gather daily to peer into the city's open wound, trying, I expect, to wrap their minds around what has come to pass.

But I have been doing medical ethics for decades, focusing regularly on "scarce resource problems." So even as the towers were pancaking into memory, I began to fixate on the challenges New York's health care system would face caring for the wounded.

Later on, it was sobering to contemplate that the city was able to respond as well as it did, in part, because so many of the victims were killed outright. As violent as the attack had been, only a few seriously injured survivors came to nearby hospitals. The stories I heard described hundreds of clinicians and volunteers waiting for the waves of wounded who never arrived. What if it had been different? What if, as had been expected, the wounded had been many?

We have now seen anthrax turned into a weapon and are warned that even deadlier agents are out there: smallpox and other pestilential scourges, nuclear and chemical weapons, and the terrorists who would use these against us. As a teacher and consultant, I had often rehearsed the dilemmas that arise in military and disaster medicine, strategies doctors have developed for managing things when ordinary routines fail. But September 11 could have been a medical catastrophe overwhelming even backup plans. I had a professional responsibility to comprehend the management of very large numbers of civilian casualties, but I didn't know my way around that topic, nor did I know any medical ethicists who did. While the attack left a smoking crater in lower Manhattan, it also exposed a gaping hole in our understanding. This is my effort to fill it.

Distributive Justice

As it happens, philosophers have thought quite a bit about the general problem of allocating scarce resources. In the background is the unhappy truth that, under conditions of scarcity, some will not receive what they need when they need it. The field of social philosophy treats this issue as a central concern: the problem of distributive justice. Think, for example, about dividing a birthday cake at a children's party. Who gets the flowers? The biggest, the best, or the first piece? What accommodation should be allowed for the birthday child, and the diabetic? Whereas most would agree that everyone is entitled to some fair and reasonable share of a collective good (here, the cake), what exactly is fair, and what is reasonable, what counts as a share, and which goods are collective? Health care wrestles with these same questions. How, for example, should we queue those who desperately await transplantable hearts? This is not merely a philosopher's problem.

As it happens, we draw on many familiar strategies in distributing limited resources. Movie theaters rely on first-come, first-served at the box office. Get in line early enough and you can select the choicest seat. (What about those who let their friends jump the queue?) Merit can also play a role: medical schools, for example, aspire to offer places to those best qualified. Lotteries are a third approach: random selection. Selling to the highest bidder (or pricing to clear the market) is a fourth. "Women and children first" played a memorable role on the *Titanic* but is a less plausible criterion today. These procedures, although richly varied, are commonly taken for granted.

Buses offer a complex and surprisingly pertinent model. Alhough capacity is limited, the passenger load varies. As the bus fills, a dynamic process plays itself out along the route: seated passengers offer their places to the elderly and infirm, and standees move to the rear and squeeze together in the aisle. Eventually the driver allows no more passengers on, and those lined up at the curb must either wait there until the next bus comes or find an alternative.

In health care, the term "triage" refers to procedures used in queuing prospective patients for treatment. There are three basic variations. The first is clinical triage, a familiar practice in the emergency department. The second is battlefield triage, a special case. The third is disaster triage, a civilian cousin to its military counterpart. A review of these will frame the problem of catastrophe.

Clinical Triage

In the emergency department the task of queuing prospective patients typically falls to a nurse with responsibility for initial interviews and assessments. Those with the greatest need can see the doctors at once; the lady with crushing chest pains receives attention before the football player with the injured knee, even if he showed up first. Allocating care on the basis of need is consistent with medicine's clinical orientation, is consummately fair under the circumstances, and is easily understood.

On one side of the triage nurse is what can be called the burden of patient need: the stream of medically treatable conditions entering the hospital. On the other side is the institution's carrying capacity: resources that can be brought to bear on those treatable conditions. In between these elements is the triage nurse, choreographing their engagement. When things go well, patients receive the care they need, although perhaps not when they want it, and the hospital does its most important job— preventing technically avoidable deaths and disabilities.

The stream of medically treatable conditions can be mapped along three scales. The first is the *rate* at which patients appear. How many are coming into the system per hour? The second is *urgency*. Medical conditions can arrive with a countdown timer. Alhough some ailments are self-limiting—patients are stable or can be expected to improve on their own—others require timely care. Too much delay and the patient will deteriorate, suffering permanent loss or requiring more care than would otherwise have been necessary. The third is *complexity*. What resources (time, staff, equipment, supplies, etc.) must be allocated to improve a patient's prospects? Taken together, rate, urgency, and complexity define the burden of patient need. When things go well, the hospital's therapeutic resources will be equal to its clinical responsibility. Clinical triage reconciles these two elements as they engage each other.

The hospital's goal is to ensure that patients receive the treatments they need, that there are no technically avoidable bad outcomes, but it is easy to see how temporary staff shortage or sudden surge of urgent and complex medical problems can overwhelm carrying capacity. What hospitals must have is a backup plan, a fallback position. (The bus is full, and new passengers can't board until others get off.) As often as several times a month some medical centers call a "code red," close their doors, and go to "divert" or "bypass." Ambulances are redirected to other regional medical centers, reducing the flow of incoming patients until the imbalance is corrected. Although there may be delays, the goal is still to ensure that patients receive necessary care and that bad outcomes are prevented insofar as medical and nursing skills can make it so.

Battlefield Triage

In contrast with the everyday rituals of the emergency department, military medicine has characteristically contended with large numbers of casualties. Clinically, war is the mass production of wounds. The modern idea of rationally giving priority to the injured has its roots in French military medicine during the Napoleonic era (Winslow 1982, 2). More than a century later, American doctors came into contact with European battlefield triage at casualty clearing stations near the trenches of World War I (Winslow 2001). At least 19 million men were wounded during that conflict and a single station could see 2000 in a day (Winslow 1982, 4). Under battlefield triage (in contrast to clinical triage), the most seriously injured soldiers were set aside to die even if, technically, many of them could have lived if treated. Many lives might be saved in the time necessary to manage a single complicated injury with a poor prognosis. Preventing every technically avoidable death was not an option (Winslow 1982, 5).

Even more striking were priorities sometimes given to men with minor ailments, soldiers who, if treated, could readily return to the front. During World War II, when the first supplies of penicillin reached American forces in North Africa, a decision had to be made whether to use it for men with battle wounds or those with venereal disease. Soldiers with VD won out because, unlike the others, they could quickly return to duty. On the battlefield, the interest in maximizing fighting strength (and so prevailing in battle) could trump the interest in saving the most lives and limbs (Winslow 1982, 6–8). Together with some others, this distinctive feature of military medicine sets it apart from its civilian counterpart.

Disaster Triage

Civil disasters—plane crashes, tsunamis, earthquakes, and so on–also cause mass casualties. When clinical triage is overwhelmed in these unusual cases, diversion fails as a fallback position: hospitals cannot go on bypass and redirect ambulances elsewhere when other regional centers are overwhelmed too. Disaster triage is the fallback position, one that relies on rapid initial assessment—ninety seconds is the goal—and a dynamic tagging process that registers and continues to monitor the urgency and complexity of injuries.

Those presenting for care are characteristically assigned to one of three categories. Think of the injured as falling along a horizontal scale, with the most seriously injured toward the right and the walking wounded on the left. Disaster triage reduces hospitals' clinical responsibility by lopping away the patients at both ends: those at the right, who will likely die even if treated, and those at the left, who will likely live even if not treated. After a disaster, clinicians must firmly narrow their focus to casualties in between: those who will live if treated but die otherwise. As with battlefield triage, it is not an option to prevent every technically avoidable death: the resources simply are not there.

Within the middle group, priority should go to those whose conditions are the most urgent and the least complex. (I am told that a patient with an otherwise fatal sucking chest wound can be stabilized temporarily with a piece of plastic wrap.) One can think of disaster triage as the solution to a mathematical problem. It specifies what clinicians must do to save the maximum number of lives.

Mass casualties and professionalism force a transformation of everyday moral intuitions. Two errors are common in implementing disaster triage, both traceable to understandable and ordinarily praiseworthy character traits: the virtue of compassion in the first case, and perseverance in the second.

The first error involves failure to appreciate the importance of firm professionalism at intake. It is easy to accede to the everyday moral imperative to accord greatest attention to worst-off victims, but this compassionate response cascades into major problems later on. On any ordinary day clinicians would do whatever it took to save this patient's life. Today she must be black-tagged as "expectant" and left to die, even as those with lesser wounds are treated. Necessary though they may be, these counterintuitive and unsympathetic choices can strain the sensitive conscience. Hence the need for firm professionalism.

The second error is failure to anticipate staff exhaustion. Although it may seem noble and heroic to persevere despite exhaustion, doctors and nurses cannot function indefinitely without sleep. The managerial key is, in advance, to adjust the use of human resources to a level that is sustainable for the anticipated duration of the crisis. To fail to do this is to risk erosion of staff functionality starting at the twenty hour mark.

Justifying Firm Professionalism   It is common to justify disaster triage by appealing to the simple utilitarian obligation to achieve optimum outcomes: do whatever it takes to realize the greatest good for the greatest number. But the crude idea that worthy ends can legitimize any means has rightly fallen on hard times. Fortunately, there are two other justifications for firm professionalism at intake, two better routes to the same destination. These are arguments from social contract and stewardship.

The Social Contract Argument   This justification aims at showing that reasonable persons would agree to disaster triage under conditions of uncertainty. Consider a thought experiment. Suppose we are on an airplane that will crash, but none of us knows how extensive anyone's injuries will be (*i.e.*, where they will end up on the horizontal scale). Suppose we must agree on a procedure for queuing casualties after the crash. Each of us wants to maximize the likelihood of our own survival, but our need for agreement and out uncertainty about the outcome together make it impossible to rig the procedure for personal advantage. Under those circumstances, rational negotiators would favor disaster triage on the grounds that it gives everyone the best chance of survival.

Should any passenger be allowed to jump the queue? If health care professionals and other rescue personnel are on board, they should be treated for minor injuries first, *but only if doing so will readily increase the supply of vital resources during the period of dire scarcity.* This would give other passengers an even better chance of survival.

Are the most seriously injured entitled to anything? If someone were going to decide that my wounds are too grave to treat, I would want that person to be the most competent professional around. I would want fair access to pain-control drugs. And I would want passengers with minor injuries to care for me while they awaited delayed treatment and awaited death. All reasonable persons would want those things, in case they ended up among the dying; but only as long as those accommodations did not detract from the effort to save lives, just in case they ended up among those who could survive. Rational social contractors hedge their bets in this way.

The Stewardship Argument   The second argument for firm professionalism is grounded in the responsibilities of stewardship. Among other duties, health care professionals have custody of supplies and services that become critically important to the community after disaster. These custodians have a duty to ensure that vital resources are employed efficiently and, above all, that they are not wasted. Life-saving resources are culpably wasted when they are knowingly used for patients who are likely to die, or for those who do not require them to avert death, and when using them in these ways results in more patients dying for want of those same resources.

Disasters call for a distinct ethical paradigm, one within which responsibilities fly in the face of everyday moral intuitions. Compassionate attentiveness must give way to firm professionalism and ninty-second assessments, both of which are critical when clinical triage is overwhelmed regionally.

Catastrophe

Some Preconditions

We can now begin to consider the problem of September 11: how can catastrophe overwhelm the second fallback position? What happens when the burden of patient need exceeds a region's *disaster-level* carrying capacity? And what would a third fallback position look like? Consider six preconditions that have to be satisfied for hospital staff to implement disaster triage:

1. Staff must be able to assess prospective patients as they enter the hospitals.

2. Staff must be able to monitor patients for whom treatment has been delayed.

3. Staff must be able to care for patients who most urgently require simpler treatment and provide follow-up care as necessary.

4. A sufficient number of staff must be on the job for the duration of the crisis; not drawn or kept away by injuries, competing obligations, or exhaustion.

5. Hospitals' physical infrastructures must be kept functionally free of crowds, contamination, and damage.

6. Untreated seriously ill patients and their accompanying loved ones must cooperate with the process, accepting why treatment has been delayed or denied.

Because it is understood that mass casualties can strain disaster-level carrying capacity, clinicians typically implement certain well-known measures to improve preparedness. Empty as many beds as possible, sending patients home. Add more beds. Assemble supplies for ease of use. Bring in more health care workers: dentists, veterinarians, hospice nurses, retired doctors, and volunteers. Set up showers outside the hospital. Increase security staff to keep order and protect physical facilities. Call out the National Guard if necessary to prevent riots. Prepare to evacuate casualties to distant centers.

But experience with three very large disasters suggest that the effort to tweak and preserve hospital capacity has only a limited utility. Consider the following.

Tokyo, 1995

At about 8 AM on March 20, members of a Japanese religious cult released a quantity of dilute nerve gas, sarin, at several locations on the crowded Tokyo subway system. Within minutes, those exposed to the vapors began to sicken with headache, nausea, weakness, and other symptoms. Of 641 casualties who were treated at St. Luke's International Hospital, near several of the affected subway stations (Ohbu et al. 1997), 498 arrived during the first hour (Defense Research Establishment 2001). Assuming ninety-second initial intake and assessment, twelve health care professionals would have been required just for those preliminary tasks. Since most of the casualties (361) showed up on foot or in private automobiles, diversion would have done little: only 35 patients arrived in ambulances (Okamura et al. 1998, 614). Secondary contamination was a significant problem. About 10 percent of emergency medical technicians were affected by the nerve gas (Okamura et al. 1998, 615) and 23 percent of medical staff at St. Luke's complained of symptoms (Ohbu et al. 1997). Hours elapsed before doctors understood which chemical agent was involved (Okamura et al. 1998, 615). In the end, over 5,500 were injured and 11 died (Ohbu et al. 1997). Although the casualties challenged the carrying capacity of Tokyo hospitals, they did not overwhelm it.

Bhopal, 1984

Early in the morning of December 3, an immense plume of deadly methyl-isocyanate gas escaped from a tank at a Union Carbide plant in Bhopal, India. Cool breezes held the heavy cloud close to the ground and moved it across the city, blinding, choking, and sickening tens of thousands as it proceeded. Clinicians were initially misinformed about the hazard. Alfred De Grazia (1985) wrote:

All five hospitals of the City became crowded quickly. The first victim staggered into Hamidia Hospital at 1:15 A.M. and within an hour thousands appeared. Hamidia was the largest of the five hospitals and is joined to a medical school and research center. The beds filled everywhere; then there were two to a bed. The prior bed tenants were bundled off to their homes unless gravely ill. Then the floors were lined with mats and no one could move about without difficulty. So tents were set up on the grounds. . . .

It may never be known what the human toll was at Bhopal. Records were not kept during the disaster and corpses were disposed of without official notice. Whole families vanished. Union Carbide's compensation offer assumed 2,600 deaths (Unger 1994, 72) but estimates ranged as high as 10,000 dead and more than 300,000 injured (Bogard 1989, viii).

Hiroshima, 1945

At 8:15 A.M. on August 6, an atomic bomb was detonated over Hiroshima, Japan. Nearly 100,000 died, many immediately, others after the emergence of perplexing symptoms hours, days, and weeks later; 100,000 more were injured (Hersey 1985, 25). Of 200 nurses who worked at Hiroshima's Red Cross Hospital, about a mile from the epicenter, 10 were able to function (Hersey 1985, 24, 14). John Hersey's

Hiroshima, first published in 1946, chronicled the experience of Dr. Terufumi Sasaki, the hospital's sole uninjured physician. In a supply room that had been wrecked by the blast, he found bandages and an unbroken bottle of Mercurochrome.

Dr. Sasaki worked without method, taking those who were nearest to him first, and he noticed soon that the corridor seemed to be getting more and more crowded. Mixed in with the abrasions and lacerations which most people in the hospital had suffered, he began to find dreadful burns. He realized then that casualties were pouring in from outdoors. There were so many that he began to pass up the lightly wounded; he decided that all he could hope to do was to stop people from bleeding to death. Before long, patients lay and crouched on the floors of the wards and the laboratories and all the other rooms, and in the corners, and on the stairs, and in the front hall, and under the porte-cochere, and on the stone front steps, and in the driveway and courtyard, and four blocks each way in the streets outside. Wounded people supported maimed people; disfigured families leaned together. . . . At least ten thousand of the wounded made their way to the best hospital in town, which was altogether unequal to such a trampling, since it had only six hundred beds, and they had all been occupied. (Hersey 1985, 25–26)

Failure of Disaster-Level Health Care

Events such as these illustrate how catastrophe can compromise the preconditions for disaster triage. Somewhere between the scales of Tokyo and Hiroshima, and depending on the region and the nature of the insult, the number of injured will exceed the number that can be assessed, stabilized, and monitored–essential tasks even if the goal is merely to evacuate casualties. It will be worse if health care professionals are succumbing to whatever hazards are present, especially if the nature of the agent is obscure and it is frighteningly unclear what protection is required. It will be worse if hospitals are damaged, if large crowds of casualties and loved ones are assembling there, if those waiting for care are contaminated or infectious or unruly, and if those outside believe that essential resources are being hoarded inside.

In the worst case, hospitals become health hazards. The effort to make one's way through the crowds seeking hospital care may be fraught with grave and avoidable risk.

Whatever is done to manage such a crisis, hospitals will have to effect a transition to a third fallback position well before the growing burden of patient need overwhelms the region's disaster-level carrying capacity.

Catastrophe-Level Health Care

In catastrophe, problems reach a level of intensity that compromises the very institutions we have created to deal with them. It is not enough to lop away even more of the injured, not enough to process selected ones with greater efficiency. Rather, the problems are built into the hospital-centered paradigm of health care.

The skilled attention hospitals can give to a handful of patients with inhalational anthrax cannot be offered to 100,000 of them. When the bus service can no longer transport passengers safely and effectively, it is time to shut it down and consider alternatives. Months ago, when I began my inquiry, I could not have anticipated the conclusion that would emerge: *during a catastrophe, hospitals cannot serve as the primary locus of health care. Accordingly, regional hospitals must close their doors before they reach disaster-level capacity, diverting prospective patients and transferring staff and supplies to peripheral emergency health care venues.*

Although the details must be filled in by those better informed than I am, here is a sketch of catastrophe-level health care: health care without hospitals.

First, we should be emulating the Israelis who, concerned about gas attacks, have implemented a strategy called shelter in place. During a terrorist attack, it may be better for people to remain where they are. If a deadly plume is passing over my city, I am at greater risk if I move about; safer if I stay put, especially in a windowless room or closet with the door taped shut (Sorenson and Vogt 2002), with food and water for several days, a radio, and a telephone.

Second, we should be designating locations as peripheral health care venues, with provision for supplies, decontaminating showers, floor space, and robust communication links. Instead of attracting the ill to a medical center, it is better if help is available nearby, at a school, fire station, pharmacy, neighborhood clinic, cafeteria, or hotel. If casualties are staying put, the outposts can support house calls and home care. The overriding goal is to eliminate crowds and reduce travel, preventing infection and cross-contamination. Whereas hospitals should continue to serve as regional coordination centers, they should resume patient care responsibilities only when it is known they can operate safely and effectively.

Third, we should openly preassign the broadest range of health care personnel to these designated venues so they can report there and know what to do when a "code black" is called. Perhaps the most heartening aspect of the New York disaster was the public-spiritedness it exposed. I expect health care professionals will want to register for emergency duty and ordinary citizens will want to learn to serve as volunteers. We must hear more about registries, training programs and community practice drills, about caching locally usable medical supplies and communication equipment, and about procedures in case of catastrophe. Above all, people must know where to go if, as is likely, hospitals are to be avoided.

I vaguely recall a cautionary tale about the battle of Stalingrad, how Soviet officials had stored the city's food supply in a single warehouse. The Nazis blew it up, causing terrible starvation. Had the Soviets distributed the food, they could have averted enormous suffering. Scattering vital resources creates a more robust system.

Doctors in America take an understandable pride in their devotion to the needs of individual patients and in the sophisticated technologies they have learned to use. But both of these have limitations. Terrorism and catastrophe cry out for a different conception of goals, techniques, and organization of health care. At the forefront is a transformative responsibility in the face of mass casualties and medical scarcity. We are at the beginning of a learning curve. We know we have work ahead of us. We do not know how much time we have.

Acknowledgments

Work on this project was undertaken while a Visiting Senior Scholar at the American Medical Association. Although I am grateful for their support, this chapter is not an expression of AMA policies. Special thanks are owed to Mike Davis, Sam Huber, Kenneth Iserson, Harvey Kipnis, Faith Lagay, Erich Loewy, Leanne Logan, John Moskop, Gerald Winslow, and Matthew Wynia for helpful comments and suggestions.

References

Bogard, William. 1989. *The Bhopal Tragedy: Language, Logic, and Politics in the Production of a Hazard.* Boulder, Co: Westview Press.

Defense Research Establishment. 2001. First Responder Course. Aum Shinrikyo: Chemical and Biological Terrorism. Available at http://www.dres.dnd.ca/Meetings/FirstResponders/ 3%20-%20Aum%20Shinrikyo_final.pdf (visited March 8, 2002).

De Grazia, Alfred. 1985. *A Cloud over Bhopal*. Bombay: Kalos Foundation. Available at http://www.grazianarchive.com/governing/bhopal/Bhopal_C3.html (visited March 8, 2002).

Hersey, John. 1985. *Hiroshima*, New York: Vintage Books.

Ohbu, Sadayoshi et al. 1997.

"Sarin Poisoning on Tokyo Subway." *Southern Medical Journal*. June. Available at http://www.sma.org/smj/97june3.htm (visited March 8, 2002).

Okamura, Tetsu et al. 1998. "The Tokyo Subway Sarin Attack: Disaster Management. Part 1. Community Emergency Response." *Annals of Emergency Medicine*. 5(4): 613–617.

Sorenson, John H. and Barbara M. Vogt. 2001. "Will Duct Tape and Plastic Really Work? Issues Related to Expedient Shelter-In-Place." Oak Ridge; TN: Oak Ridge National Laboratory. Available at http://emc.ornl.gov/EMC/PDF/TM2001_154_duct_plastic.pdf (visited March 8, 2002).

Unger, Stephen H. 1994. *Controlling Technology: Ethics and the Responsible Engineer*, 2nd ed. New York: John Wiley & Sons.

Winslow, Gerald R. 1982. *Triage and Justice*. Berkeley: University of California Press.

Winslow, Gerald R. 2001. Personal communication from Kenneth Kipnis. October 26.

III

Health Care Workers

7

Emergency Health Professionals and the Ethics of Crisis

Lisa A. Eckenwiler

A special subset of health professionals has long been called on to respond to emergencies or sudden, calamitous events that demand urgent attention.[1] Yet, at least two things are new. First, rather than responding to natural disasters, they increasingly confront complex emergencies in which human action (attributable to inexhaustible possible explanations) contributes to or exacerbates crisis and hinders efforts at remedy. More than ever before, these professionals address the health consequences of conflict and violence (Bok 1999; Lindenberg 1999). Second, since September 11, privileged nations such as the United States have developed a heightened sense of vulnerability to catastrophic events. In the wake of these shifting circumstances, sizable caches have been set aside to support emergency preparedness and design action plans and education for all—including emergency—health professionals. We should also bring our considerable resources to raising, and in some respects reassessing, questions of ethics that arise in and around their professional practice.

Exploration of ethical issues for emergency health professionals presents an opportunity to analyze questions that span domains of medical, research, and public health ethics, institutional and organizational ethics, and ethics in health, social, and economic policy. Indeed, this exercise in moral excavation attests to the need for analyses in bioethics to embrace a perspective that is broad and encompasses fields that inevitably intersect yet are often discussed in isolation from one another. Serious reckoning with these intersections is especially important when it comes to considering ethics in emergencies in light of new relationships forming institutions and disciplines, and possibly of our roles as professionals and citizens.

In addition, issues raised in this chapter reveal the importance of developing methodologies in bioethics that incorporate a global perspective. Such a perspective will acknowledge that firm boundaries between nations are less real than perceived when it comes to matters of health. As well, it might avoid what some have seen as a tendency toward myopia in much Western bioethics, in its frequent attendance to concerns for the affluent.

Above all, raising these issues presents an opportunity to contemplate moral reasoning and choice carried out by committed people in complicated contexts that leave us most always in awe. If any joy at all is to be found in the events that occasioned this anthology, it might be in stories of emergency health workers. They help us to find inspiration in what can be achieved in the moral character of persons in the most adverse of conditions. What's more, they urge us to find answers to ethical questions that will best serve them and the public health.

Questions highlighted here concern whether emergency health professionals have a duty to face danger; the meaning of fairness in allocating moral attention and health resources; and implications for ethics of links forged among medicine, public health, law enforcement, and private industry in emergency assessment, response, and preparation. In addition, how best do we resolve tension between the ideals of self-determination, voluntarism, privacy, and justice, and the demands of sometimes secretive and nearly always hierarchical social institutions? What constitutes just decision-making processes, and is neutrality an appropriate ideal of professional practice as opposed, say, to taking stands on moral and political matters? But first some background details.

Who and How?

Any attempt to evaluate ethical issues in crises is difficult because there are so many kinds of emergency health professionals. They include federal health officials working in the Department of Health and Human Services (DHHS), Centers for Disease Control and Prevention (CDC), and state and local public health departments as epidemiologists, laboratory staff, and clinicians. Some operate dispatch centers, serve as emergency medical services (EMS) team members, fire services professionals, environmental health experts, evacuation and transport personnel, and command post coordinators, while still others care for patients in emergency departments, offer mental health services, and tend the dead.

When emergencies occur, generally local governments are responsible and act first by calling on local medical and public health professionals, EMS teams, and others. State and federal assistance may be provided depending on the capacity of a given locality to respond. Should a national emergency occur, DHHS is responsible for coordinating operations among other federal agencies and departments, and providing health and medical resources such as evacuation services, beds, direct medical care, personnel, and health-related social services.[2] The CDC responds whenever a state agency requests its assistance, and now, in the event of the use of biological and chemical weapons.[3]

In international crises, local response comes when available, followed by government, again where functioning and available. But increasingly, United Nations agencies intervene, though they are often delayed due to political constraints and demands of wealthy donor governments. Non-government organizations (NGOs) have the advantage of being able to respond with minimal delay. A central question is whether the sovereignty of a nation in crisis should be respected and a principle of non-interference honored, or whether other nations or independent agencies have universal jurisdiction when, for example, human rights violations occur and contribute to emergency health conditions. Making crises all the more complicated is that agencies must now often negotiate with many combatants—with some functioning independent of the state—to provide emergency health services (Leaning 1999).

Beyond general commitments expressed by a range of agencies and associations[4] related to respecting human dignity and equality, preventing and reducing harm and suffering, promoting health, safety, and cooperation, and fairly allocating resources, what are the particular ethical dilemmas faced by emergency health workers? What might be said about their obligations in crisis and, more broadly, in the contemporary social and political context?

Given that catastrophes most often have serious social implications, a public health perspective is warranted for addressing these questions. A proposed ethical framework for evaluating interventions and policies calls for selecting those that are most likely to be effective in achieving an identified public health goal (reducing morbidity and mortality), whose risks of harm are minimized and reasonable in relationship to anticipated benefits, that promote justice (or more minimally, that do not promote injustice), and that are decided on using fair procedures (Kass 2001).[5] As we will see, these criteria are often elusive and call for further elucidation.

The Call to Action: Ethics and the Decision to Respond

Is It an Emergency?

We have become familiar with many forms of crises on a continuum of possible devastation: drought, hurricanes and monsoons, and human-wrought tragedy: the use of "smart" bombs and poison, nuclear weapons, genocide, systematic torture, starvation, and symbols of commerce and prowess transformed into lethal incendiary devices. Characterizing an event as an emergency, catastrophe, or crisis follows judgments that intense and widespread human suffering has occurred or is imminent; expert knowledge and rapid response of emergency health workers can help to alleviate it and perhaps prevent subsequent harm; and in some cases, this ought to take priority over other needs.[6] With respect to crises that occur outside of the United States, Sissela Bok observed: "Too often what is at stake is not so much levels of human suffering as whether or not the outside world becomes aware . . . and chooses to make an issue of it" (1999, 186). How do people come to recognize and understand the plight of others? As a start, we might shine the moral light in the direction of channels of communication and, in particular, concerns of justice: who has access to these, and what are their interests? This issue will resurface later.

Duty and Danger

What grounds the judgments of emergency health workers to select their professions and to respond when necessary? Perhaps a commitment to maximize benefit and reduce harm and suffering is most familiar. But what else about choices of these professionals might warrant praise from a moral perspective? It may be that their actions emerge from the motive of respecting the dignity of persons. Perhaps they should gain our respect for their capacity, built on a self-aware, keenly perceptive, and steadfast moral character, to assess particular circumstances and features of context, and identify appropriate action among alternatives, often under serious duress. In the case of international emergency health workers, one might argue that they deserve to be honored as moral exemplars, even heroes, for embracing a duty to address injustice or oppression.

Digging a bit deeper, emergency health workers' response to the suffering of others raises a perennial question in ethics. Among our many capacities as humans, which ones ground our capacities to think and act well as moral agents? Rationality? Emotion? Philosophers from Plato to Peter Singer granted privilege of place to reason. Many contemporary ethicists criticize the tendency to discount emotion, and hold that as social beings who are nurtured by and grow to care for others, emotion equips us with some important moral competencies, for example, to recognize the plight of others, to react, and to do so adequately. That is, the power of compassion enables us to appreciate the situations of others and to respond in ways attuned to their particular sufferings. Putting this issue in a more concrete context, we might ask ourselves what takes people into war zones, floods, and lands far from home? What motivated emergency health workers who were officially on duty after the attacks on the World Trade Center and the Pentagon, and countless health professionals from around the country to come forward voluntarily to help? Did they reason that this was the right course of action or were they acting also from emotion?

Whatever ethical orientation it springs from, what level of commitment is it right to expect from emergency health workers in catastrophic conditions? Do they have a duty to face great danger or risk? Should we perhaps postulate a general duty to confront danger, or no duty with some carefully tailored exceptions, say, in the event of a public health emergency? What constitutes "great" or "significant" risk? [7]

Infectious or toxic agents with unknown synergistic effects, unstable buildings and debris containing the injured and dead, and military personnel or others firing at emergency health workers and their facilities, or threatening to do so, present various levels of possible harm to health workers. In some instances, natural disasters or unknown actors generate danger, yet in others agents of the state or other authorities create and sustain risks of significant harm to health professionals and thwart their efforts. On occasions where their safety is threatened in such a manner, not only do they face risks of physical and psychological harm, but their professional commitment to avoid complicity in causing suffering to others—especially civilians—is tarnished. Perhaps most damaging is that hard-won international ethical agreements regarding appropriate treatment of health workers and other noncombatants are violated.

It would seem that emergency health workers would be likely candidates for a duty to face danger. Some might contend that the public health—especially under emergency conditions—justifies imposition of such a duty. However, where only some subset of health professionals is said to have a duty we might say this would be unfair distribution of burden. Even if emergency workers are best equipped to confront danger, they cannot respond effectively alone. Moreover, respect for bodily integrity and self-determination is compelling. Because public resources support these arrangements, citizens, together with different groups of health professionals should address these questions. Although hardly new, they have renewed force under growing threats of crisis. An important issue for deliberation is what social and institutional conditions must exist to support emergency and other health professionals who confront danger, especially given an expectation that they do so. Even more broadly, it is vital that we consider how to encourage care giving in societies.

Are There Obligations to Distant Others?

In principle, emergency health workers are committed to the idea that all persons are of equal moral worth. Yet the strength of obligations to differently situated persons is an issue that looms large on the moral landscape. Consider again that one of the awe-inspiring elements of the terrorist attacks on the United States was arrival of those who volunteered to help. International relief workers reveal their affirmative response with their decision to enlist for service. For them, not only is geographical distance an issue, so is economic and/or cultural distance. Decisions to come to the aid of others far away might be seen as reflecting a particular moral stance summed up by Howard Zinn (in an essay on those who died in Afghanistan under U.S. bombs, thereby calling up still more demand for emergency health workers to face danger): "Surely it is time, half a century after Hiroshima, to embrace a universal morality, to think of all children, everywhere, as our own" (2002, 20). The idea that all persons are of equal moral worth might be seen as demanding this quite literally.

But of course, it does matter to most of us whether a sick or injured child or elderly grandmother is the one we are trying to nurture on a daily basis or one some distance away with whom we are not acquainted. To suggest that taking care of "our own," or showing partiality toward those closest to us, is wrong, according to many, is not only counterintuitive; it would also seem to make our lives as social beings colder and less colorful, devoid of ground projects and caring relationships that, in a profound sense, constitute who we are as persons.

The appeal for equal treatment questions why it should matter, morally speaking, whether another is one's fellow citizen, neighbor, family member, or friend. To maintain that it does risks denying equal consideration to all and treating some people worse than others according to "morally irrelevant" differences. The ideal of impartiality emerges chiefly out of concern for relationships of privilege and oppression, for example, between dominant social groups and cultural minorities, and those born into poverty and affluence. Considering relations of affluence and poverty, rejecting the ideal of impartiality risks neglecting others in need of moral respect and the resources that responsive moral agents such as emergency health professionals may offer. In light of the unequal distribution of material and other resources, neglect of distant others can have serious social consequences, leaving some basking in the glow of moral attention and others, who do not have resources to show partiality, deprived of its many life-enriching benefits. "Partiality, if practiced by all, untempered by any redistribution of wealth or resources, would appear to lead to the integrity and fulfillment of only some persons, but not all" (Friedman 1993, 59). As we will see, many wish to highlight possible connections between this point and emergency prevention.

Many advocates of partiality in personal relationships agree with those committed to the ideal of impartiality to a degree in supporting the importance of showing concern for disadvantaged distant others, especially under the threat of emergency. Lingering questions concern how much is owed to others near and far; and who merits the most praise as a moral exemplar, one who favors intimates or vulnerable strangers? Perhaps one way of thinking about all this is to consider ways in which one's partiality creates or perpetuates harm, and what might be done to mitigate this. Zinn, for instance, is not necessarily suggesting that we treat our own children less well than we do currently. Perhaps his aim is for us to raise questions regarding how our perceptual and imaginative capacities are attuned, indeed, directed, in ways that privilege some and harm others. It is a matter of justice that we resist this tendency, for it can create and sustain inequalities.

"Let's Roll": Emergency Assessment and Intervention

Once emergency health workers make a decision to mobilize, the next set of ethical issues they confront pertains to crisis assessment and choice among possible interventions. From assessments of the magnitude, intensity, possible spread, likely duration and health impact of the emergency, who and/or what is at risk, and health needs of affected and potentially affected populations, comes an evaluation of available resources, the nature of affected communities, and alternatives for action. Next, they set priorities and carry out plans, sometimes, but not always, well laid (FEMA 1996, 1999; Sphere Project 2000).

Assessment

To be sure, the process of assessing a catastrophe and identifying ways to respond requires gathering and interpreting facts. However, as was made all too clear by the anthrax-laced letters and allegations that postal workers, unlike senators and their staff members, were not given due attention, this has the potential to be a difficult process, permeated with uncertainty and laden with values. Doing the "right" thing, indeed, is a moving target aimed at by persons with distinctive standpoints shaping the inquiry. This observation is of the utmost importance in that how emergency health professionals conduct assessments has implications for their other responsibilities: communication to the public, resource allocation, the choice of intervention, and disclosure of information to potential treatment populations. Yet crisis assessment is complicated by the status of science at the time, access to information, institutional norms and structures, and bureaucratic processes.

Reflection on the anthrax incidents finds these in stark relief. Especially poignant are revelations about how the secrecy of the FBI and military officials hindered the CDC's ability to determine the course of assessment and, in turn, design maximally effective response strategies (Siegel 2002). Thus scientists working in different institutional environments with divergent orientations may engage differently in, or perhaps in different kinds of, investigations during an emergency. In turn, this raises questions regarding the ethical implications of different structures of responsibility in light of ties among law enforcement, the military, and emergency health professionals.

Together with the possibility that institutional norms and organizational structures can undermine efforts, bias in moral reasoning based on class, race, or ethnicity, even unintentionally, can compromise an adequate assessment of needs. Concerns of bias emerge in the practice of international health workers, who have been criticized for misunderstanding a catastrophe and the communities involved, and perhaps causing further harm by perpetuating conflict or weakening local capacity to respond (Toole 1997).

The anthrax investigations and countless other incidents demonstrate that all knowledge, reasoning, and judgment reflect the standpoint of the knower or moral agent and his or her epistemological community; it is inevitably partial. Determinations of what are important data to gather, gathering them, interpreting them, and acting on them are all shaped by subjectivities of participants and the social and institutional contexts in which their knowledge-seeking endeavors unfold. Epistemology and ethics are tightly bound in that assessment, or interpretation and satisfaction of needs, and are central to giving people their due and promoting the ideal of justice. Determining what is happening, what it means, what could help, and what will be effective and not excessively harmful can be seen as matters of justice in the sense that they concern fair processes of decision making. Emergency health professionals, thus, face the challenge that interpretation of needs and their satisfaction are ethically and politically contestable. They will do best when they are careful to consider who interprets the circumstances and needs in question and for whom, from what perspective, and in light of what norms, interests, and assumptions. A full commitment to justice and minimal harm, furthermore, demands respect for the contributions of all participants and, where possible, affected communities. We have seen this in other times of crisis, during the emergence of AIDS, for instance.

Response

Resource Allocation   Reflecting commitment to equality, the presumption, a priori, is that all those in need are eligible candidates for care in an emergency. However, emergency health workers embrace different distributive principles depending on available resources and the level of catastrophe. Most codes of ethics hold that if no resource scarcity exists, it is right to do the greatest good for each individual. In conditions of scarcity, however, it is usually said that the ethically correct resource distribution is the one that maximizes the effectiveness of the available resources; that is, saves the maximum number of victims and best preserves resources (World Medical Association 1983, 1994; Pesik, Kleim, and Iserson 2001). In most of the world, scarcity is a very real constraint (Wetter, Daniell, and Tresor 2001). Public health and health care systems worldwide face shortages of trained health professionals, beds, drugs, and laboratory and other positions. Even where there is no scarcity per se, efforts to contain costs shape choices. So once again, to maintain that all persons are of equal moral worth is not to say that all are entitled to or will receive the same treatment.

Although other possible schemes can be identified, principles for emergency medical triage, evacuation triage, and allocating emergency medical care in disaster are widely shared among agencies and institutions. Based on considerations including the urgency of the condition, likelihood of benefit and its duration, and amount of resources necessary for successful treatment, care is given first to those who can be saved and whose lives are in immediate danger; then to those who can be saved who need urgent but not immediate attention; and last, those in need of minor treatment or psychological care. The final category, those who are "beyond emergency care," includes those whose needs exceed available resources (World Medical Association 1994; Pan American Health Organization 1995; Pesik et al. 2001). Tension may arise for health professionals accustomed to putting their patients first. Evacuation teams, for example, might have to stagger the flow of patients to hospitals if capacity is limited, or physicians might be called on to choose among their own patients for discharge to create room for disaster victims.

All emergency health professionals express a commitment to impartiality, that is, to treating patients according to their medical condition and available resources, and not considering age, ethnicity, or perceived social worth. Some, including designers of the MSEHPA, suggest at least one important possible exception to the principle of nondiscrimination: emergency workers, including health care providers and disaster response personnel, should perhaps receive priority treatment. They contend that this may be justified as it is likely to result in greater benefit to others. Others might suggest that some in positions of leadership in government or the military should move to the head of the queue. Those planning for emergencies face the dilemma of making such judgments themselves or involving others in decisions concerning fair resource allocation. Would schemes that allow for distinctions according to estimated social worth be deemed acceptable in open and fair public decision-making processes?

A related concern is how to uphold the ideal of impartiality and avoid perpetuating harm in allocating resources. Circumstances wherein, for example, food is distributed in a way that serves to strengthen combatants or, under threat of harm, health professionals are called on to favor military personnel and/or refrain from treating "enemies," can challenge this ideal. They can also find these workers feeling compromised in their commitment to neutrality, which holds that they should not act as instruments of government policy or in ways that favor a particular group.

Administering Interventions Health professionals aim to avoid harm, but how does this weigh against possible harms to public health in an emergency? In some cases, an adequate evidence base may exist to support particular interventions, such as prophylaxis or treatment. But how does limited knowledge regarding the safety and efficacy of proposed interventions affect decisions? Proportionality suggests that the greater the harms posed by an intervention, the stronger the evidence should be that it will work. In a public health emergency, where the probability of substantial harm to the common good is high but data are scant or controversial regarding a proposed intervention's safety and effectiveness, should we administer it, and if so, on what scale? Would its use be deemed voluntary or mandatory? What about situations—quite likely indeed—in which informed consent is unobtainable due to the patient's condition? Perhaps we might take a lead from regulations concerning emergency research, in which not only expert deliberation but also community consultation is required in advance of using experimental interventions. It is possible that public consent following fair deliberative processes could allow for timely response without tarnishing respect for bodily integrity, self-determination, or justice.

Even once it is decided who should get what, how much, and when, there are no guarantees that care will be provided. Differences in the structure and financing of health care for senate staff and postal workers, for example, led to differences in treatment for those exposed to anthrax. Resources are allocated according to complex economic structures and processes, many of which undermine optimal care and the ideal of fairness.

One other set of issues involves instances in which individuals hesitate to embrace or even outright refuse what is recommended, be it medical examinations, testing, prophylaxis, or treatment. In a case of anthrax exposure, this raises one sort of worry. Yet in cases of contagious disease, under what conditions might mandatory measures such as forced treatment, vaccination, quarantine, or isolation be justified?[8] Again, how many data are sufficient to justify an intervention? From an international perspective, lack of knowledge regarding the efficacy of interventions renders it difficult for health professionals to have confidence that their choices will have the desired results (Bantvala and Zwi 2000).

Time will tell whether the often tenacious commitment to autonomy will hold, or more communitarian-minded responses (or others under their guise) will gain influence, and allow for more public health paternalism aimed at preventing harm or even affirming a commitment to certain collective goods such as health and national security. Other urgent issues to be resolved concern ethical considerations in the structure within and relationships between responsible agencies and institutions (public health, hospitals, industry, law enforcement) with distinct pressures and objectives in emergency response.

Management of Information: Privacy and State Secrecy   As we have seen, accurate information about emergencies is not easy to come by for emergency health professionals, a reality that greatly constrains the need and responsibility to communicate with the public and local health professionals who require guidance. Together with their revelations regarding ethical implications of divergent professional orientations for assessment, the anthrax cases revealed the difficulties this can pose for communication. Ostensibly, all are concerned about benefiting the public's health, but some are also concerned about reassurance, and still others about social control, punishment, and national security. Again, the ethical significance of structures of responsibility emerges with respect to acquisition, exchange, and dissemination of information. Not to be overlooked are questions regarding resources; that is, what capacities in terms of technology and infrastructure emergency health professionals have to manage information.

Persons under the care of health and medical professionals rightly expect that identifying information, including their medical information, will be protected by security measures and held in confidence by professionals. Maintaining confidentiality shows respect for persons, for the relationships within which private information is shared, and for benefits that may accrue to the vulnerable in need of aid or sanctuary. Although the presumption in favor of it is strong, the duty to protect confidences and other private information is not absolute. Yet who has the authority to release medical information, to whom, and under what circumstances? Carefully circumscribed releases are permissible when required by law, and to avert serious and (most often) imminent harm to other identifiable persons, when it is thought that the release will be effective in achieving its aim and will not result in even greater harm.

In an emergency, especially one with serious public health and/or national security implications, would the same justificatory conditions hold, or might the burden of proof be easier to meet? Could the presumption shift in favor of release under certain circumstances? According to the MSEHPA, where public health authorities possess protected health information, they can disclose it only to those who require it for purposes of treatment, epidemiological research, or investigating transmission. Consent, according to the proposal, is not necessary if the information goes to the individual, his family, or "appropriate federal agencies or authorities," or in response to a court order (Center for Law and the Public's Health 2001, 34). Are all of these exceptions justifiable? Once again, we can envision tensions arising between what is alleged to be for the common good and individual privacy, and among the moral commitments of public health professionals, health care providers, and criminal justice authorities.

On the other hand, what about instances in which authorities seek to keep health data secret? For example, might certain health data for some groups have to be classified; say, whether military personnel have been given a particular vaccination in or in preparation for an emergency?[9] One might imagine a national security argument being offered to justify such a practice. Yet serious scrutiny is warranted given the implications for patient care outside of a military context should the need for it arise. Depending on the nature and extent of adverse effects, how would classified information affect attempts at seeking compensation for harm? The plot thickens considerably when interventions have been administered without informed, voluntary consent, which is likely in an emergency and maybe inevitable for members of the military.

With respect to dissemination to the public, we have seen that absent a clearer understanding of who has the expertise and authority to speak, individual health professionals and members of the public face confusion, misunderstanding, and serious threats of harm. When appropriately designated emergency health officials do disclose information to the public, how should they go about it? How should they communicate what is known about the risks of harm, and using what channels of communication?

Before embarking on a communication campaign, emergency health workers should call up their capacity for moral perception and assess contextual features of the crisis, including the level of concern in the public, perhaps the emotional climate, political conditions, and so on. When they communicate information about the nature of the catastrophe, what is being done to control it, and what people can do to protect themselves, an approach aimed at accuracy and truthfulness, even when this involves uncertainty, indicates respect for persons' capacity to determine their actions and the conditions of their actions, and is most likely to yield desired health benefits and encourage trust. For the sake of social justice, communication initiatives must also be mindful of who are the populations known and suspected to be at risk, and how they typically obtain, understand, and react to health information and authorities. As so much history in research, medicine, and public health reveals, biases concerning others, inequities of access, and relations of distrust are possible barriers to effective disclosure, understanding, and uptake.

Accountability and Advocacy

Questions of accountability to beneficiaries and donors, and advocacy concerning social and political affairs, have arisen often in discussions of international relief agencies. However, after September 11, health officials and others in the United States, together with international authorities, have brought them to the fore.

A source of significant moral distress for many health professionals is the danger that, under the threat of emergency, and moreover, in the thick of one, they might become agents of law enforcement. As well, many find serious tensions in links being forged between public health system and national security. Of special interest is whether strengthening these relationships is consistent with the mandate and mission of public health, a field committed to open and independent inquiry in research and setting public health priorities. Some wonder whether these ties threaten the ideals not merely of public health professionals, but more broadly of all health professionals, and perhaps make them complicit in harming health by bolstering military preparedness and perpetuating an arms race (Cohen, Gould, and Sidel 1999).

Many wonder, indeed, how emphasis on preparing for crisis, particularly bioterrorism, will affect public health more broadly. Such preparation is vital, some say, because we do face serious health threats from chemical, biological, and other weapons. In their view, failure to prepare would "constitute a massive 'malpractice' error of omission on the part of public health and medical authorities" (Henretig 2001, 719). Moreover, emergency preparedness initiatives will lend strength to public health infrastructure and, for example, enhance our understanding of the human immune system and ability to address toxicologic disasters and new or reemerging natural infectious diseases. George Will stated, "[b]ecause of today's war against terrorists, tomorrow's Americans will live better and longer" (2002, A25).

A strong concern in public health, however, questions whether increased government support for domestic bioterrorism initiatives is (dis)proportionate. They point to lack of data on which to base risk assessments, and above all, remark on the contrast between the vigor with which these high-cost initiatives have been pursued, and lack of conviction that characterizes federal support for such reforms as more inclusive health coverage and addressing social determinants of health (Sidel, Cohen, and Gould 2001; Cohen et al. 1999). The worry is that bioterrorism initiatives and other emergency response planning will limit the scope of public health and divert resources from other more urgent public health endeavors, and therefore harm health and perpetuate inequalities in the United States and globally (Fee and Brown 2001; Wetter et al. 2001). In the meantime, consider the psychological effects of preparation for crisis on the public's health. Anxiety, fear, and depression are clear threats to health and well-being, and may affect more people than any catastrophe.

Fairness in decision making figures prominently on the agenda of emergency health professionals concerned about accountability both to their respective disciplines and to the public at large. The notion that those affected by decisions involving the structure of responsibility in crisis response or health interventions should have a say in making them demands participation of local public health officials, emergency department nurses, and citizens (Wetter et al. 2001; Fraser and Brown 2000; Nicoll et al. 2001; Marwick 2001). Moreover, these endeavors should be international in scope. Community involvement in decision making, is now identified as crucial by numerous agencies and organizations (for example, Federal Emergency Management Agency, International Red Cross, Sphere Project). This suggests that narrow conceptions of "expertise" and institutions and officials operating in secrecy violate international consensus and tarnish ethical ideals.

Linked to the ideal of impartiality, neutrality has long been embraced explicitly by many health professionals, including the International Committee of the Red Cross. Yet agencies such as the Medecins sans Frontieres (MSF) and many others engaged in emergency health efforts reject this position and embrace a commitment to advocacy (Perrin 1999; Tanguy 1999; Fink 2000; Alberti et al. 2001). In the United States, where, citing Nazi doctors and eugenicists, health professionals (purportedly) have tried to keep politics out of medicine, science, and public health, renewed attention is being paid to whether this is possible or ethically acceptable. Recent years have seen emergency physicians iden-tify duties to oppose violence, promote public health, and advocate for the uninsured, and others, appealing to human rights and social justice, calling for global peace and equality, and restrictions on global arms sales and weapons development (Alberti et al. 2001; Cohen et al. 2001; Gellert 1995; Lindenberg 1999). Much of this activity draws attention to the fundamental causes of complex health emergencies and hopes to avoid medicalizing what are fundamentally social, economic, and political problems. The commitment to neutrality seems to be weakening in some quarters. The question remains open for bioethics.

Conclusion

Whereas others have already endured this and many continue to, those of us living in the United States find ourselves in a new world where the threat of emergency is ever present, or so we are told. Effective and eth-ically sound response compels us to give careful consideration to the issues raised here concerning the duty to face danger, our obligations to differently situated others, ethical implications of ties among medicine, public health, the state, and most important, designing just decision-making processes. These considerations cannot proceed adequately without appreciation for intersections among medical, public health, research, and organizational ethics, ethics in policy design, or global economic and political realities.

But too, we should pause to reframe the debate. Indeed, other matters deserve to be addressed. What really makes us safe and healthy? Perhaps we can do little to prevent earthquakes, hurricanes, and floods; yet we can do much to mitigate the devastation they might cause by making certain social, economic, and political choices as individuals, institutions, and governments. With respect to emergencies brought about by human actions, especially violence, social justice would have us devote at least as much attention as we give to emergency planning to supporting— through education, social programs, universal health coverage, and redis-tribution of wealth, perhaps—the capacity for all people to live well and to give expression to their ideals. Prevention of a health catastrophe, then, may be more a matter of making just social, economic, and political choices than spending scarce social resources on enhancing laboratories and stockpiling vaccines.

Notes

1. This definition is derived from the ones offered by the World Medical Association (1994) and the Pan American Health Organization (1995).

2. The Office of Emergency Preparedness within DHHS coordinates the National Disaster Medical System, a network that includes the Departments of Defense (DOD), Veterans Affairs (DVA), Transportation (DOT), Energy (DOE), U.S. Department of Agriculture (USDA), Environmental Protection Agency (EPA), Federal Emergency Management Agency (FEMA), as well as the private sector.

3. Well before September 11 the U.S. government and federal agencies, in collaboration with state and local health departments and medical and professional associations, were working to establish a protocol for response in the event of a terrorist attack. The Federal Bureau of Investigation (FBI) is designated as the lead agency for implementing a crisis plan, and DHHS has been working to develop partnerships with localities to develop a Metropolitan Medical Response System (MMRS). The CDC's National Bioterrorism Preparedness and Response Initiative (CDC 2000a, b) aims at building federal, state, and local response capacity. States and local jurisdictions also have their own preparedness initiatives under way (CDC 2002), as do individual institutions such as hospitals (American Hospital Association, DHHS 2000).

4. The International Red Cross, World Medical Association, National Association of Emergency Medical Technicians, American College of Epidemiology, and American College of Emergency Physicians, for example.

5. Indeed, the Model State Emergency Health Powers Act (MSEHPA) invoked this framework. Its language calls for the use of emergency health powers to promote the common good and to avoid injustice, as well as unnecessary constraints on such ideals as liberty, bodily integrity, and privacy (Center for Law and the Public's Health 2001, 8).

6. A public health emergency, in one proposed definition, is where there is or where will exist an imminent threat of illness or health condition—the result of bioterrorism, a new or old infectious agent or biological toxin, natural disaster, or chemical or nuclear release—that presents a high probability of causing substantial harm to a large number of people (Center for Law and the Public's Health 2001, 11).

7. Here I note some of the questions raised by panelists Leslie J. Blackhall, Walter S. Davis, Eric A. Feldman, and Ann B. Hamric at the bioethics and bioterrorism conference, sponsored by the Center for Bioethics at the University of Pennsylvania and Center for Biomedical Ethics at the University of Virginia, and held in Washington, D.C., February 28, 2002.

8. The MSEHPA allows for coercion, specifically, confinement (subject to review and appeal) but not examination, vaccination, or treatment, if a person's refusal poses a danger to public health.

9. I owe this point to the editor.

References

Alberti, George et al. 2001. "Open Letter: Health Professions on the Aftermath of Terrorism." *British Medical Journal*. 323: 1004.

American Hospital Association, and Office of Emergency Preparedness, Department of Health and Human Services. 2000. *Hospital Preparedness for Mass Casualties*. Chicago: American Hospital Association.

Bantvala, Nicholas and Anthony B. Zwi. 2000. "Public Health and Humanitarian Interventions: Developing the Evidence Base." *British Medical Journal*. 321: 101–105.

Bok, Sissela. 1999. "The New Ethical Boundaries." In *Humanitarian Crises: The Medical and Public Health Response*, edited by Jennifer Leaning, Susan M. Briggs, and Lincoln C. Chen, 179–93. Cambridge: Harvard University Press.

Centers for Disease Control and Prevention. 2002a. *Local Emergency Preparedness and Response Inventory*. Atlanta: Centers for Disease Control and Prevention.

Centers for Disease Control and Prevention. 2002b. *State Emergency Preparedness and Response Inventory*. Atlanta: Centers for Disease Control and Prevention.

Center for Law and the Public's Health. 2001. *Model State Emergency Health Powers Act*. December 21.

Cohen, Hillel W., Robert M. Gould, and Victor Sidel. 1999. "Bioterrorism Initiatives: Public Health in Reverse?" *American Journal of Public Health*. 89(11): 1629–1631.

Federal Emergency Management Association. 1996. *Guide for All Emergency Operations Planning*. Washington, DC: Federal Emergency Management Association.

Federal Emergency Management Association. 1999. *Emergency Response to Terrorism: Self-Study*. Washington, DC: Federal Emergency Management Association. Available at *www.usfa.fema.gov/pdf/ertss* (visited March 21, 2002).

Fee, Elizabeth and Theodore M. Brown. 2001. "Preemptive Biopreparedness: Can We Learn Anything from History?" *American Journal of Public Health*. 91.5: 721–726.

Fink, Sheri L. 2001. "Physician Groups and the War in Kosovo: Ethics, Neutrality, and Interventionism." *Journal of the American Medical Association*. 283.9: 1200.

Fraser, Michael R. and Donna L. Brown. 2000. "Bioterrorism Preparedness and Local Public Health Agencies: Building Response Capacity." *Public Health Reports.* 115.4: 326–330.

Friedman, Marilyn. 1993. *What Are Friends For?: Feminist Perspectives on Personal Relationships and Moral Theory.* Ithaca, NY: Cornell University Press.

Gellert, George A. 1995. "Humanitarian Responses to Mass Violence Perpetrated Against Vulnerable Populations." *British Medical Journal.* 311: 995–1001.

Henretig, Fred. 2001. "Biological and Chemical Terrorism Defense: A View from the 'Front Lines' of Public Health." *American Journal of Public Health.* 91.5: 718–719.

Leaning, Jennifer. 1999. "Emergency Care." In *Humanitarian Crises: The Medical and Public Health Response,* edited by Jennifer Leaning, Susan M. Briggs, and Lincoln C. Chen, 81–93. Cambridge: Harvard University Press.

Lindenberg, Marc. 1999. "Complex Emergencies and NGOs: The Example of Care." In *Humanitarian Crises: The Medical and Public Health Response,* edited by Jennifer Leaning, Susan M. Briggs, and Lincoln C. Chen, 211–245. Cambridge: Harvard University Press.

Marwick, Charles. 2001. "Transatlantic Agreement Signed on Health Care and Emergency Measures." *British Medical Journal.* 323: 890.

Nicoll, Angus et al. 2001. "Managing Major Public Health Crises: Lessons from Recent Events in the United States and the United Kingdom." *British Medical Journal.* 323: 1321–1322.

Pan American Health Organization. 1995. *Establishing a Mass Casualty Management System.* Washington, DC: Pan American Health Organization.

Perrin, Pierre. 1999. "Supporting Sharia or Providing Treatment: The International Committee of the Red Cross." *British Medical Journal.* 319: 445–447.

Pesik, Nicki, Mark E. Keim, and Ken V. Iserson. 2001. "Terrorism and the Ethics of Emergency Medical Care." *Annals of Emergency Medicine.* 37.6: 642–646.

Sidel, Victor, Hillel W. Cohen, and Robert M. Gould. 2001. "Good Intentions and the Road to Bioterrorism Preparedness." *American Journal of Public Health.* 91.5: 716–718.

Siegel, Marc. 2002. "The Anthrax Fumble." *Nation*, March 18, 14, 16, 18.

Sphere Project. 2000. *Humanitarian Charter and Minimum Standards in Disaster Response.* Geneva: Sphere Project.

Tanguy, Joelle. 1999. "The Medecins sans Frontieres Experience." In *A Framework for Survival: Health, Human Rights, and Humanitarian Assistance in Conflicts and Disorders,* edited by Kevin M. Cahill, 226–244. New York: Routledge.

Toole, Michael. 1997. "Frontline Medicine: The Role of International Medical Groups in Emergency Relief." In *World in Crisis: The Politics of Survival at the End of the Twentieth Century,* edited by Medecins sans Frontieres. 16–36. London: Routledge.

Wetter, Donald Clark, William Edward Daniell, and Charles David Tresor. 2001. "Hospital Preparedness for Victims of Chemical or Biological Terrorism." *American Journal of Public Health*. 91.5: 710–716.

Will, George. 2002. "War and Health." *Washington Post*. February 7, A25.

World Medical Association. 1983. *International Code of Medical Ethics*. Geneva: World Medical Association.

World Medical Association. 1994. *Medical Ethics in the Event of Disasters*. Geneva: World Medical Association.

Zinn, Howard. 2002. "The Others." *Nation*, February 11, 16–20.

8

Emergency Medicine, Terrorism, and Universal Access to Health Care: A Potent Mixture for Erstwhile Knights-Errant

Griffin Trotter

For at least two decades American health care reformers have been tilting at windmills. Consistently, they have sought to enhance federal powers while targeting "inequality" and "market forces" as the twin scourges of the system. The American public, quite enamored of economic competition with its correlative forms of inequality, has been unsympathetic, more interested in cutting back welfare than in proliferating health care rights, and more inclined to for-profit managed care than to government oversight.

Amid the melee, meaningful reform has been virtually nonexistent. Clinton-Care was stillborn, and since 1986 Congress has managed nothing more drastic than a paltry pair of patients' rights bills. Now there is a much-publicized War on Terrorism, and health care reform seems to have dropped from the political landscape. Patients' rights bills languish. And health care has dropped precipitously from third to sixth on the public's list of priorities for government (Blendon et al. 2002). The old windmills—inequality and market forces—remain, but they are no longer front and center, even in bioethics, public health, and other former bastions of medical knight-errantry. As we face the specter of sudden, violent death from unseen malefactors, our health care system (should we be so bold as to call it a system) guarantees little more than access to crowded emergency departments, achieved by Congress in 1986 through the Emergency Medical Treatment and Active Labor Act (EMTALA). This system is friendly neither to the poor and uninsured, who have few suitable options for routine health care, nor to potential victims of terrorism, whose designated rescuers are more engaged with holding up the mangled EMTALA safety net than in creating a more appropriate kind of safety net, suitable for disaster response.

Despite these gloomy realities, prospects for meaningful health care reform are perhaps brighter than ever. My thesis is that the War on Terrorism and accompanying shift in political priorities present a golden opportunity for strengthening our health care infrastructure and establishing universal access to a basic package of benefits in America. Rather than sallying against inequality and market forces, erstwhile knight-errants can face off against a real fire-breather: the threat of disaster and mass casualties. National security, I submit, is the new banner for health care reform. Under this standard we can eliminate the counterproductive older solution (EMTALA) and fill the void with something more comprehensive and effective.

Of Past Reforms: A Tale of Medical Knight-Errantry

I am a knight of La Mancha and my office and profession is to go through the world redressing injuries and making crooked things straight.
—Don Quixote

It doesn't take a bioethicist to conclude that something is crooked in American health care. For some time now, ordinary folks have been disgruntled about high prices, long waits, opaque jargon, and bad manners that seem to infect contemporary medicine. They are incensed over experiments at Tuskegee and appalled at how medical arrogance constrained Quinlan, Cruzan, and many others to unwanted life support. Even before the first textbook on bioethics and health care reform came out, my Aunt Norma discerned the crookedness. So did my barber, my son's football coach, and (I suspect) the green-haired lady at Schnucks. Bioethics and other exalted academic disciplines were not required.

Where bioethics excels, especially in distinction to ordinary common sense, is in crafting grand narratives about crookedness and ingenious schemes for straightening things out. In this regard, the bioethicist-health care reformer has been an essentially quixotic figure. For this school of health care reform, as for all knight-errantry, there is a needy Dulcinea: she is the unwashed public. Following Cervantes's example, the narrative has Dulcinea enchanted by an evil force that instills in her the delusion that something besides good health in choiceworthy. Even the World Health Association, with its clever strategy of defining health as "a state of complete physical, mental and social well-being and not merely the absence of disease or infirmity," has been unable to wipe out this belief (World Health Organization 1946). In her delusional state, Dulcinea engages in every manner of folly. She smokes cigarettes, carouses past midnight, bikes without a helmet, copulates with unsheathed strangers, and (most unfortunate) fails to make adequate financial arrangements for doctors' visits. Second, we have an evil force—the market. Before the Elysian idols of economic prosperity and insatiable consumption, Dulcinea trembles helplessly. Thus rendered, she is oblivious to the stethoscope and the mammogram.

In response to this peril, health care reformers offered a consistent strategy: get her to the doctor! Through the febrifuge of friendly health care workers, our Dulcinea could be cured of her frenzied adventurism. Given access to the clinic, she would learn about tobacco-related illness, highway safety, and condoms. She would receive early intervention for potentially chronic maladies, and her tumors would be detected early, then eradicated. Indeed, access to health care the Holy Grail of old-style health reform.

This crusade, undertaken from the age of Truman to the dawn of second Bush, has produced few salient effects. Apparent early successes—Medicare, Medicaid, and tax-free employee-sponsored health care—boomeranged. Medicare languishes in inefficiency. Medicaid struggles for breadcrumbs. And tax law has mushroomed into America's single greatest health policy boondoggle, disempowering consumers as it saps the middle class of will for serious health care reform.

The most problematic recent accretion to this patchwork campaign is EMTALA, enacted in 1986. Ostensibly based on a noble antipatient-dumping platform, it provides a back door for universal access: every individual who arrives at an American emergency department is entitled to a medical screening examination. Should the examiner document that the individual does not have an emergency medical condition, legal obligations are fulfilled. However, is an emergency condition, or a possible emergency condition, exists, the staff is legally beholden to stabilize the patient before transfer or discharge.

The mandate to document the absence of an emergency medical condition amounts to an imperative to prove a negative. Although emergency physicians are constantly faced with proving negatives, usually by ruling out likely positive diagnoses, this process is much more feasible as a clinical exercise than it is as a bureaucratic one. Under the glare of suspicious (and, in my experience, often poorly trained) Medicare inspectors, physicians are apt to strive beyond reason to document the absence of an emergency. In most cases, this enterprise amounts to a complete clinical workup and treatment, even for those with minor illnesses such as upper respiratory viruses or dry skin. For those with nowhere else to go, this development is an improvement, however paltry. Under EMTALA, the emergency department (ED) becomes their surrogate primary care clinic. Those with true medical emergencies, on the other hand, have less to cheer about.

The EMTALA Debacle

During times of crisis, all roads lead to the emergency department.
—James K. Church, Jr. (2002)

I am an emergency physician at a level I trauma center at a university hospital in urban Saint Louis, Missouri. In our ED we see about eighty patients a day, admitting about twenty-two to wards or intensive care units. This modest influx is enough to stress our resources. Because our intensive care units are often full, critically ill patients may spend many hours in the ED and we are frequently forced to divert ambulances. Our attending physicians spend almost twice as much time documenting, arranging, or discussing their activities as they do at the bedside engaging in them. When patients are transferred out of the ED (an event that is mercifully less common in our tertiary center than in most EDs) this ratio tips even further in favor of documentation over action. Under EMTALA, transferring facilities are responsible for generating a veritable sheaf of paperwork, much of it redundant and clinically unhelpful. Although it is permissible to postpone some of the paperwork when unstable patients would clearly suffer from delaying their transfer, EMTALA provides no guidance for predicting when moderately unstable patients will deteriorate and no provision for bucking the system on behalf of other patients (i.e., those not being transferred) who go untended during the bureaucratic shuffle.

Should we encounter a terrorist incident or a natural disaster, our ED would be quickly stressed to the breaking point. Suppose, for instance, that terrorists release sarin gas in a downtown Saint Louis mall on a scale similar to the Tokyo incident. And suppose we are lucky enough to be notified immediately of this event, before the arrival of casualties to our ED. In our chronically overcrowded state, the effort to set up decontamination areas and to free up treatment areas is extraordinarily difficult. All routine and semiurgent treatments are suspended. Several patients are dispatched to holding wards. Within twenty minutes, a half-dozen critically ill patients are brought by the emergency medical service (let us suppose these patients have been decontaminated in a staging area near the mall and that treatment has been initiated), followed by a number of woozy, vomiting individuals who arrive in the back of a pickup truck. The latter individuals have not yet been decontaminated, and they are herded outside for decontamination. By the time they finish, the ED is full of seriously compromised individuals who have tied up staff together with their reinforcements. Meanwhile, a little over 600 ambulatory patients (seven times our normal daily ED volume) have staggered to our doorstep seeking help. Our sweating, thirsty, moon-suited triage personnel diligently sift out the small numbers among these who require immediate treatment. They want to transport the remaining patients as quickly as possible to alternative facilities where they can be treated expeditiously. If the hundreds of nonurgent, "green" patients stay at our facility, they will wait interminably. Then the question arises: should we or shouldn't we transfer them?

Strictly interpreted, EMTALA forbids expeditious transport of these patients to alternative facilities. Triage does not include an adequate EMTALA screening examination, being a little too sparse on medical evaluation and far too sparse on documentation. Even in the simplest, most uncomplicated cases, adequate EMTALA pretransfer screening and paperwork will take at least ten minutes of clinicians' attention per patient. For 600 patients, this amounts to 100 hours of work. Even if it were possible to assign four doctors to this function, it would take them over twenty-four hours to effect the transfers legally. Casualties would grow restless.

Actually, this example is optimistic. In Tokyo, there were 12 sarin deaths, but over 5,000 walking wounded streamed into nearby emergency departments and clinics. As in other terrorist incidents such as the bombings in Oklahoma City and Nairobi, and both of the World Trade Center events, most patients in Tokyo (over 80%) arrived on their own, generally transporting themselves to the nearest facility rather than to more distant, less over-burdened facilities. In past terrorist incidents in the United States, doctors gave priority to patient safety and prudently neglected transfer regulations. Although such actions have yet to be challenged or litigated under EMTALA, the existence of inhibitory regulations remains a concern.

In fall of 2001 federal regulators tried to ameliorate some of this concern with the following announcement (Healthcare Financing Administration 2001):

There may be cases in which state or local governments have developed community response plans that designate specific entities (hospitals, public health facilities, etc.) with responsibility for handling certain categories of patient in bioterrorism situation. The transfer or referral of these patients in accordance with such a community plan would not violate the hospital's EMTALA obligations.

Despite this reassurance, several legitimate worries remain. First, given its incongruence with current legislation, the authority of this directive is suspect. Second, disjunction between directives of federal regulators and interpretation of these requirements by state inspectors and Medicare carriers is notorious (Hawryluk 2002). Finally, it is ambiguous as to what would count as being in accordance with a community plan, especially in the all-too-common instance in which such plans are vaguely written and/or poorly disseminated.

Quite simply EMTALA is a security risk. Under normal conditions, it places patients at risk because it delays care. In the ED, all delays are potentially dangerous. Given the war on terrorism and heightened risk of large-scale medical disasters, the danger is amplified. Specifically, EMTALA threatens national security in the following ways. It contributes to ED overcrowding. It forces ED physicians to focus their practice (and hence also much of their attention, training, and study) on evaluating nonurgent conditions rather than on emergency conditions and disasters. It enacts bureaucratic protocols that preclude effective disaster medicine. And by providing a vestige of (albeit inadequate) health care access for uninsured patients, it deflects attention from designing and implementing important infrastructure changes.

The Overcrowded ED

Since 1992 United States ED visits are up more than 14 percent to 103 million a year (McCaig and Burt 2001), yet the number of departments themselves is down by 8 percent (11 percent in rural areas) (Shute and

Marcus 2001). Much of the increased ED volume is due to an increasing number of visits for nonurgent illnesses, although the departments are also seeing more urgent and emergency cases (McCaig and Burt 2001; McCabe 2001). Because the total number of available hospital beds, especially intensive care unit beds, has declined markedly, critically ill patients are spending greater periods of time in EDs waiting for open beds. But these abstract numbers do not effectively describe the phenomenon of ED overcrowding. For this, one must simply be there. One must see the gurneys piled up in hallways, filled with men and women with broken bodies and grimacing, anxiety-ridden faces. One must behold the physician who is drawn and quartered by ten cases at once. And one must join an ambulance crew for an evening in limbo, bounced about by one hospital diversion after another.

The root causes of ED overcrowding can be classified into several categories: factors related to more ED visits; factors related to decreased ED efficiency; factors that impede ED patients from leaving the premises. Of course, there is some overlap. For instance, when patients do not leave the premises (factor 3) it has an effect on efficiency (factor 2). Although certainly not the sole culprit, EMTALA has contributed to each of these causes. It has increased the number of visits by transforming the ED into a default primary care clinic. It has decreased ED efficiency by generating paperwork and by shifting the focus away from rescue medicine. And it has impeded ED patients from leaving the premises by generating time-consuming discharge and transfer protocols.

The Default Primary Care Clinic

Currently over 40 million Americans lack health insurance. For these individuals, the ED is the only health care game in town. Many millions of others are inadequately insured and are forced into the ED when necessary services are not covered or when providers do not accept their insurance. Patients on Medicaid (the federally subsidized, state-administered indigent health insurance) are generally covered for basic services, but often have no relationship with or realistic access to primary care providers. Even these patients are now experiencing difficulty finding physicians who will accept their insurance (Pear 2002). Such patients look to the ED physician for a large proportion of their health care needs (McCaig and Burt 2001).

The typical contemporary ED sees three times as many nonemergency conditions as it does emergencies,[1] and ED physicians are often thrust into the position of providing continuing care for chronic conditions. It is not unusual for the physicians to do their own follow-up on sutures, infections requiring antibiotics, and other minor problems, but often their involvement runs much deeper than this. In Saint Louis, I recall seeing an uninsured man with advanced metastatic prostate cancer who had managed to find a irradiation oncologist willing to provide irradiation therapy free of charge. Unfortunately, he was less successful at making it to the office of an internist or oncology subspecialist. My colleagues and I treated him in the ED for virtually all the complications that attended his protracted demise, including partial bowel obstructions, bony pain, and skin lesions. This man and many like him persisted, despite protestations, in listing their favorite ED physicians as their primary care physicians or their family physicians, and with good reason.

Because EMTALA enforces an unfunded mandate that every ED will evaluate all comers, use of these departments as primary care clinics is inevitable. This EMTALA effect is subtler than one might think. Emergency departments have always been important safety nets and the best, most responsible ED physicians have always been willing to see all comers, despite the occasional triviality of their complaints. None of this changed with EMTALA. What changed was the public perception of the role of the ED, and the political will for finding other sources of primary care. As EDs came to be regarded as government-designated surrogate primary care clinics, the impetus to find other, more adequate venues dissipated. And the census rose.

The Effect on Disaster Preparedness

Common sense tells us that if emergency physicians spend most of their time seeing routine ambulatory medical cases and little time treating genuine emergencies or drilling for disasters, they will be more competent at delivering routine care than at responding to medical catastrophes. On the other hand, if emergency-medicine focused on responding to emergencies, ED physicians would be a lot more like firemen and less like family practitioners. They would drill frequently, and they would spend most of their time thinking about bad things that rarely happen.

Effective disaster medicine requires emphasis on efficiency rather than comprehensiveness. It requires a relatively detached rescue mentality rather than a more engaged caring mentality. This mandate runs counter to crucial values that have animated bioethics since its inception. Bioethicists have undertaken to dethrone rescue medicine, especially as it manifests itself in intensive care units and other dehumanizing, ultratechnical intervention zones. Because bioethics has been so obsessed about investing treatment of critically ill and dying patients with compassion, wisdom, and narrative exchange, the discipline has tended to portray detachment as one of medicine's greatest vices. It is no surprise that bioethicists have had relatively little to say about emergency medicine, and what they do say usually emphasizes the need for ED physicians to be more caring than they traditionally have been. And EMTALA continues in this tradition, viewing the emergency physician as harboring an essentially boundless reservoir of time and energy, convertible by adroit bureaucrats into large dollops of compassionate treatment and precise documentation.

In a disaster, this mindset is disastrous. The triage officer sorting through 100 patients in an hour has no time for eliciting personal narratives, or even for conversation. Paperwork is truncated into tag-work. And emotions should be, as far as possible, temporarily suspended.

A prudent disaster physician, that is, one who clearly understands the task (saving as many lives as possible with as little disability as possible) and who adroitly discerns the necessary constituents of this task (speedy transfer of large numbers of patients from hospital triage areas to secondary assessment centers), will disregard EMTALA entirely. She or he knows that if the hospital is close to a disaster area that it will probably be deluged with large numbers of walking wounded and worried well who can be treated elsewhere. The job is to ensure that these patients are triaged effectively, that they are not allowed to contaminate treatment areas or interfere with treatment of seriously injured patients, and that they are transported quickly as possible to an acceptable secondary assessment center (SAC). The SAC could be another building such as a local gymnasium, remote site in the hospital, or makeshift facility created under the direction of the incident command. It is not a hospital and its providers are, for the most part, not physicians. In the SAC, temporizing therapy or guidance is provided by paramedics, nurse practitioners, and others trained in disaster care, with the objective that patients can return home quickly and safely. Emergency physicians, meanwhile, remain in the ED treating serious casualties.

As EDs struggle to integrate their efforts with a larger public mission to protect citizens against terrorist attacks and other disasters, EMTALA-generated liabilities will become untenable. To function efficiently, the emergency-management system must employ emergency physicians who are readily available and trained for the management of mass casualties. Currently, this objective is impossible. Emergency physicians are unavailable because they are submerged in overcrowded EDs and burdened with paperwork. They lack expertise in rescue medicine because they have been forced to practice comfort medicine.

From the policy perspective this unfortunate situation is a byproduct of the old windmill campaign. Once upon a time—not so long ago—health care reformers set out to slay the perpetrators of patient dumping. In the process, they skewered every emergency physician, every emergency nurse, every critically ill patient, and every potential disaster victim in the country. In the name of equality, everyone has been wounded.

The Road to Universal Access

Does this hermit by any chance keep chickens?
—Sancho Panza

In the campaign for universal access to health care, victory will be partial and it will arise out of compromise. Bioethics is dominated by strong egalitarians who despise multitiered health systems, systems where citizens at different wealth and income levels receive different levels of medical service. To assist in making the quantum leap to the next level of access, these thinkers will have to set aside their aspirations for a unitary, single-tiered system. Similarly, libertarians and free-market advocates will have to concede a higher degree of government involvement than they view as optimal.

I will make no predictions or recommendations about how we will or should construct a specific template for universal access, except to predict (as above) that access will be partial; it will be access to a basic package rather than to the full gamut of effective or possibly effective treatments. My thesis is, instead, that universal access to a basic package of health benefits is justifiable on the basis of national security. As such, it is to be viewed as an important improvement to the national infrastructure, rather than as a moral entitlement of individuals.

Perhaps the most obvious link between universal access and national security is the consideration that to maximize survivability in a terrorist attack we need healthy, well-informed citizens. According to this line of reasoning, access to health care is important because it will enhance the overall health of the population and it will produce an informed citizenry, ready to act. In my opinion, this argument is weak. I find little reason to believe that increased access to health care will result in a significantly healthier population. As public health officials have been telling us for years, the most important causes of ill health and mortality are not greatly affected by doctor visits. Genes, lifestyles, and environment are more important. Dulcinea will continue to carouse, ignoring her doctors and other advisors. And there is even less reason to think that access to health care will enhance the savvy with which patients face terrorist threats. Most health care providers are woefully ignorant about NBC (nuclear, biological, chemical) warfare and its medical consequences. Witness the irrational prescription of Cipro during the anthrax scare.[2] There is little reason to think that doctor visits will significantly affect citizens' knowledge about what to do in the face of a NBC event or other terrorist attack. Public announcements, advertisements, and news are more effective and efficient when it comes to educating the public about responding to disasters.

The connection between national security and universal access to health care is mediated by the political imperative for solidarity. As I have proposed elsewhere, it is neither feasible nor desirable that Americans achieve solidarity by forging a thick common morality (Trotter 2002). We have too many diverging moral communities to achieve such an ideal without coercion. Nevertheless, solidarity is important, and if it is to be meaningful it requires mutual moral commitment. In the United States, as in any libertarian society, these commitments center on the provision of a political, social, and physical infrastructure that enhances the quality and security of ordinary lives and promotes the activities of ordinary social units in a manner that cuts across many creeds and cultures.

Basic health care can be a solid constituent of such an infrastructure. Individuals from virtually every American moral community live better when they have access to it. They live better because they feel more secure and because they are more socially integrated. To be needful of health care and to be turned away, on the other hand, is perceived as suffering an indignity. Systems that generate such indignities are offensive to the Hippocratic ideal, as well as to patient sensibilities.

In addition to these general considerations, disaster preparedness might be enhanced by universal access in several other specific ways. First, an effective disaster response requires kinship and trust between rescuers and victims. This relationship is cultivated with universal access to health care because health care personnel are more apt to be viewed in this instance as public servants, available to all. Second, systems of universal access would provide political pathways for disaster preparedness. That is, the disaster-response system could be built into the health system. Third, if the federal government ensured universal access to health care, citizens might develop a sense of ownership and common responsibility for the health care system. This attitude would translate into increased participation in disaster preparedness, an effect that would go much further than actual doctor visits toward producing citizens who are competent to survive a terrorist attack. Fourth, even apart from its effect on EMTALA, establishment of universal access to health care would mitigate ED overcrowding and hence help lay the foundation for better disaster preparedness. Better access to primary health care means better continuity of care, which should translate into fewer ED visits and fewer hospitalizations (Christakis et al. 2001).

However, the most important benefit of establishing universal access to health care from a disaster preparedness perspective is that it would provide a stimulus for bagging EMTALA. Effective disaster triage and rapid treatment protocols could be designed and implemented without running into a regulatory brick wall. No doubt, some bureaucrats and liberals will urge us to retain EMTALA even if we do achieve universal access. So long as there are incentives to transfer the most poorly insured or financially unpromising patients, these commentators will warn, there is an imperative for EMTALA protection. But other less intrusive and dangerous ways of addressing patient dumping are available. Even before EMTALA, a burgeoning tide of litigation was growing against patient dumping (Frank 1985). Now that evaluation and stabilization before transfer are clearly established as standards of care for emergency medicine, it will be even more feasible to prosecute negligent dumping in civil court.

For bioethics, establishment of a system of universal access, even a compromise-generated, two-tiered system of basic services, is a worthy venture. Should they assist in this endeavor, bioethicists would earn a great victory. Within their own ranks, many warring strands could be united in a common project. In the long run, today's compromise would likely produce the kind of stable consensus that so many bioethicists crave, consensus that health care, like education, is an important pillar in the national infrastructure. The cleavage between public policy and professional medical values would shrivel. And erstwhile knight-errants, feasting on success, could gaze on the horizon of better, nobler crusades.

Notes

1. Data from 1999 (McCaig and Burt 2001) indicate that 17 percent of United States emergency department visits were for patients triaged as emergencies. In this study, emergency visit was defined as a "visit at which the triage practitioner determines that the patient should receive care immediately to combat danger to life or limb, and where any delay would likely result in deterioration." The actual percentage of emergency visits is probably higher, however, because 27 percent of visits recorded in 1999 contained no triage designation. Hence, about 23.5 percent of emergency department visits in which a triage category was listed were triaged into the emergency category. The most common illness-related diagnosis for ED visits is "acute respiratory infection"—i.e., the common cold.

2. Prescriptions for Cipro were up 42 percent nationwide, and 203 percent in the New York area (Furmans 2001). The proliferation of prescriptions for Cipro was irrational because the drug was prescribed in many instances in which chances of deleterious side effects greatly eclipsed any possibility that patients actually harbored anthrax, and because there was little reason to believe that Cipro would be more effective than doxycycline for postexposure prophylaxis against anthrax. Cipro costs $4.25 a tablet, doxycycline costs $0.80. Both agents are given in the dosage of one tablet twice a day. In the only study that compares these agents for postexposure prophylaxis against anthrax (in rhesus monkeys), doxycycline did better than Cipro. The military, which acquires Cipro at a steep discount, added Cipro rather than doxycycline to Gulf War soldiers' first-aid kits. This decision was based on the dubious consideration that Iraq was more likely to have engineered doxycycline-resistant than Cipro-resistant strains of anthrax.

References

Blendon, Robert J. et al. 2002. "The Impact of Terrorism and the Recession on Americans' Health Priorities." *Health Affairs*. Available at *http://www.healthaffairs.org/WebExclusives/Blendon Web Exclusive 011602* (visited January 16, 2002).

Christakis, Dimitri A. et al. 2001. "Association of Lower Continuity of Care with Greater Risk of Emergency Department Use and Hospitalization in Children." *Pediatrics*. 107 (March): 524–529.

Frank, Cheryl. 1985. "Dumping the Poor: Private Hospitals Risk Suits." *ABA Journal*. 71 (March): 25.

Furmans, Vanessa. 2001. "Its Image Under Fire, Bayer AG Scrambles to Meet Cipro Demand." *Wall Street Journal*. October 22, A1, A8.

Hawryluk, Markian. 2002. "CMS Help Lines, Bulletins, Offer Little Help, GAO Says." *American Medical News*. 45 (March 18): 5, 7.

Healthcare Financing Administration. 2001. "Bio-Terrorism Questions and Answers." Available at *http://www.hcfa.gov/medlearn/terrorqa.htm* (visited April 4, 2002).

McCabe, John B. 2001. "Emergency Department Overcrowding: A National Crisis." *Academic Medicine*. 7: 672–674.

McCaig, Linda F. and Catherine W. Burt. 2001. "National Hospital Ambulatory Medical Care Survey: 1999 Emergency Department Summary." *Advance Data*. 320: 1–36 (June 25).

Pear, Robert. 2002. "Doctors Shunning Patients with Medicare." *New York Times*. [Web version] (visited March 17).

Shute, Nancy and Mary Brophy Marcus. 2001. "Code Blue: Crisis in the ER." *U.S. News and World Report*. September 10, 54–61.

Trotter, Griffin. 2002. "Bioethics and Healthcare Reform: A Whig Response to Weak Consensus." *Cambridge Quarterly of Healthcare Ethics*. 11 (Winter): 37–51.

World Health Organization. 1946. Preamble to the Constitution of the World Health Organization adopted at the International Health Conference, New York, June 19–22.

IV
Industry Obligations

9

The Rightful Goals of a Corporation and the Obligations of the Pharmaceutical Industry in a World with Bioterrorism

Evan G. DeRenzo

The Rightful Purpose of a Corporation

Proposing that corporations have moral obligations beyond not breaking the law flies in the face of what many consider the only necessary corporate ethos—seek profits for stockholders. According to this view, most notably articulated by Milton Friedman (1970), the primary responsibility of a corporation is to produce profits for its owners to the greatest extent possible within the limits of the law. Given that corporations do make profits for their owners, on the face of it, Friedman's assertion sounds plausible. It is an assertion that has held sway for a long time across a great number of persons and institutions.

Strengthening the grip of this viewpoint on corporate and public assumptions about the morally appropriate ordering of business goals is that it is consistent with legal opinion. The classic example is the case of Dodge v. Ford Motor Co. in which Justice J. Ostrander (1919) of the Michigan Supreme Court opined, "A business corporation is organized and carried on primarily for the profit of the stockholders. The powers of the directors are to be employed for that end." If, however, one thinks seriously about the implications of what Justice Ostrander and Milton Friedman are saying, they do not make moral sense.

Just because persons act and judges opine in such a fashion does not mean that they are right. To the act or the opinion and the ethics is to fall prey to the classic philosophical problem of conflating the "is–ought" distinction; that is, facts—the "is" part—with what should be the case—the "ought" part. In the present matter, confusion is over what is versus what ought to be the primary moral goal of a corporation.

Robert Solomon (1993) made a convincing argument that misconceptions about the profit motive have supplanted the rightful goals of business and that the profit motive is merely a euphemism for abstract greed. Solomon cited Anthony Flew (1976), who attacked the reasonableness of the profit motive, wondering if it was reasonable to elevate it to the status of a primary goal. He sked rhetorically why it would not be reasonable also to elevate the notions of a "wage motive" or a "rent motive" or an "interest motive" to a morally acceptable primary business goal.

The silliness of Flew's question lays bare the conceptual absurdity. Completing the destruction of the (il)logic that profit motive is the morally acceptable primary goal for the conduct of business, Solomon concluded sardonically, "Of course, people work for profits, in a system that encourages profit making. But it does not follow that there is a profit motive. . . . So, too, we could speak of a 'theft motive' or a 'murder motive,' but no one would thereby conclude that the actions that follow such motives are thereby justified or even excusable ('I'm sorry, Your Honor, I just had this overwhelming murder motive')" (Flew 1976, 40). Or consider sexuality; the next time your neighbor says that it is ethically acceptable to engage in adultery because he or she is motivated to have sex, take pause. It may be that your neighbor's adulterous motives are focused on your partner.

What, however, can be said to refute the supposed wisdom of the court? Here, again, we have to avoid confusing fact and value. Just because something is legal does not make it ethical. Let us use one of the darkest examples in United States history still in the memories of living Americans to demonstrate this fact. Jim Crow laws made it legal for restaurants to deny serving African-Americans and for hotels to deny African-Americans lodging, and forced African-Americans into separate, substandard public bathrooms, schools, and housing. Legal, yes. Ethical, no. It is critically important to recognize how often we conflate law and ethics, saying, "Well, it's legal, isn't it?," assuming that makes performing or withholding some action ethically acceptable. Instead, we must remember that judges and juries are composed of humans who are influenced by social customs and morals of the times in which they live. There is nothing immutable about earthly laws, which can be just as flawed and inconsistent as the humans making them.

Fortunately, however, humans and the institutions they create are capable of ethical evolution. Whether resulting from respectful questioning, vocal, angry debate, or even violent protest, insightful analysis can produce advances in the moral norms accepted by persons and institutions. Think, for example, about evolving notions of what is required for ethical conduct of human subjects research. When physicians first conducted research, they did it with little or no consent. Probably this omission was not because these early investigators consciously, explicitly conspired to keep the information from subjects, but more likely because it simply did not occur to anyone that such a thing as consent was required. Today, it is generally accepted that consent is essential. Not only do individual investigators know that, but institutions have substantial infrastructure and organizational mechanisms to ensure that consent is appropriately obtained and documented, consistent with international and national rules, regulations, and other guidance documents supporting this evolution in ethical reasoning.

It is this same kind of moral evolution that now has to be applied to the everyday thinking and workings of the business world. It is time to dispense with the moral nonsense that the appropriate primary goal of business is to produce profit for its shareholders.

The idea that seeking profits ought not be the primary goal of business ought not be confused with the unsupportable position that making profits is immoral. Profit is necessary for businesses to grow. Profit, defined as "the outcome of a monetary transaction, an 'investment,'" what is left over after all expenses are paid, subject, of course, to considerable creative finagling over what is to count as an "expense" and, accordingly, what is "left over" (Solomon 1993, 39), plus margin for risk—all are required to allow businesses to expand and flourish.

To suggest, however, that the primary purpose of a corporation ought to be to accrue profit is to miss the ethical point. Profit, as an end unto itself, may be what some people work toward, but that does not make it a morally justifiable primary end, a point well appreciated by two of the most successful pharmaceutical companies. Merck and Johnson & Johnson (J&J) understand that the ethically appropriate ordering of a corporation's moral goals requires putting production of goods and services first.

In the words of George Merck (2002), "We try never to forget that medicine is for the people. It is not for the profits. The profits follow, and if we have remembered that, they have never failed to appear." The J&J Credo, first published in 1943, begins by stating: "We believe our first responsibility is to the doctors, nurses, and patients, to mothers and fathers and others who use our products and services." The rest of the document orders corporate responsibilities to employees second and being a good community and world citizen third. Fourth and last is J&J's responsibility to its shareholders. This section of the Credo acknowledges that, "Business must make a sound profit." But it is clear that J&J understands well where profit making fits into the scheme of appropriate business goals. The Credo's concluding statement is, "When we operate according to these principles, the stockholders should realize a fair return." This ordering is consistent with the best of the corporate world, and threats of modern life, such as bioterrorism, demand that it become standard.

There is merit in the traditional idea that the primary ethical goal of business is production and exchange of goods and services necessary to advance the good life for the citizenry. The good life is not meant to be either utopian or to characterize a society in which government or special interests impose uniform conceptions of what a good life might be. To talk about the good life is to characterize a free and open society in which its members have the opportunity to strive for their individual desires and potential. As a society becomes increasingly diversified and evolves ethically in such a way that it fully honors that diversity, the beauty of a market economy becomes ever more obvious. As shown by the resounding failure of the economies of Communist countries around the globe, government attempts to serve as the sole arbiter of what goods and services ought to be produced for a society do not produce a healthy, vibrant economy. Instead, the genius of the mythology of the invisible hand continues to serve human progress and prosperity (Smith 1937).

That means that for the most part, allowing goods and services to be produced and exchanged in accordance with self-interested preferences of a community's individual and institutional purchasers is justified on the basis of a utilitarian analysis. Yet it is also obvious on the same ethical grounds that, left totally unrestricted, a free market can result in harms to a community that are inimical to the good life. Thus, to achieve the primary moral ends of living the good life, laws are created to constrain the free market system where the body politic deems necessary. A few examples should suffice.

Although providing products at the lowest cost ordinarily is the ideal for both buyer and seller, under certain circumstances, such as general global needs for environmental protections, this is not invariably the case. When it comes to having clean air and fresh water, companies that produce environment-harming wastes are compelled by public policy to have waste-disposal processes to protect the environment. Creating public policy in this area, however, has been and continues to be a struggle. Defining what is a fair balance between reasonable and unreasonable burdens on business will depend on where the viewer stands. Delineating the degree to which corporations ought to be held responsible has resulted in considerable public debate, with little consensus achieved. Nonetheless, few believe that business ought to be permitted to pursue even rightful ends in such a way as to disregard harms that such pursuit may cause to the planet's air, soil, and water.

A less controversial example concerns illicit drugs and child pornography. Virtually every country in the world could have a thriving market in recreational narcotics and child pornography if the invisible hand were left to manage vice. But because of the grave harms that would ensue, most countries make both products illegal. Here, too, these matters are not without controversy and disagreement. Public debate continues about which nonmedical drugs ought to be placed beyond consumer's reach and over what lengths we should go to block access to child pornography.

In both examples, tempering a strict utilitarian calculus by Kantian concepts of duty and obligation is tolerated on the ethical reasoning that a government has an obligation to protect its citizens. In an unsafe world, the good life is beyond everyone's grasp. When it comes to public safety, consensus is easily reached that government interference in the free market is not only ethically acceptable but also obligatory. Especially since September 11, virtually no debate has been held in the United States about the need for securing our borders from foreign invasion or from foreign or domestic terrorist attack. The one area that seems indisputably the domain of a government to regulate and control, even if it constrains free markets, is protecting its citizens and supporting military action required to do so.

Interference in free markets by government on behalf of homeland security and enhanced global intelligence-gathering capabilities are not always only constraining. As a result of the public's support of the United States government's expansion of its antiterrorist military and quasi-military activities, new businesses sprang up and existing businesses expanded and moved into new market areas. If the primary moral purpose of a corporation is not simply profit, what might be implications for the pharmaceutical industry?

The Rightful Purpose of a Pharmaceutical Corporation

The moral purpose of a pharmaceutical corporation is to produce and exchange pharmaceutical goods and services necessary to pursue the good life. Although it is beyond the scope of this chapter to tackle the question of where on the list of human goods health sits, we know it is fundamental to living well. Pharmaceutical corporations, by virtue of the types of goods and services they produce and exchange, are central to human well-being. These goods and services cover the full range of agents, interventions, and related activities involved in prevention, diagnosis, treatment, and cure of diseases or medical conditions that produce physical and mental impairment, pain, suffering, or death. The stakeholders cover the globe. This is not only because many pharmaceutical companies are multinational, but also relates to the kinds of goods and services produced and exchanged. Research to develop pharmaceutical goods and services is increasingly global, and disease does not honor national boundaries.

Although the numbers and kinds of goods and services are vast, the scope is not infinitely elastic. That is, conditions other than those amenable to pharmacologic intervention produce disease, debilitating conditions, pain, suffering, and death. But unless such conditions are remediable by activities involved in the production and exchange of pharmaceutical goods and services, we should not set unreasonable expectations of the degree to which the industry is held accountable. Consider the intertwined problems of poverty and violence, such as critical injury from gang attack, to a patient without health insurance.

It is regularly the case that persons who lack health insurance in the United States receive substandard medical care. Subspecialty care is frequently difficult to obtain. Discharge from hospitals to community care often means discharge to no care at all. For a patient, or family member, or other caregiver, it is distressing that sound medical care is denied because of social injustice in a country with arguably the best medicine available in the world.

The pharmaceutical industry has a moral obligation to be a good faith participant in public policy debates required to resolve health problems such social injustices cause. But we should demand only implementation of those parts of the solution that involve production and exchange of pharmaceutical goods and services. Working with international and national government, patient, and citizen groups to develop and implement industry-wide fair pricing strategies for pharmaceuticals is an example of a reasonably expected corporate responsibility (Brody 1996; Pecoul et al. 1999; Durbin 2002; Freudenheim 2002). Developing, supporting, and participating in community programs to reduce crime that results in injuries requiring medical care, however, is not.

Of course, it might be in the strategic interests of a pharmaceutical corporation to participate in such programs. Supererogatory corporate behavior is to be applauded. It has always been a point of pride for me that my family's firm, Saginaw Furniture Corporation, converted its Saginaw, Michigan, furniture-manufacturing plant during World War II to produce tank body parts for the Army. Nonetheless, neither Kantian considerations of duty nor utilitarian notions of personal sacrifice for the greater good can be stretched to suggest convincingly that corporations have an obligation to move well beyond their primary focus on goods and services.

Instead, one can set reasonable limits on the obligations of the pharmaceutical industry and on any particular pharmaceutical corporation. In addition, accepting this premise allows us to avoid the complex debate about whether or not corporations are moral agents in the same sense as individuals. We need not spend time here in lengthy rebuttal of Milton Friedman's (1970) claim that corporations have no social responsibilities because "only people can have responsibilities." The relevant point is that in meeting what is surely its primary moral purpose, the corporation can take various routes to achieve that purpose. In deciding on the routes, the obvious requirement is to choose those that are moral.

Special Obligations of the Pharmaceutical Industry and Its Separate Corporations

Because its products protect or enhance human or animal health, the pharmaceutical industry is a central player in the new horror film of bioterrorism. Regardless of how macabre the film might be, the industry can not avoid participating in antibioterrorist efforts. This role can be played well or ill. Aristotelian notions of virtue, reiterated in contemporary philosophy (MacIntyre 1981) and modern business ethics (MacIntyre 1977; Solomon 1993), are instructive. These ancient notions of right behavior well serve efforts at clarifying particular obligations created by the performance of particular activities. That is, companies that produce and exchange pharmaceutical goods and services have obligations connected to virtuous performance of these functions. "So, too, in business ethics, the Aristotelian view takes ethics to be not an imposition from above (reason or the divine law), nor a matter of internal, individual conscience and consciousness, but a set of virtues and values that are formed by the practice of business and cultivated (whether or not formulated) by the business community" (Solomon 1993, 202). Although philosophers have long argued about what a reasonable list of virtues might include, general consensus is that trustworthiness, integrity, and conscientiousness belong on everyone's list. The following example is illustrative.

Amadeo Peter Giannini, born 1870, in San Jose, California, was the son of Italian immigrants. As a bank board member who encouraged making loans to immigrants, he was at odds with the banking establishment that mainly served business and the rich. In 1904 he opened the bank of Italy and staked his claim on making loans to the little guy. When the great earthquake struck in 1906, and San Francisco was in rubble, he again found himself at odds with his colleagues. They wanted to keep banks closed and wait to see if the area's economy would collapse along with the buildings. Giannini disagreed, believing that if loans were not made immediately the economic collapse would be a result of bankers' self-fulfilling prophesy, not of the earthquake.

Putting the money from his bank into a horse-drawn wagon and making a desk out of a wooden plank and two barrels, he set up shop on the docks of San Francisco's waterfront. He made loans to small businesses and individuals and is credited for much of the city's redevelopment. Thereafter, Giannini went on to buy Bank of America, today the second largest bank in the United States (Kadlec 2002).

This story of is relevant also for another reason. Not only does it appear that Giannini grasped the core moral notion of banking as providing banking services to assist customers to pursue the good life, he did so under conditions of environmental catastrophe. When disaster hit, rather than hunker down, he innovated. He was more than innovative in the traditional sense of creativity in product development, he was creative in organizational response. "Innovative companies are not only unusually good at producing commercially viable new widgets; innovative companies are especially adroit at continually responding to change of any sort in their environments" (Peters and Waterman 1982, 12).

Achieving their primary moral purpose in a world of bioterrorist threat calls on pharmaceutical companies to respond to this new catastrophe in moral ways. The goods and services the companies produce and exchange are linked to ways in which bioterrorism or the threat thereof may affect industry activities.

Security

The bioterrorist threat demands that security for laboratory facilities and corporate communications systems be at an all-time high. Security has always been necessary to protect against accidents, industrial piracy, and sabotage. Now, however, the new threat demands that it be tightened. Animal and plant laboratory facilities and transport systems must take exceeding care to protect against threats from theft or contamination. This should be each corporation's highest priority.

Recommendation   Bioterror security consultants should be brought into all pharmaceutical corporations to evaluate facilities and operations related to vulnerabilities to bioterror threat. Reassessment should be performed on a regular basis to ensure that previously identified vulnerabilities have been reduced and/or removed and to capture new once that may have developed.

Research and Development

Deciding where to put research and development resources has implications for antibioterrorist strategy development. Blockbuster drugs, devices, and biologics produce huge profits for their manufacturers and the promise of better health for patients. Producing a new drug merely to gain market share, a strategy often called "me-too" drugs, however, is morally unacceptable. The reason to develop new drugs, devices, or biologics is because real improvement is required.

What is interesting about this issue is that if only one drug is available for a particular indication, vulnerability increases. Having effective alternatives is important; however, this is not an argument that favors development of me-too drugs. What bioterrorist vulnerability favors is true innovation.

The common position in support of me-too drugs is that even for a blockbuster agent, in a subset of patients it will be ineffective or produce unacceptable side effects. No question, this point is convincing; it makes good strategic sense to diversify diagnostic and therapeutic interventions. But as a support for developing me-too drugs, the position does not hold up. When only one drug is available for a particular indication, and when the alternatives are improvements based on completely different diagnostic or therapeutic strategies, clinical and antibioterrorist efforts support drug development. Pursuing such innovations addresses both the issue of subpopulation efficacy-side effects and antiterrorist demands for diversified defenses.

Recommendation   Pharmaceutical corporations must establish structured mechanisms for rigorous and internally open discussions about the moral purposes and goals at the earliest stage of drug, device, or biologic development. These discussions should be multidisciplinary and occur at the highest levels of corporate decision making—clinical, commercial, and regulatory. They must analyze ways in which legitimate moral justifications for moving forward with or terminating a drug, device, or biologic program may conflict.

Patents

Patent protection is reputedly the life blood of research and development. Industry dogma is that without it, companies will lack competitive motivation to put in substantial up-front resources necessary to bring new products to market. Without such protection, the debate goes, the pace of medical progress will slow or stop dead in its tracks. Much controversy surrounds the ethical acceptability of patent practices and it does not appear to be abating (McGee 1998; Rifkin 1998; Merz 1999; Resnik 2001; Attaran and Gillespie-White 2001).

Issues of the patent debate crystallize in the Cipro story (Friscolanti 2001; Vedantam 2001; West 2001; Mantz 2001). Cipro is the only drug licensed by the Food and Drug Administration (FDA) to treat anthrax infection. When anthrax was sent through the U.S. mail, exposing postal workers and those connected to the intended recipients, panic set in and there was a rush on the drug. To quell concern and ensure availability of Cipro, the United States and Canadian governments moved to break the patent held by Bayer, the German pharmaceutical company. Panic subsided and negotiations with Bayer resulted in production and purchase arrangements that avoided takeover of the patent.

We should not be caught so unprepared a next time. As legal, business ethics, and social policy scholars become more mindful of ways in which increasingly complex relationships between patents and regulations affect innovation (Eisenberg 2001), we must look for ways to refine patent laws that preserve legitimate corporate interests that also make moral sense for a world threatened by bioterrorism.

Recommendation   When only one FDA-approved drug for an indication exists, mechanisms should be created immediately for compromise between total unwillingness to relax or relinquish patent protection temporarily and a fair alternative means of compensation. One possibility would be to create an amendment to the existing patent laws that allows for a "stop-the-clock" interruption on the basis of national security. What is envisioned is something akin to a similar mechanism that allows tenure-track university faculty women to take maternity leave without continuing to run the tenure clock during that career suspension. This would involve creating a fair process to determine that an emergency was of such national or global security importance as to merit this drastic step. During the time the disaster called for lifting the patent, other issues, such as who else would be allowed to produce the drug and placing constraints on competitor product development, would require agreement and public policy development. Substantive review, and possibly refinements, of patent laws relating to pharmaceuticals and bioterrorism are warranted.

Fair Pricing

When considering issues of exchange of pharmaceuticals, the Cipro story is again illustrative. During the hearings about possibly breaking Bayer's patent, Rep. Henry A. Waxman of California, ranking Democrat on the Government Reform Committee, was reported as saying, "The disparities in Cipro pricing show that drug prices have become so complicated that even the largest purchasers are groping in the dark to try to figure out what is a fair price and what is unreasonable" (Vedantam 2001). Although it is credibly maintained that price disparities across patient populations and nations have been exaggerated, public interest groups and published data raise serious justice concerns about how drugs are priced and marketed globally (Kleinke 2001; Reinhardt 2001; Burton et al. 2001). The Cipro story has brought renewed vigor to the debate about fair pricing that we should not squander.

Recommendation   Efforts at all levels of government should establish formal ways to bring all stakeholders together. Such coordinated systems must focus sustained deliberations, conducted in good faith, on the goal of developing fair pricing strategies for drugs, devices, and biologics in the event of another bioterrorist attack. Several nascent models indicate how this might work. The Institute of Medicine roundtable is one (Institute of Medicine). The pharmaceutical industry has created its own Task Force on Emergency Preparedness (Pharmaceutical Research and Manufacturers 2001). Neither entity, however, has the breadth of membership, explicit mandate, or formal bioterrorism agenda necessary to resolve some of the most intractable problems related to development of industry-wide fair pricing standards.

Systems Coordination

Without significantly greater coordination of government entities and the pharmaceutical industry, in the event of bioterrorist attack, preparative effects will come to little. Bioterrorism and its threat sow panic, and when casualties and destruction of property occur, the effects are almost unimaginable. Our best hope is to create coordinated systems of communication and decision making immediately. Data and experience consistently show that confusion over decision making and lines of authority increase chaos in response to a disaster (Vastag 2001). We must create mechanisms now that can be activated promptly and that will set in motion arrangements that were already worked out in principle.

Recommendation   Government agencies at federal, state, and local levels must move to highly coordinated, systems of internal communication. Policies and procedures should be developed and disseminated, clearly identifying who and how authority is to be managed and communicated throughout all response systems. Maryland's legislation (Mosk 2002) is a good example of what local measures should look like. It is incumbent on the federal government to produce linking legislation to create a seamless network of coordinated agency response. It is important to call for rapid progress in government interagency coordination in communication. What might be asked of the pharmaceutical industry ought not be more than is asked of, and obtained from, public agencies.

Education

The pharmaceutical industry must be educated and trained concerning bioterrorist threats to their research and manufacturing facilities, distribution processes, and communications systems. Employees must understand the vulnerabilities of their corporations and specifics related to their own job responsibilities. This education is beyond internal corporate capabilities and should be provided by outside entities. Because protection against bioterrorist threat is a government responsibility, the federal government ought to shoulder significant portions of the burden of this additional training.

Recommendation   Consistent with a recommendation by Thomas Frazier, President of GenCon of Montross, Virginia, "Associations, agribusinesses, and pharmaceutical companies should be provided with cooperative private courses and workshops by law enforcement, defense, and intelligence agencies to educate and inform them about current and prospective threats and defense measures they can take. These courses and workshops should include protecting company facilities and critical infrastructures from chemical and biological terrorism and biocrimes"

(Frazier 1999, 7). Antibioterrorist education will have to be integrated into regular corporate in-service training programs.

Reducing Unnecessary Corporate Secrecy

It is time to reevaluate and refine corporate policies on secrecy and proprietary information. Corporations have legitimate and morally acceptable needs in these areas to protect their competitive advantage, but it is time to bring a greater degree of reasonableness and proportion to such practices. Protection of proprietary information need not be breached in an effort to communicate more transparently across the industry and with the public.

The importance of breaking down anachronistic, overly secretive modes of thinking is demonstrated by the story told by Frazier of his e-mail exchange with a European colleague. In this e-mail note, Frazier's correspondent wrote, "Based here in the UK as European Secretary of the Animal Transportation Association I am acutely aware of attacks on all sorts of commercial biological targets from GM crops to livestock haulers, veterinary laboratories, breeding establishments, and veterinary surgeries, to name but a few." Frazier laments, "We are working more or less in the dark because governments and companies use very compartmentalized security measures to keep one another and the public in the dark" (Frazier 1999, 2). These often counterproductive practices are typified by one bad example. When Schering-Plough Corporation was accused of bad ethical judgment, efforts by the press to obtain a copy of its corporate code of conduct were unsuccessful. The press reported that Schering-Plough said that the code was "an internal document meant for employees and could not be provided to outsiders" (Verschoor 2001). Pharmaceutical companies must innovate in the Giannini sense, recognizing that the Cold War is over and that the industry should update its secrecy practices accordingly.

Recommendation Industry-wide standards of practice that call for keeping secret only information that realistically can be expected to impinge directly on the production or exchange of a company's goods and services should be developed. This process of standard setting should be coordinated through the industry's professional associations.

Finally, the industry must become internally more alert to issues related to bioterrorism. That means not only increasing security but also being aware of business opportunities that this new threat creates for developing drugs, devices, and biologics, or distribution systems that will serve antibioterror ends as well as the primary moral purpose of a pharmaceutical company.

Recommendation   Persons with bioterror expertise or interests should be added to the company payroll, and bioterror experts might be asked to serve on boards of directors.

Conclusion

The surest road to achieving pharmaceutical corporations's purpose is innovation. Changes in the fabric of moral communities of the United States and those around the world as a result of September 11 can be expected to produce substantial innovations in pharmaceutical products and exchange mechanisms, as well as in the business environment itself. The winds of such change can already be felt. Fundamental differences in ways in which the pharmaceutical industry interacts with government are already taking place. Although the industry and the FDA have always had a cozy working relationship, evolving relationships that turn pharmaceutical companies into biodefense contractors are new. Reports of high-level industry discussions about how to work with the United States government to produce pharmaceutical-defense systems have appeared in the press (Hensley and Winslow 2001). Debates related to change in response to bioterrorism must forge new corporate and industry-wide patterns of more open communication and disclosure of processes, policies, and procedures. For example, although most published discussions focused on ensuring greater preparedness for future attacks, vigorous debate about just where resources are most appropriately and profitably placed are emerging (Cohen et al. 2001). Such conversations and many others required to adapt to a changed world must be more open than those the pharmaceutical industry conducted in the past. Unnecessary secrecy prevents optimal policy development, public or internal, by reducing the voices and perspectives brought to bear on such highly complex problems as protection of populations against bioterrorist attack.

The events of September 11, 2001, and the bioterror attack on members of the U.S. Congress, postal workers, private citizens, and the media indelibly altered the way the world works. As business, and the public whose needs it meets, struggle to adjust to the new and unwelcome problems bioterrorism brings, the importance of adapting to new rules of practice becomes obvious (Wilson 2000; Gardner et al. 2001). As society works out who is responsible for which parts of the problem (Fletcher 1999), staying focused on what the moral goals of business ought to be will serve everyone.

Acknowledgments

I thank the following persons for their assistance during various stages of the development of this chapter: Gail Waldman of Waldman Financial Advisors, Fairfax, Virginia for her research related to the Cipro story; Dianne Howell, of FreemanWhite, Inc., North Carolina for her review of a previous draft of the chapter; Al Derivan, MD and Rick Martinez, MD, Johnson & Johnson, for their discussions in the conceptual stage of this chapter; and Emil DeRenzo, my husband, for serving as the backboard for my thinking throughout the whole process.

Disclaimer. The thoughts contained in this chapter are mine only, and the only material support that I received in the preparation of this chapter from any institution or organization with which I am affiliated was in the form of the outstanding skills of Carol Lever, librarian, Union Memorial Hospital, Baltimore, MD.

References

Attaran, Amir and Lee Gillespie-White. (2001). "Do Patents for Antiretroviral Drugs Constrain Access to AIDS Treatment in Africa?" *Journal of the American Medical Association*. 286. 15: 1886–1892.

Brody, Baruch. (1996). "Public Goods and Fair Prices: Balancing Technological Innovation with Social Well-being." *Hastings Center Report*. 26 (March/April): 5–11.

Burton, Stephan L. et al. (2001). "The Ethics of Pharmaceutical Benefit Management. *Health Affairs*. 20. 5: 150–163.

Cohen, Hillel W., Victor W. Sidel, and R.M. Gould. (2001). Preparedness for Bioterrorism? *New England Journal of Medicine*. 345. 19: 1423–1424.

Durbin, Dee-Ann. (2002). "Drug Firms Fights Prescription Plan." *Washington Post*. January 7. Available at http://www.washingtonpost.com/ac2/wp-dyn/A9616-2002Jan7?language=printer.

Eisenberg, Rebecca S. (2001). "The Shifting Functional Balance of Patents and Drug Regulation." *Health Affairs*. 20. 5: 119–135.

Fletcher, Robert H. (1999). "Who Is Responsible for the Common Good in a Competitive Market?" *Journal of the American Medical Association*. 281. 12: 281, 361–367.

Flew, Anthony. (1976). "The Profit Motive." *Ethics*. 86: 312–322.

Frazier, Thomas W. (1999). "Natural and Bioterrorist/Biocriminal Threats to Food and Agriculture." *Annals of the New York Academy of Sciences*. 894: 1–9.

Freudenheim, Milt. (2002). "Spending on Prescription Drugs Rises Sharply." *New York Times*. March 29. Available at http://www.nytimes.com/2002/03/29/health/29COST.html?pagewanted=print&position=top.

Friedman, Milton. (1970). "The Social Responsibility of Business Is to Increase Its Profits." *New York Times Magazine*. September 13. Reprinted in Beauchamp, T.L. and Bowie, N. (1993). *Ethical Theory and Business*, 56. Englewood Cliffs, NJ: Prentice-Hall.

Friscolanti, Michael. (2001). "Ottawa Tilts Rules to Get Anthrax Pill: Maker of No-name Drugs Says It Has Order to Produce 900,000 Pills by Early November." *National Post*. Available at http://www.elibrary.com/s/edumark/getdoc.cgi?id=213491592x127y60780w0&OIDS=0Q001D025&.

Gardner, Howard, Mihaly, Csikszenthmihalyi, and William Damon. (2001). *Good Work: When Excellence and Ethics Meet*. New York: Basic Books.

Hensley, Scott and Ron Winslow. (2001). "Drug Companies Must Contemplate New Role as 'biodefense contractors.'" *Wall Street Journal*. November 12. Available at http://interactive.wsj.com/archive/retrieve.cgi?id=SB1005523942796771360.djm&template=doclink.

Institute of Medicine. "Pharmaceutical roundtable." Available at www.iom.edu/crr.

Johnson & Johnson. (2002). "Credo." May 3. Available at http://jnj.com/who_is_jnj/cr_usa.html.

Kadlec, Daniel. (2002). "American's Banker A.P. Giannini." *Time*. May 3. Available at http://www.time.com/time/time100/builder/profile/giannini.html.

Kleinke, J.D. (2001). "The Price of Progress: Prescription Drugs in the Health Care Market." *Health Affairs*. 20. 5: 43–60.

MacIntyre, Alasdair. (1977). "Why Are the Problems of Business Ethics Insoluble?" In *Proceedings of the First National Conference on Business Ethics*. Waltham, MA: Bentley College.

MacIntyre, Alasdair. (1981). *After Virtue*. Notre Dame, IN: University of Notre Dame.

Mantz, Beth M. (2001). "Tales of the Tape: Drug Makers Enlist in Bioterror Fight." *Dow Jones Newswires*. December 9. Available at http://interactive.wsj.com/archive/retrieve@0.cgi?unionm/text/autowire/data/BT-CO-20011109-0048.

McGee, Glenn. (1998). "Gene Patents Can Be Ethical." *Cambridge Quarterly of Healthcare Ethics.* 7: 417–421.

Merck, George. (2002). Available at http://www.merck.com/about/ (visited May 3).

Merz, Jon F. (1999). "Disease Gene Patents: Overcoming Unethical Constraints on Clinical Laboratory Medicine. *Clinical Chemistry.* 45. 3: 324–330.

Mosk, Matthew. (2002). "Glendening Expands Bioterrorism Health Coverage." *Washington Post.* April 9. Available at http://www.washingtonpost.com/ac2/wp-dyn/A20105-2002Apr9?language=printer.

Ostrander, J. 1919. "Majority Opinion." Michigan Superior Court, 204 Mich. 459, 170 N.W. 668, 3 A.L.R. 413. Reprinted in Beauchamp, T.L. and N. Bowie. (1993). *Ethical Theory and Business,* 95. Englewood Cliffs, NJ: Prentice-Hall.

Pecoul, Bernard et al. (1999). "Access to Essential Drugs in Poor Countries: A Lost Battle?" *Journal of the American Medical Association.* 281. 4: 361–367.

Peters, Thoma J. and Robert H. Waterman. (1982). *In Search of Excellence: Lessons from America's Best-Run Companies.* New York: Warner Books.

Pharmaceutical Research and Manufacturers. (2001). "America's Pharmaceutical Companies Create a Task Force on Emergency Preparedness." Available at http://www.phrma.org/press/print.phtml?article=299.

Reinhardt, Uwe E. (2001). "Perspectives on the Pharmaceutical Industry." *Health Affairs.* 20. 5: 136–149.

Resnik, David B. (2001). "DNA Patents and Human Dignity." *Journal of Law, Medicine and Ethics.* 29: 152–165.

Rifkin, Jeremy. (1998). *The Biotech Century.* New York: Putnam

Smith, Adam. (1937). *The Wealth of Nations.* New York: Modern Library.

Solomon, Robert C. (1993). *Ethics and Excellence: Cooperation and Integrity in Business.* New York: Oxford University Press.

Vastag, Brian. (2001). "Experts Urge Bioterrorism Readiness." *Journal of the American Medical Association.* 285. 1: 30–31.

Vedantam, Shankar. (2001). "HHS's Varying Cost for Cipro Criticized: US to Pay 95 Cents a Pill under One Program and 43 Cents under Another." *Washington Post.* October 26. Available at http://www.elibrary/com/s/edumark/getdoc.cgi?id=213491592x127y60780w0&OIDS=0Q002D053&.

Verschoor, Curtis C. (2001). "Alleged Unethical Behaviors and Schering-Plough." *Strategic Finance.* 83. 1: 18.

West, Diane. (2001). "More Antibiotics Seek to Ride on Cipro's Wake." *Drug Store News.* 23. 16: 1,2p,1c.

Wilson, Ian. (2000). "The New Rules: Ethics, Social Responsibility and Strategy." *Strategy and Leadership.* 28. 3: 12–16.

10

After the Terror: Health Care Organizations, the Health Care System, and the Future of Organization Ethics

Ann E. Mills and Patricia H. Werhane

Over the past two decades concerns about the United States health care system have generally fallen into two broad categories: cost and quality. Many observers of the health care industry believe that cost concerns have overwhelmed efforts to focus attention on quality, and as a result quality of care has suffered. This should not surprise even the most casual observer. Payers, providers, and consumers of care do consider cost a legitimate and urgent issue. More fundamental, American citizens do not seem able to make up their minds whether health care is a basic right or an earned privilege. They have done nothing to resolve this conflict, and so a hybrid and fragmented delivery system has developed. Payers are not consumers of health care, and two different sources, public and private, drive funding. Thus consumers and payers have different visions about what should constrain costs and what should count as quality.

September 11 and the new potential for bioterrorism altered the importance of these issues. We are being forced by circumstances to ask new questions and develop new paradigms. Rather than juxtaposing cost and quality issues (and making decisions based on whichever side of the relationship most immediately claims our attention), we are now forced to think more systemically about public health, public policy, and health care delivery. Bioterrorism threatens our public health system as well as the organizations that deliver care. When public health and lives are at stake, cost can no longer be the primary concern, and a certain level of quality of delivery is essential for survival. The recent crises remind us that health, health care payment, and health care delivery are part of a system, a set of networks of relationships between the public and individual health, public and private payers, and public and private health care delivery. In times of crisis, priorities can alter and previously established balances are quickly disrupted.

Recent History

Ralph Stacey calls a paradox the simultaneous presence of two self-contradictory, essentially conflicting forces. It is possible in some instances simply to remove the paradox by reframing the problem or by consistently choosing one force all the time. In other instances it may not be possible to remove one or the other force; both must be accommodated at the same time and it is possible to do this only by continually rearranging them (Stacey 2000, 12). This has been the case with cost versus quality issues in health care, which formed a paradox that before September 11 could not be removed by reframing the problem or by consistently giving one value priority over the other. The problem was the provider mission of excellent patient care and the goal of delivering it at a reasonable cost. Since no consensus existed on what these terms meant to either consumers or payers, for the past two decades all facets of the health care system wrestled with the contradictions, conflicts, tensions, and sequential alternatives engendered by this paradox.

From the standpoint of forces working for health care reform in the 1980s, the quality of medical care available through the existing system in the United States was unproblematic, but society deemed the cost excessive. Payers targeted providers, both institutional and individual, as one important contributing element in driving costs, and so providers were made to shoulder some of the burden. This was a radical departure from the traditional norm in which payers of benefits simply absorbed increases in costs, allowing, at least theoretically, quality of care to take precedent.

Health care organization leaders, faced with revenue squeezes, looked to other industries to derive techniques that could help restrain the costs of care. These techniques included merging, both horizontally and vertically, "downsizing," consolidating to eliminate duplicate structures and excess capacity, financial incentives to control clinician behavior, quality initiatives to change or coordinate core functions of health care delivery, and so forth.

These techniques were all employed in one fashion or another by different industries and with greater or lesser success. Health care organizations, forced into a turbulent market and inexperienced in dealing with turbulence, seemed determined to repeat the mistakes other industries had made in reacting to similar pressures. Horizontal mergers swept the country as hospitals sought to achieve some kind leverage in markets dominated by payers of health care. But the public demand for efficiencies in scale and scope, leading to smaller prices for payers, proved largely illusionary. In reality, these systems often acted to dampen competition, and some such as HCA/Columbia were eventually investigated for fraudulent billing practices (Friedman and Goes 2001, 3–28). Health care providers learned, just as other businesses learned, that there are generally limits to decreasing costs of scale and that product pricing below marginal costs is, in the long term, a suicidal marketing strategy.

Taking their cue from the automobile industry, health care managers began to look to vertical integration as a cost-cutting and marketing strategy, just at the time that manufacturing and service industries were abandoning the practice of building large, complex, vertically integrated industries. Other health care organizations attempted full-blown mergers in spite of the fact that associated difficulties are well known and mergers are often unsuccessful (Beer and Nohria 2000, 133–141).

Lay-offs were associated with each type of reorganization. Nursing staffs, in particular, were cut deeply despite advice from other industries, which learned through corporate restructuring of the 1980s that firing large numbers of key employees hurts the ability to retain core staff and provide appropriate goods and services.

Financial incentives that introduced a conflict of interest in the physician-patient relationship were employed to reward the individual or collective for achieving financial goals. These techniques were used in spite of the fact that patients soon understood that physicians or health care organizations could financially gain through policies that encouraged undertreatment, and that those policies would undermine and perhaps destroy the physician-patient relationship—a core commitment of the health care professions. These techniques were employed just at the time that other businesses were refocusing their attention on core functions and their "reason for being."

The dominant logic of the for-profit health care industry changed from providing care to providing quarterly profits. Changing conditions in the market also challenged nonprofit organizations and some nonprofits changed to for-profit status. Some were absorbed by for-profits and others emulated the behavior of for-profits. The basic assumption seemed to be that health care could be manufactured and delivered just like cars and airplanes, and that physician labor was just another factor of production, to be used in the most frugal way possible. Thus, health care organizations began their transformation to manufacturing models, and in the process, damaged their relationships with their most important stakeholders: health care professionals, patients, and the larger community.

Many physicians, nurses, and other professionals reacted in fury to overt efforts of payers to control their behavior through financial incentives. Nurses left the field in droves, either because they were laid off or they because they felt unable to give what they perceived as appropriate quality of care to patients. Regardless of the resulting national shortage of nurses and consequent upward pressure on nursing compensation, nurses seem to be in no hurry to return to the profession. Most worrying, however, was the effect of this turmoil on the American public's perception of health care providers and organizations (Kleinke 1998).

Some health care organization-accrediting agencies realized that the "quality" pole of the cost versus quality relationship was being ignored and made efforts to introduce, define, and measure notions of quality for the general public, health care professionals and organizations, and payers of benefits. The Joint Commission on Accreditation of Healthcare Organizations (JCAHO) evaluates and accredits more than 19,000 of these organizations in the United States. Accreditation is required for Medicare and Medicaid reimbursement, and most health care organizations and many managed care organizations have received it. The Commission adopted the theory of continuous quality improvement in the late 1980s and early 1990s. It was hoped that this would restore balance to the cost-quality equation and allow providers to deliver high-quality, reasonably priced care (Westphal, Ranjay, and Shortell 1997).

Efforts were also made to focus the attention of payers to the quality of care. The National Committee on Quality Assurance (NCQA) is an independent, nonprofit organization whose mission is to evaluate and report on the quality of the nation's managed care organizations. The HEDIS dataset developed by NCQA is an attempt to encourage payers to use quality of care as a criterion in purchasing; that is, to have and apply data that correlate the cost of a plan with its quality (Blumenthal and Kilo 1998).

Other organizations such as the Health Care Financing Administration (recently renamed the Centers for Medicare and Medicaid Services), the Foundation for Accountability, and the National Patient Safety Foundation sought to develop or refine quality indexes (Bodenheimer 1999). Despite these efforts and those of the Institute of Medicine (IOM) whose vision of the twenty-first century health care system rests on well-established quality characteristics (Committee on Quality and Health Care in America 2001), there seems to be wide consensus that efforts to improve quality have not achieved the results envisioned by its early advocates (Shortell, Bennett, and Byck 1998; Bailit 1997). Various explanations for this failure have been offered, including physician resistance and persistence of more traditional management approaches (Blumenthal and Kilo 1998). In our view, a more likely explanation is that a fragmented system, continuing to think of cost containment and quality care as trade-offs, prevents consensus on appropriate cost constraints and quality measures. This lack of consensus allowed cost issues to overwhelm quality issues and led to widespread acceptance of ethically problematic processes and outcomes in the delivery system.

Introduction of Organization Ethics
Realizing that turmoil in the market was damaging health care organization relationships, and perhaps that quality of care may be more than a simple resource issue [(in 1990 the IOM defined quality as appropriate resource usage in medical care; this allows distortions in quality to be classified as mistakes attributed to waste, underuse, or overuse of resources) (Lohr 1990)] the JCAHO, in 1995, introduced a mandate that requires health care organizations to conduct their business and patient care practices in an "honest, decent and proper manner." The JCAHO called this mandate "organization ethics" (1996). A broader more process-oriented definition was laker advanced by the Virginia Bioethics Network:

Organization ethics consists of [a set of] processes to address ethical issues associated with the business, financial, and management areas of healthcare organizations, as well as with professional, educational, and contractual relationships affecting the operation of the healthcare organization. (Spencer et al. 2000, 212)

This definition encompasses all aspects of the organization's operation and includes articulation, application, and evaluation of the organization's mission and values statements. Each approach represents an important step in quality movement because both acknowledge that quality of care depends in part on relationships the health care organization has with its stakeholders. Both approaches insist that organizations pay attention to these relationships by creating positive ethical climates throughout their structure.

A positive ethical climate has at least two important characteristics. First, it is a culture in which the organization's mission and vision inform expectations for professional and managerial performance and are implemented in actual practices. Second, a positive ethical climate embodies a set of values that reflects societal norms for what the organization should value, how it should establish priorities for its mission, vision, and goals, and how it and the individuals associated with it should behave. Such a set of ethics directs attention to the how the mission to provide excellent care at reasonable cost is carried out in the organization's business, clinical, and professional practices, and works to bring its activities at all levels of function in line with that mission (Spencer et al. 2000). Of importance from our perspective, the JCAHO mandate acknowledged tensions, conflicts, and temptations surrounding the cost-quality relationship. Rather than summarily dismissing one element or the other, JCAHO left it to individual organizations to work out how to rearrange the elements as necessary in the context of a positive ethical climate that encourages supportive relationships, promotes discussions of conflicts, and provides a model for difficult decision making in the context of the organization's mission and values. Since attention is directed to the values and ideals associated with the intersection of management, clinical, and professional roles of the health care organization, many believe that an ethics program can serve as a constraining force (or quality control mechanism) as the organization seeks to provide patient care in a resource-scarce environment.

Health Care Organizations after September 11

These are platitudes we have all heard. We are in a war that lacks visible enemies and visible targets, and we have been assured that it will be long one. There are no rules, an attack could be overt or covert, or it could not come at all. Thus planning is a nightmare and readiness is going to be costly.

The American Hospital Association (AHA) said that it will cost $11.3 billion to increase the ability of the nation's 4,900 community hospitals to respond to a chemical, nuclear, or biological attack (AHA 2001). The AHA recommends that metropolitan hospitals be ready to treat 1,000 casualties for 48 hours and that nonurban hospitals should prepare for 200. Under this plan, $3 million has to be spent for each metropolitan hospital and $1.4 million at each nonurban hospital. Regardless of whether or not these figures are accurate, hospitals and other health care organizations are looking at the costs of stockpiling drugs, preparing decontamination plans, training staff, and ensuring increased and secure communication and transportation. But what effect do these new demands have on the balance of cost and quality?

Revisiting the Cost versus Quality Paradox

The paradox was formulated in the context of the provider mission of patient care. Attention focused on what "care" was, what it meant to the individual patient or to a defined population (often meaning those insured under a specific health plan), and how to provide it in the context of appropriate mechanisms to constrain costs. But terrorist threats shift our attention from organizations's mission of excellent patient care to their mission of community service. This brings to forefront a number of issues in both public health and provider organizations with which the system has been wrestling: shifts in what we mean by basic health care, who is to be served, in how care is delivered and payment is carried out.

The mission of most provider organizations has been to provide patient care at a reasonable cost to a defined population and, through a variety of mechanisms, to make some efforts at community service for the uninsured. Some providers even define their mission as maintaining and improving the health of their patient populations. The mission of public health is to protect, maintain, and improve health, and prevent disease or the spread of disease to the whole population. With threats of bioterrorism, the missions of these two sectors have become more closely aligned. Bioterrorism threatens the survival of a large part of our population. The mission of public health combines with national security efforts and becomes focused on preventing terrorism and on survival mechanisms for those who are targeted by such acts; that is, on life or death, in addition to its base functions of health and disease prevention (Coates 2002). So basic health is now redefined as living or surviving. But whereas public health and public defense initiatives in the anthrax episodes, for example, focus on preventing further episodes, drug treatments (antibiotics), and vaccination, actual patient care for those who are stricken falls to health care providers, most of whom, for-profit or nonprofit, are in the private sector.[1] The mission of providers dealing with these patients, or preparing to deal with bioterrorist victims, becomes more aligned with public health, that is, survival of these patients. And the expectations of public health, and of the community however conceived, are that these provider organizations will be engaged in saving the lives of all those in that community who are victims, whether or not they fall under some defined health or insurer plan.

This alignment of missions also has another outcome that affects how bioterrorist victims and threats are dealt with. Public health agencies, with few exceptions, cannot provide health care. Provider organizations are not medically or fiscally equipped for bioterrorism disasters. These two sectors must align mission, research, funding, and delivery missions in order to meet this challenge. The cost versus quality paradox in these drastic situations, or under their threat, when survival is at stake is no longer an issue. The goal is to enable the most people, ideally the whole population, to avoid, become immune to, or survive bioterrorism with the best means available.

That shift from providing care to a defined population to massive protection and treatment for everyone decommodifies health care. Private insurers and providers alone, who even earlier were hard pressed to meet the health demands of the uninsured, cannot now meet the demand to prepare, provide, and pay for possible bioterrorist attacks on the market model. The public sector, with its relative paucity of provider organizations, also cannot. Only by working together can these two sectors create viable responses.

Toward a Systems Perspective

The bioterrorism threat suggests that we must rethink operative models for health care research, payment, delivery, and public health. The free market alone cannot deal with this threat, nor can government, public health agencies, or public policy alone. This became clear when the government, in an attempt to garner enough Cipro for anthrax victims, threatened to suspend Bayer's patent protection (and thus its exclusive license to produce Cipro) in order to increase production and reduce the cost of the antibiotic. Market mechanisms alone were seen as vulnerable when such a crisis occurred.[2]

We suggest that we have to think of health care, in all its dimensions, more systemically.

A truly systemic view [of health care] . . . considers how [this set of individuals, institutions, and processes] operates in a system with certain characteristics. The system involves interactions extending over time, a complex set of interrelated decision points, an array of [individual, institutional, and government] actors with conflicting interests . . . and a number of feedback loops. (Wolf 1999, 1675)

For the purpose of this discussion, a health care system can be defined as "assemblages of interactions within an organization or agency, or between organizations, agencies, governments and individuals" (Emanuel 2000, 152). A system is "a complex of interacting components together with the relationships among them that permit the identification of a boundary-maintaining entity or process" (Laszlo and Krippner 1998, 51). Under this rubric health care systems are networks of relationships between individuals, between individuals and organizations, among organizations, and among individuals, organizations, institutions, agencies, and government. Our system has another important characteristic. Like most human-generated systems, it is what Paul Plsek (2001) calls a "complex adaptive system," because it consists of individuals and organizations who have the liberty to interact with, respond to, and change it.

The threat of bioterrorism adds new urgency to systems thinking about health care. We can no longer, if we ever could, separate private-sector, market-driven, and nonprofit payers and deliverers whose foci were primarily on a defined patient population, from issues of public health and the total population. This does not mean the end either of private health insurance and delivery or the demise of public health initiatives. Nor is this an argument in favor of a single-payer system. It implies, rather, that each sector has to think of itself as part of a system in which no one single payer, organization, agency, or government body can deal adequately with health (or in this case, survival). It is obvious that no one of these institutions by itself can deal with the financial burdens of bioterrorism. But it is clear, too, that no one agency, research institute, insurer, payer, or delivery organization, and certainly not the present commitments and support of the United States government for public health can presently deal with all the relevant health, illness, or survival issues. Cross-pollination of research between the National Institute of Health and private institutes that has gone on for some time is a model of systemic cooperation that should be extended to all elements of the system.

Systems thinking demands what was called a "multiple perspectives" approach (Mitroff and Linstone 1993). It is never possible to take into account all the networks of relationships involved in a particular system, especially given that these systems interact and change over time. A multiple perspectives approach forces us to think more broadly and to look at particular systems or problems from different points of view. This is crucial in trying to deal with threats of bioterrorism, because each perspective—those of the threatened population, public health agencies, researchers, drug manufacturers, and health care providers—usually "reveals insights . . . that are not obtainable in principle from others" (Mitroff and Linstone 1993). A multiple perspectives approach is essential if, for example, for-profit health care providers are to understand what is at stake in dealing with a survival threat for a large population, and for policy makers and insurers to realize what is at risk if there are not adequate drugs or vaccines, or what costs are required for public health, public policy, payment, and delivery; that is, the whole system is threat-ready. This kind of approach is critical for public health, public policy, insurers, and health care organizations to help them deal with the complex dynamics of policy, and it is important for health care consumers as well.

A multiple perspectives approach might involve describing the system and subsystems in question, and examining and evaluating the network of organizational, relational, and individual perspectives. One investigates how a particular configuration of a system or subsystem affects individuals, in this instance, health care delivery, public and private insurers, community and public health, as will as microissues such as patient autonomy, access, informed consent, privacy, and other important matters of concern to those delivering and receiving care. Then one evaluates both by giving priority to goals of the system and indeed, by evaluating those goals (including professional, organizational, economic, and sometimes, political norms) implicit in the system.

In analyzing the ethics involved, an evaluative grid sets out the purpose, structure, processes, and outcomes of a particular system against professional, political, and economic models (Emanuel 2000, 161). Whereas the details of that grid are certainly subject to more debate, this approach pushes us into the direction of more broad-based thinking and into more creative and imaginative ways to analyze and evaluate health care systems. The aims are threefold: to understand the system and its complex interrelationships; to evaluate its concomitant moral responsibilities; and to think through possible solutions or resolutions of issues in question that take into account these multiple perspectives. Accountability relationships exist between each stakeholder and element of the system in question. It is tempting to conceive those dyadically, and from an organizational or public health perspective a dyadic description of accountability may be adequate. But health care is embedded in a complex (and changing) system, and these relationships are much more overlapping and interlocking than either approach alone can accommodate. Being clear about these relationships, and how each individual and each element is or should be accountable to the others helps to clarify where decisions go wrong.

Embedded in this process are the goals or purposes of the system, or in the case of health care or a subsystem, what goals it should have and how they are ranked in priority, since the goals will affect the system's structure, interrelationships, and outcomes. These goals then become the evaluative elements overlaid on the descriptive grid. Notice that when threatened with bioterrorism, the goals are reordered and all elements of the system move into a survival mentality.

One other perspective must be considered in a systems approach: individual responsibility—responsibilities of policy makers, Medicare, and other insurers, health care professionals, managers, public health officials, drug manufacturers, and each of us as individuals. The approach should not be confused with some form of abdication of individual responsibility, if, as stated earlier, our health care system is adaptive or changeable. As individuals we are not merely the sum of, or identified with, these relationships and roles. We can evaluate and change our relationships, roles, and role obligations, and we are thus responsible for them. That is, each of us is at once a by-product of, a character in, and an author of, our own experiences. Each one of us has responsibilities to be familiar with our health alternatives and the system in which we find ourselves, and responsibilities to work for constructive change.

Implications for Organization Ethics

Nothing that we have said suggests or implies that organization ethics programs should be disbanded or that they are no longer relevant after September 11. Organization ethics was formulated as a reaction to how tensions and contradictions generated within a cost versus quality paradigm affect individual patient care. Concerns included the rights and responsibilities of the individual patient and other stakeholders in the institution, including providers and managers, and how the institution could delineate and protect them.

We suggest, however, that the threat of bioterrorism forces the focus of attention from the health care organization's mission of patient care to an enlarged mission of community service that is more closely aligned with the mission of public health agencies. For instance, the organization must include the uninsured and community as primary stakeholders. How it interacts with an enlarged community and how it can accommodate public health goals within its own financial constraints in times of crisis raises questions about the viability of all such organizations as market-driven institutions. The answers to these questions will change the structure, interrelationships, and outcomes associated with both nonprofit and for-profit health care organizations. These changes will affect the ethical climate of these organizations, which is the responsibility of the ethics program.

We said that a positive ethical climate has at least two important characteristics. It is a culture where mission and vision inform the organization's expectations for professional and managerial performance and are implemented in practices; and it embodies values that reflect societal norms for what the organization should value, how they should set priorities for their mission, vision, and goals, and how the organization and the individuals associated with it should behave. Bioterrorism has altered the mission and vision of health care organizations and so altered the organizations' expectations of stakeholders. In taking on more responsibilities to the community in which it operates, the social role of the organizations has changed and the values associated with their changing role have to be identified and given priority. This too is the work of organization ethics committees.

Conclusion

The focus on cost containment and market segmentation over quality has encouraged a disjointed approach to health care in which public health issues have largely been ignored. Turmoil in the market prevents a true systems approach to health care. Individual and institutional issues and agendas have occupied center stage, and at the same time, we have been unable to deliver good quality care to those who are insured. Bioterrorism did not remove the need to align cost and quality. It changed its context by reminding us of the importance of other elements of the health care mission. But changing the context may allow us to reformulate the problem.

The hope is that bioterrorism and its threat will allow us to become more creative and less individualistic, and begin to address other health care issues from a systems approach. We are forced to question the adequacy of either the private sector or the public sector separately to deal with pubic and private health and to deliver health care. Neither market mechanisms nor public policies are adequate by themselves to handle this overwhelming systemic issue. The threat forces us to think again about universal minimum health care provisions, funding mechanisms, and disease prevention as well as care, the role of intellectual property in disaster situations, and global health, all of which affect each of us individually and can affect us as a nation if we do not take a more systemic approach.

Acknowledgment

We gratefully acknowledge the advice and comments of Mary V. Rorty in the preparation of this paper.

Notes

1. According to data from its 2000 annual survey, the AHA reports that of 5,810 registered hospitals in the United States, 3,752 are nongovernment or noncommunity-owned and 1,408 are local community or federal hospitals. The remaining are long-term care hospitals or prison institutions. See www.aha.org/resource/newpage.asp (1/9/2002).

2. Bayer responded by massive increases in production and cost reductions, but the threat to their intellectual property rights was real. The underlying assumption of the government appears to be that intellectual property rights are prima facie rights that could be set aside when lives were at stake. Of interest, that argument is not used by the United States policy makers in the global HIV crisis.

References

American Hospital Association. 2001. *Hospital Resources for Disaster Readiness Update*. Available at http://www.aha.org/Emergency/EmIndex.asp (visited November 1, 2001).

Bailit, M. 1997. "Ominous Signs and Portents: A Purchaser's View of Health Care Market Trends." *Health Affairs*. 16.6: 85–88.

Beer, M. and N. Nohria. 2000. "Cracking the Code of Change." *Harvard Business Review*. 78.3: 133–141.

Bodenheimer, T. 1999. "The American Health Care System—The Movement for Improved Quality in Health Care." *New England Journal of Medicine*. 340.6: 488–492.

Blumenthal, D. and C. Kilo. 1998. "A Report Card on Continuous Quality Improvement." *Milbank Quarterly*. 76: 625–648.

Coates, T. 2002. "Review of Betrayal of Trust: The Collapse of Global Public Health, by Laurie Garrett." *Journal of the American Medical Association*. 287.3: 381–382.

Committee on Quality and Health Care in America. Institute of Medicine. 2001. *Crossing the Quality Chasm: A New Health System for the 21st Century*. Washington, DC: National Academy Press.

Emanuel, Linda. 2000. "Ethics and the Structures of Health Care." *Cambridge Quarterly*. 9: 151–168.

Friedman, Leonard and Jim Goes. 2001. "Why Integrated Health Networks Have Failed." *Frontiers of Health Services Management*. 17.4: 3–28.

Joint Commission on Accreditation on Healthcare Organizations. 1996. *Patient Rights and Organizational Ethics: Standards for Organizational Ethics. Comprehensive Manual for Hospitals*, 95–97. Oakbrook Terrace, IL: Joint Commission on Accreditation on Healthcare Organizations.

Kleinke, John. 1998. *Bleeding Edge: The Business of Health Care in the New Century*. Gaithersburg, MD: Aspen Publishers.

Laszlo, A. and S. Krippner. 1998. "Systems Theories: Their Origins, Foundations and Development." *In Systems Theories and a Priori Aspects of Perception*, edited by J. Scott Jordon, 47–74. Amsterdam: Elseviere.

Lohr. K.N., ed. 1990. *Medicare: A Strategy for Quality Assurance*. Washington, DC: National Academy Press.

Mitroff, I. and H. Linstone. 1993. *The Unbounded Mind*. New York: Oxford University Press.

Plsek, Paul. 2000. *Redesigning Health Care with Insights from the Science of Complex Adaptive Systems. Crossing the Quality Chasm: A New Health System for the 21st Century*. Washington, DC: National Academy Press.

Shortell, S., C. Bennett, and G. Byck. 1998. "Assessing the Impact of Continuous Quality Improvement on Clinical Practice: What It Will Take to Accelerate Progress." *Millbank Quarterly*. 76: 593–624.

Spencer, E. et al. 2000. *Organization Ethics for Healthcare Organizations*. New York: Oxford University Press.

Stacey, Ralph. 2000. *Strategic Management and Organizational Dynamics: The Challenge of Complexity*, 3rd ed. Essex UK: Pearson Education Limited.

Westphal, J., G. Ranjay, and S. Shortell. 1997. "Customization or Conformity? An Institutional and Network Perspective on the Content and Consequences of TQM Adoption." *Administrative Science Quarterly*. 42: 366–394.

Wolf, Susan. 1999. "Towards a Systemic Theory of Informed Consent in Managed Care." *Houston Law Review*. 35: 1631–1681.

V

Research and Genetics

11

Research Involving Victims of Terror—
Ethical Considerations

Alan R. Fleischman and Emily B. Wood

All disasters are tragic. The often-unpredictable nature and inability to prevent major disasters that result in destruction and loss of life are associated with feelings of sadness, loss, and fear by those affected. Most disasters are unintentional consequences of natural or technological events. Terrorism, however, is intentional creation of death and destruction in order to instill fear and feelings of uncertainty, intimidation, demoralization, vulnerability, chaos, and helplessness among those targeted. Because of its characteristics and the maliciousness that motivates its aims, there are many important reasons to study the environmental, clinical, and psychosocial effects of terror on individuals, families, and populations. Such research can provide important information that may improve long-term survival, help prepare for subsequent incidents, affect mental health management of victims and other affected persons, and increase understanding of the human experience (Lundin 1984; Murray Parkes 1997; Camino et al. 1990; Dreman and Cohen 1990). In the long term, information gained from such research may help to refine treatment and crisis intervention strategies for present and subsequent disaster affected populations.

After September 11 it rapidly became clear that many well-intentioned investigators wished to do studies to elucidate the impact of this disaster on the victims, their families, and other populations. The magnitude and potential consequences (mental, physical, emotional, environmental) of the events justified the need for clinical, epidemiological, and social science research involving various populations. Anecdotal evidence suggests that researchers from within and outside New York initiated well over 100 such studies.

This outpouring of interest raised questions about whether ethical issues surrounding the design and implementation of this type of research have been addressed adequately. Specific concerns were raised by the city administration, in particular the Commissioner of Health, for the potential of such studies to be redundant, insensitive, and overly burdensome to an acutely vulnerable and extremely distressed population. Despite previous efforts in disaster-focused research, little systematic guidance was available to answer their concerns and address many of the ethical issues that arose.

The most recent human-made disaster that took place in the United States before September 11 was the bomb explosion at the Alfred P. Murrah Federal Building in Oklahoma City on April 19, 1995. Research that was undertaken to assess the impact of that disaster on victims and the local population resulted in substantial knowledge about post-traumatic stress, the effect of terrorism on children, and various approaches to healing the wounds of the community. All research projects in Oklahoma City were reviewed and approved through a special process put in place by the University of Oklahoma Health Sciences Center with the imprimatur of the governor (Pfefferbaum 1996). Perhaps the smaller city or the smaller number of victims or other circumstances of the disaster made this approach possible in Oklahoma, but such a mechanism was not put into place in New York.

Much, if not most, postterror-related research is undertaken by thoughtful and sensitive investigators and reviewed by institutional review boards. Little focus is placed on whether specific safeguards should be established to protect the interests of the subjects of such studies. Human-made disasters, including terrorism, have profound effects on its victims that vary depending on the individual and proximity to the event. These victims are vulnerable and require special protection that cannot be afforded solely by the good intentions of the research community and the review of proposals by an institutional review board.

Research on Disaster-Affected Populations

Previous episodes of terrorism and disaster dramatically affected communities and nations. A great deal of research has been undertaken to examine short- and long-term physical, psychological, and psychosocial consequences of such events. Although different types of disasters occurred in culturally diverse populations, findings are consistent. For example, in a review of the literature for the years from 1981–2001, which consisted of 177 articles describing results for 130 samples composed of over 50,000 individuals who experienced 80 disasters, six common outcomes were observed (Norris et al. 2001a). Specific psychological problems such as posttraumatic stress or depression were identified in 74 percent of the samples, nonspecific distress in 39 percent, health problems and concerns in 25 percent, and chronic problems in living and loss of psychosocial supports in 10 percent. Fifty-two percent of studies reported moderate psychological impairment of subjects that resulted in prolonged but subclinical distress, and 24 percent showed severe impairment with 25 percent to 49 percent of the sample suffering from criterion-level psychopathology.

In addition to affecting short-term mental health, disasters have a long-term impact. Life often changes in ways that increase distress for individuals, families, or a population. For example, economic hardship and loss of employment, deterioration of significant relationships, or deterioration of physical health due to the disaster add to an already stressful situation (Camino et al. 1990). Such events may have insidious and unsuspected long-lasting consequences. One study revealed that encounters with terror during adolescence have a pervasive and long-lasting effect on survivors' adult life in both intrapersonal and interpersonal areas (Desivilya, Gal, and Ayalon 1996). The authors concluded that such events inflict a notable setback in psychosocial development and have ramifications for the frequency and type of therapy that is effective. Hence, research not only contributes to understanding how disasters and trauma affect individuals and communities, but can also result in development of improved mental health interventions.

The research community that deals specifically with trauma and disaster-focused research has given some thought to ethical considerations related to studying acutely ill trauma survivors, refugees, and others who experienced extreme situations (Ruzek and Zatzick 2000; Leaning 2001; Richman 1997; Raphael, Lundin, and Weisaeth 1989). It was found that those who have been witnesses to or victims of extreme disaster may be so emotionally upset as to be unable to provide fully informed consent to participate in research (Newman, Walker, and Gefland 1999; Pope 1999). In addition, they may be unable to anticipate accurately the degree of distress that they may encounter, or to weigh the risks and benefits of participating in a meaningful way (Newman et al. 1999). Researchers noted the importance of sensitivity to victims and the potential for retraumatization that may occur during research, as well as the utility of attempting to coordinate research efforts after disaster.

Ethical Principles Guiding Human Subjects Research

Shortly after September 11 many investigators proposed studies involving the victims, their families, and others. Aside from federal regulations that address research with human subjects, no specific guidelines are in place to ensure that these individuals are adequately protected from redundant, possibly insensitive, and overly burdensome inquiries.

Federal regulations (U.S. Department of Health and Human Services 1991) are the framework used to protect the interests of research subjects. They define standards for ethical conduct of research, including the process for proposal review, assurance of voluntary informed consent, and protections that should be afforded vulnerable subjects such as children, prisoners, fetuses, decisionally impaired, and economically and educationally disadvantaged. The origin of these regulations is the National Commission for the Protection of Human Subjects of Biomedical and Behavioral Research, which was convened in the 1970s in response to several ethically questionable practices that had occurred in the United States. The commission articulated three principles that inform ethical decision making in research involving human subjects: respect for persons, beneficence, and justice (U.S. Department of Health, Education, and Welfare 1979).

Respect for persons obligates investigators to ensure that each individual subject is given the opportunity to make a voluntary and uncoerced decision about participating in the study. Potential subjects are entitled to a full explanation of the study, including possible risks and benefits. Ultimately, their consent or refusal to participate is to be respected. The principle of respect for persons has a second aspect: the investigator is obligated to ensure the protection of individuals with diminished autonomy, such as those who do not have the capacity to exercise the right to choose.

Respect for persons is operationalized through informed consent. Considered by many to be the cornerstone of protection of research subjects, it is the autonomous authorization of a competent, fully informed individual to participate in a study (Beauchamp and Childress 1994, 142–46). It requires that certain elements be in place to ensure that authorization by the participant is both informed and voluntary. Such elements consist of disclosure of all relevant information such as the purpose of the research, procedures involved, perceived benefits, potential risks of pain, discomfort, indignity, and breach of confidentiality, and assessment that the potential subject has the capacity adequately to evaluate the risks and benefits associated with participating.

Beneficence obligates the investigator to design and conduct the study to maximize possible benefits and minimize harms or risks. Thus the researcher must not merely ensure that no harm is intentionally inflicted on the participant, but also create the additional duty to prevent harm, protect welfare, and promote good for the subject. These duties are in place even when a project is not intended to benefit its subjects directly. When the purpose is to benefit society or future others by accruing new knowledge, without the intention of benefiting actual subjects, the investigator is obligated to explain all potential risks and ensure these risks are understood before participants are permitted to volunteer.

The principle of justice requires that individuals be given fair, equitable, and appropriate treatment based on what is due or owed to them (Beauchamp and Childress 1994, 327). It requires that the study be fair in its procedures and processes, including recruitment methods and mechanisms, to ensure that participants are allowed to ask questions and voice concerns about any aspect of the research. Distributive justice refers to the proper distribution of benefits and burdens across populations. Subjects must be recruited from all populations who will likely benefit from the research and not merely from those most easily available. The potential benefits should also be fairly distributed. In the past, women, children, and racial minorities were underrepresented in research and were missing out on potential benefits. Justice requires that steps be taken to rectify those inequities, and several initiatives are in place to address these concerns.

Research Burden

Another aspect of the principle of justice obligates the investigator to consider the overall burden to specific individuals or populations that participation entails. The burden of participation may be in addition to other burdens such as institutionalization or infirmity. When such otherwise burdened populations are recruited, the study should relate to their specific disease, disorder, or condition. Excessive burdens may also occur when individuals or populations are overstudied. There are both ethical and statistical reasons not to recruit an individual into several similar studies or to allow redundant studies to be performed on the same population (U.S. Department of Health and Human Services 1993, vol. 22).

Institutional Review Boards

Federal regulations require institutional review to ensure that all research involving human subjects is given careful scrutiny. Institutions are responsible for the creation of institutional review boards (IRBs) to review and approve proposals and monitor their implementation. They obtain federal-wide assurance from the Office for Human Research Protections (OHRP) of the U.S. Department of Health and Human Services certifying that their institution will be bound by federal regulations for all human subjects research conducted under their auspices.

Although ethical responsibility ultimately lies with the investigator, it is the role of the IRB to ensure that each proposal is consistent with ethical principles, balance potential risks and compensating benefits, approve the process for informed consent, and provide continuing monitoring of the study. This local review process is generally effective in protecting subjects' interests. The IRBs are asked to make judgments concerning the ability of potential subjects to provide voluntary and uncoerced informed consent. If a question arises about the capacity of individual subjects to consent, the IRB must approve a process of surrogate decision making or consent monitoring to ensure that subjects' interests are protected.

The IRBs are also responsible to ensure that subjects are not overly burdened by research as a result of redundancy of proposals or oversampling of a specific population. The local review process is generally quite effective in this in as much as the IRB understands the populations studied and usually reviews all proposals being considered for each one.

In the case of September 11 it was difficult for local IRBs to ensure that victims and their families were not subjected to several studies dealing with the same questions. What was clear from the outset was that investigators from all over the country wanted to study these events and their aftermath. It is assumed that individual IRBs reviewed and approved these projects, but no local IRB in the Bronx, Baltimore, Boston, or Berkeley would have known about studies being reviewed by other IRBs. Nor would IRBs necessarily have been knowledgeable about specific circumstances of research involving victims of trauma and the need for certain protections.

Some might argue that autonomous individuals could simply refuse to participate in redundant projects if they felt overly burdened or distressed. The informed consent process with the right of refusal in research with no additional safeguards may be an insufficient and insensitive way to protect distressed potential subjects from inappropriate intrusions into their lives.

Vulnerability

Federal regulations for protection of human subjects of research do not specifically address populations that experience terror or disaster, nor do they imply that such populations ought to be considered particularly vulnerable and therefore subject to special consideration for additional protections. Regulations do define several groups for whom the ability to make voluntary and uncoerced decisions about participation may be impaired (U.S. Department of Health and Human Services 1991). These groups, deemed vulnerable, are children, prisoners, pregnant women, adults who are cognitively impaired or mentally disordered, and persons who are economically or educationally disadvantaged. When individuals from these groups are potential subjects, limitations may be imposed on the permissible level of risk to which they may be exposed without compensating benefit. In addition, investigators must create special protections to ensure the voluntary nature of informed consent by the individual or surrogate, and IRBs must give special scrutiny to such proposals and may create procedural safeguards to protect the interests of the subjects.

Some contend that to describe these federally protected populations as vulnerable is pejorative and potentially stigmatizing. In the parlance of social scientists, those who are vulnerable are at risk of harm; in the context of research ethics, such subjects may not be at greater risk of harm from procedures in the project; rather they require additional protections because their ability to provide free and informed consent is impaired. This may be due to age, cognitive impairment or mental illness, or social circumstances in which voluntary and uncoerced consent may not be possible (U.S. Department of Health and Human Services 1991). The federal regulations were created to protect all subjects of research so it ought not be surprising that some level of paternalism is embedded in the beneficent motivation to protect subjects' welfare and minimize harm to them. The regulations augment the investigator's moral virtue with a process of oversight and review in order to reveal potential conflicts of interest and balance the welfare of present subjects with those of future patients (Moreno 2001). Whether or not a group of potential subjects fits into one of the designated categories of those deemed vulnerable, all subjects because of individual characteristics or social circumstances who may be susceptible to increased risks or unable to provide voluntary and uncoerced consent ought to receive special consideration and necessary protection.

Whether recognized or not, terror victims and their families frequently suffer from severe psychological and emotional distress. Acute anxiety, depression, posttraumatic stress, and severe grief may affect their ability to make authentic choices about research participation. They may be vulnerable or even considered "doubly vulnerable" because of their potential to experience several factors that may diminish their autonomy (Weaver Moore and Miller 1999). Psychological impairments may be coupled with additional stresses of permanent dislocation, social disruption, family and financial strains, environmental worry, and ecological stress that may create a circumstance that renders individuals significantly vulnerable (Norris et al. 2001b).

It is unclear what level of closeness to the trauma or its victims is required to create such psychological distress as to render an otherwise competent individual subject to the need for special protection with regard to research participation. It is known that proximity increases the psychological impact. Therefore, at a minimum those who are injured, their families, those who escaped, direct observers, first responders, rescue workers, and recovery personnel should be afforded additional safeguards and protection.

Recommendations

Without requiring additional federal regulations, the research community in the United States could agree to a series of recommendations to protect the interests of victims of terror who may become potential participants in studies without unduly affecting the efficiency and integrity of the research. The following recommendations require the collaboration of clinicians, social scientists, academic institutions, public health officials, government leaders, and research regulators in responding to this problem.

Declaring a Serious Episode of Terror

Regional public health officials in collaboration with local political leaders such as the mayor of the affected city should declare that an event has occurred and request assistance from the director of OHRP. The director of OHRP should confirm the serious nature of this episode and contact all IRBs that hold federal-wide assurance for research involving human subjects, asking them to review each proposal related to this terror and grant only provisional approval based on special recommendations in effect in such circumstances.

Coordinating and Reviewing Research Proposals

The state or city commissioner of the department of health in collaboration with local university and medical school deans should create a small blue-ribbon panel consisting of senior academicians and local leaders in research ethics. Local IRBs would forward provisionally approved proposals to this panel for review and final approval. The panel should encourage collaboration among investigators to decrease redundancy of research and oversampling of those affected by the event. Since the panel will have ultimate authority concerning which proposals are approved, it must make every effort to be fair and impartial, keeping the interests of the subjects as the primary focus. The panel must work diligently and expeditiously to ensure that research is not unduly delayed. Although research intended directly to benefit the victims of terror should be given priority, high-quality studies that provide information on the response to trauma of several populations, mechanisms and protective factors that determine the psychological response, and longitudinal research to measure short- and long-term effects and predict outcome are also relevant and should be encouraged.

Specific Protections for Research Subjects Who Are Victims of Terror
Local IRBs should review research proposals to ensure that the following issues have been adequately addressed.

Informed Consent   Subjects should be informed that, like others who had experience with terror, they may be retraumatized by participation, and may have difficulty making decisions. They should be given the opportunity to consult with family members and others before they consent to participate.

Privacy and Confidentiality   All IRBs should be cognizant of the fact that the privacy of subjects may already have been breached by the media or others who made their names and personal identifiers public. Research proposals should include methods to allow subjects to reject participation and control access to themselves by others. Provisions for confidentiality of collected data should be explicit and effective, and subjects should be informed whether personal identifiers will remain linked to the data and what level of identifiers will accompany any publications.

Characteristics of Research   Research proposals should be sensitive to the psychological fragility of subjects and have explicit mechanisms to refer them immediately to mental health professionals as necessary.

Training of the Research Team   Relationships among investigators, field workers, and subjects is always important but takes on new meaning in these circumstances. Research proposals must reflect that the team will be trained to interact with victims of terror in a sensitive manner and be aware that they are likely to confront situations and dilemmas that may conflict with their traditional role as unbiased and objective investigators. Proposals should also reflect that explicit mechanisms are in effect for decompression of the research team and referral of team members for mental health support as necessary.

Additional Procedural Protections The IRBs may wish to require special procedural protection consistent with specific provisions or risks of individual research proposals, such as involving family members in the informed consent process, providing independent consent or research monitors, and frequently reviewing the progress of the research.

Informing Victims and the Public

The blue-ribbon panel should inform victims and the public about research proposals that have been approved. Victims should be informed that they may or may not agree to participate, but they ought to consider only proposals that are officially approved. The panel should also ensure that victims and the public are informed about research findings when data become available.

Review of Complaints and Adverse Events

The blue-ribbon panel should remain available to respond to complaints from investigators or subjects, and to review adverse events related to approved proposals.

Conclusion

Recent events create new questions about the adequacy of protection afforded victims of terror and disaster by the regulations and processes that govern research involving human subjects in the United States. The principles articulated by the Belmont Report support the obligation of investigators and IRBs to ensure that potential subjects who have been affected by terror are fully informed and adequately protected in implementing their autonomous right to decide about participation. Concern for the welfare of victims argues for additional protections than are presently in place.

Present and future victims, their families, and others affected by terror may be greatly benefited by important research. To ensure that such projects are encouraged and consistent with the highest ethical standards, additional protections are necessary that are adequate and respectful of victims. Without the need for new regulations, a special process of voluntary compliance by researchers and academic institutions could be invoked by local governments in concert with OHRP in the event of future disasters or events of terror.

References

Beauchamp, Tom L. and James F. Childress. 1994. *Principles of Biomedical Ethics*. Oxford: Oxford University Press.

Camino, Glorisa et al. 1990. "The Impact of Disaster on Mental Health: Prospective and Retrospective Analyses." *International Journal of Mental Health*. 19: 51–69.

Desivilya, Helena Syna, Reuven Gal, and Ofra Ayalon. 1996. "Long-Term Effects of Trauma in Adolescence: Comparison Between Survivors of a Terrorist Attack and Control Counterparts." *Anxiety, Stress, and Coping*. 9: 135–150.

Dreman, Solly and Esther Cohen. 1990. "Children of Victims of Terrorism Revisited: Integrating Individual and Family Treatment Approaches." *American Journal of Orthopsychiatry*. 60 (April): 204–209.

Leaning, Jennifer. 2001. "Ethics of Research in Refugee Populations." *Lancet*. 357: 1432–1433.

Lundin, Tom. 1984. "Morbidity following sudden and unexpected bereavement." *British Journal of Psychiatry*. 144 (January): 84–88.

Moreno, Jonathan. 2001. "Protectionism in Research Involving Human Subjects." In *Ethical and Policy Issues in Research Involving Human Participants*, vol. 2. Background paper prepared for the National Bioethics Advisory Commission, Bethesda, MD.

Murray Parkes, Colin. 1997. "A Typology of Disasters." In *Psychological Trauma: A Developmental Approach*, edited by Dora Black et al., 81–93. Glasgow: Bell and Bain Ltd.

Newman, Elana, Edward A. Walker, and Anne Gefland. 1999. "Assessing the Ethical Costs and Benefits of Trauma-focused Research." *General Hospital Psychiatry*. 21: 187–196.

Norris, Fran H. et al. 2001a. *50,000 Disaster Victims Speak: An Empirical Review of the Empirical Literature, 1981–2001. Part I of a three-part series: Range, Magnitude and Duration of Effects*. Prepared for the National Center for PTSD and the Center for Mental Health Services. Available at www.musc.edu/cvc/norris1.html (visited October 3, 2001).

Norris, Fran H. et al. 2001b. *50,000 Disaster Victims Speak: An Empirical Review of the Empirical Literature, 1981–2001. Part III of a three-part series: Psychosocial Resources in the Aftermath of Disasters*. Prepared for the National

Center for PTSD and the Center for Mental Health Services. Available at www.musc.edu/cvc/norris1.html (visited October 3, 2001).

Pfefferbaum, Betty. 1996. *The Oklahoma City Bombing: Organizing the Mental Health Response*. American Academy of Experts in Traumatic Stress, Inc. Available at www.aaets.org/arts/art5.html (visited March 13, 2002).

Pope, Kenneth S. 1999. "The Ethics of Research Involving Memories of Trauma." *General Hospital Psychiatry*. 21: 157.

Raphael, Beverley, Tom Lundin, and Lars Weisaeth. 1989. "A Research Method for the Study of Psychological and Psychiatric Aspects of Disaster." *Acta Psychiatrica Scandinavica Supplement*. 353: 1–75.

Richman, Naomi. 1997. "Ethical Issues in Disaster and Other Extreme Situations." In *Psychological Trauma: A Developmental Approach*, edited by Dora Black et al., 374–382. Glasgow: Bell and Bain Ltd.

Ruzek, Josef I. and Douglas F. Zatzick. 2000. "Ethical Considerations in Research Participation among Acutely Injured Trauma Survivors: An Empirical Investigation." *General Hospital Psychiatry*. 22: 27–36.

U.S. Department of Health, Education, and Welfare, National Commission for the Protection of Human Subjects of Biomedical and Behavioral Research. 1979. *The Belmont Report*. Washington, DC: U.S. Government Printing Office.

U.S. Department of Health and Human Services, National Institutes of Health. Office for Protection from Research Risks. 1991. *The Code of Federal Regulations Title 45 CFR Part 46—Protection of Human Subjects*. Washington, DC: U.S. Government Printing Office.

U.S. Department of Health and Human Services. 1993. *Protecting Human Research Subjects: Institutional Review Board Guidebook*. NIH Guide 22.29. Washington, DC: U.S. Government Printing Office.

Weaver Moore, Linda and Margaret Miller. 1999. "Initiating Research with Doubly Vulnerable Populations." *Journal of Advanced Nursing*. 30: 1034–1040.

12

Genetics and Bioterrorism: Challenges for Science, Society, and Bioethics

Eric M. Meslin

It is of little use trying to suppress terrorism if the production of deadly devices continues to be deemed a legitimate employment of man's creative powers.

—E.F. Schumacher, German-born economist (1911–1977)
from *Small Is Beautiful* (Schumaker 1973)

The attacks of September 11, 2001, may have signaled the end of innocence in the United States collective psyche in that foreign-based terror could be aimed at the country's political and economic symbols. But when news broke less than a month later that anthrax had been mailed to private citizens and public officials, it did not matter whether the threat was domestic or foreign; it served notice that a new set of challenges arising from genetic technology warranted society's concern. As of this writing (April 2002), we still do not know whether letters mailed to a Florida newspaper office, to members of Congress, and to prominent media figures were intended as acts of terrorism. The latest analysis of the residue suggests that the anthrax had been turned into a weapon, meaning that the spores were deliberately altered using sophisticated scientific techniques to enhance their capacity to kill those who came in contact with them.

Whether or not the anthrax letters could be strictly defined as acts of terrorism might be a matter of dispute that we can afford ourselves the luxury of debating,[1] but we have no such luxury with regard to the prospect that the scientific capability exists genetically to alter bacteria, viruses, fungi, or other biological material and use them for military or other destructive purposes. It is clear that action is required at many levels of science and public policy. But what action? What are the ethical responsibilities of the science community, the government, or industry?

What are the consequences of acting (or not acting)? And what, if anything, can bioethics offer?

Before October 2001—The State of Knowledge and Understanding

Use of Bioweapons

We have many accounts of biologicals being unleashed upon society. Greek mythology describes Pandora, who, unable to overcome her curiosity, opened a box given to her by Zeus, thus releasing plagues upon the world. This accounts for widespread use of Pandora's box as a metaphor for the dangers of unregulated genetic technology. Plague also was used by Tartar forces invading Kaffa (now a part of the Ukraine) in 1346 when, according to most historical accounts, soldiers who died of the disease were themselves used as human bioweapons, as they were catapulted over the city walls in an effort to inflict the plague on Kaffa itself (although it was more likely the fleas carrying plague were responsible for transmission, than the corpses). In 1763 Sir Jeffery Amherst, commander of the British forces at Fort Pitt, ordered that smallpox-infected blankets used by British patients be given to Delaware Indians in order to infect them deliberately.

Such examples pale in comparison, however, with more systematic efforts to use such methods in wartime programs. The history of the twentieth century includes many examples of the use of deadly bacteria or viruses as instruments of war. The number of countries that studied or used deadly chemicals and biologicals—Germany, France, Japan, United States, United Kingdom, South Africa, the former USSR, and Iraq[2]—is as diverse as the list of diseases—anthrax, smallpox, plague, botulism, tularemia, and viral hemorrhagic fevers such as ebola virces. These diseases are classified by the Centers for Disease Control and Prevention (CDL) as category A because they cause high death rates or serious illness, are relatively easy to spread, could cause public panic, or require special steps for public health preparedness.

Fraser and Dando (2001) divided bioweapons programs into three categories. The first category includes "unscientific programs created during or in the years following World War I"; for example, when German forces in World War I used anthrax to disrupt supply lines by infecting the Allies' horses. The second category includes more effective programs created during and after World War II. Both United States and British governments conducted anthrax experiments; an example being explosive devices containing anthrax detonated on an island off the coast of Scotland. But perhaps the most horrific were experiments conducted by Japanese scientists on Chinese prisoners of war in the infamous Unit 731, the biological warfare program. The third category includes programs conducted during the Cold War, principally by the former Soviet Union, applying emerging technologies of molecular biology and genetics. These later programs, begun at a similar time as the rise of molecular genetics, accelerated the capacity and knowledge of scientists to develop more sophisticated weapons of terror and destruction.

This capacity exists to tailor existing biological weapons by making them more efficient killers and less easy to detect, thus making illnesses caused by their proliferation harder to diagnose and treat. It means that these weapons may be used by anyone with access to the same technologies and materials. But they received a significant, albeit unintended, boost from the human genome project.

Genetics and the Human Genome Project

The threat of genetic bioterrorism could not have emerged at a worse or better time from the perspective of scientific knowledge. A little more than year before the attacks, in June 2000, President Clinton and British Prime Minister Tony Blair jointly announced in a White House ceremony that the rough draft of the human genome had been sequenced. The political announcement was followed by two historic publications eight months later describing the virtually complete human sequence. But knowing the sequence was just the first step in what has now become a massive international effort to understand how genes work, how genes code for proteins that build cells, tissues, and organs, and ultimately, how genomic knowledge can be used to prevent, diagnose, treat, and cure human disease. Potential human health benefits arising from the genome project lie in the capacity to develop tools necessary to understand the function of an estimated 30,000 to 50,000 genes. Public and private research is moving quickly to do just this, and there is reason to believe that they will be successful. Many of the tools necessary to map the location and then sequence the 3 billion genetic letters of the human alphabet—faster computers, robotic sequencing machines, new assays, gene chips on which massive amounts of information could be stored—were not even invented when the project began. Researchers, governments, and a growing biotech industry (in countries around the world) are focused on the figuring out the functions of genes and how genes interact with one another and with the environment. The laudable goal is to use this information to develop better predictive tests to diagnose disease, and where prevention cannot be achieved, to treat and cure disease more effectively.

At the same time the human genome was being sequenced, and receiving the lion's share of media attention, many researchers around the world were working in relative anonymity to sequence other model organisms, such as yeast, a round worm called *Caenorhabditis elegans*, the fruit fly known as *Drosophila*, and certain viruses.[3] Reflecting on the prediction that "The power and cost effectiveness of modern genome sequencing technology mean that the complete genome sequences of 25 of the major bacterial and parasitic pathogens could be available within 5 years" (Bloom 1995), it was reported in 2001 that this goal had been surpassed, and that "genomics efforts around the world will deliver the complete sequence of more than 70 major bacterial, fungal and parasitic pathogens of humans, animals, and plants in the next year or two" (Fraser and Bloom 2001).

This prediction has proved true in many ways. The human genome project produced technologies that sped up many processes, some of which were directly applicable to detecting biological agents. For example, comparative genome hybridization allowed scientists in 2000 and 2001 to compare genetic differences in *Helicobater pylori* (Salama et al. 2000) and *Streptococcus pneumoniae* (Tettelin et al. 2001) to the point at which different strains of these bacteria could be detected, a technique that was of direct use in trying to track down type of anthrax strain sent through the mail. Similarly, development of vaccines and new antibiotics accelerated in the postsequence genome era, spurred not by the threat of terrorist attack, but principally by the possibility of military exposure during battle. DNA fingerprinting, developed in 1985 and in widespread use by law enforcement agencies, was used both to identify victims of the September 11 attacks and to provide forensic evidence to aid in the criminal investigations (Lipton and Glanz 2002).

Many in the scientific community were already well aware of the threats posed by genetic bioterrorism, as evidenced by several reports (Royal Society 2000) including one by the JASONs, a group of high-level independent scientists who provided scientific advice to the U.S. Department of Defense (Block 1999). In the late 1990s the U.S. Commission on National Security/21st Century, co-chaired by former Senators Gary Hart and Warren Rudman, issued a three-volume report, the third installment of which, *Road Map for National Security: Imperative for Change* (U.S. Commission 1999), laid out risks to the United States and strategies required to combat bioterrorism. In short, science was aware of the potential threat of genetics bioterrorism and was well on its way to making use of the array of microbiological and genetic knowledge arising from the genome project before the anthrax letters sounded the alarm.

Eugenics in State-Sponsored Terrorism

Genetics has always had a dark side. Understanding the potential for malevolent use of genetic knowledge inevitably leads to accounts of the Holocaust, one of the world's most horrific examples of state-sanctioned eugenics. The Holocaust may be the most extreme example, but full appreciation of the history of the use of genetic knowledge for malevolent means also includes more contemporary examples: involuntary sterilization policies adopted in several European countries, Canada, and many of the United States; ethnic cleansing in Bosnia, the former Yugoslavia, and Rwanda; and chemical warfare programs of the former apartheid government of South Africa. The South African example refers to Project Coast, a program designed to develop chemical weapons that would target only black opponents of the apartheid regime.[4]

The idea that genetic weapons can be targeted against racial or ethnic groups is not new but it flies in the face of solid science. Whereas geneticists have argued for years that race and ethnicity are social rather than biological constructs, it is only recently that science has amassed the data to support this position. For example, research conducted by David Goldstein and his colleagues at University College, London, found that ethnicity and race are poor predictors of drug response. They observed that comparing small changes in DNA between people using single-nucleotide polymorphisms, individual misspellings in a person's DNA, was a better predictor of drug response than ethnic or racial labels

(Wilson et al. 2001; Lewis 2002).[5] They are not the first to reveal how poor the scientific basis is for claiming race is a genetic category. Few if any polymorphisms can distinguish one racial group from another; indeed, there appears to be greater genetic diversity within than between racial groups (Jorde et al. 2000). Despite this scientific confirmation, it will not inhibit those who wish to target particular populations, the most extreme form of genetic discrimination.

The Government's Preparedness

The United States government recognized the threat of bioterrorism in several ways (a useful history is provided in Miller, Engelberg, and Broad 2001, which documents the steps President Clinton took to increase funding for bioterrorism preparedness).[6] In the fall of 1997, the Department of Defense appropriated $10 million for a study to "define" the National Guard's "role in the fight against chemical or biological terrorism." Defense Secretary Cohen directed the Pentagon to take a much more direct role in domestic defense by establishing fifteen rapid assessment and initial detection (RAID) units. On April 10, 1998, seven scientists met with President Clinton about bioterrorism and drew up a set of recommendations calling for $1.9 billion over five years.

The Clinton administration's awareness of and attention to bioterrorism preparedness may be traced to the president's own interest in science and technology. For example, Miller noted Clinton's concerns about bioterrorism to discussions he had with scientists in 1997–1998. This corresponds with Clinton's interest in the misuse of genetic technology related to other scientific developments during that same time period. Immediately after the world learned in February 1997 that a sheep had been cloned in Scotland, Clinton asked the National Bioethics Advisory Commission (NBAC) to study the ethical and legal issues and provide a report on the subject in ninety days (NBAC 1997). He also directed NBAC to study the implications of a new genetic technology after a series of reports in early November 1998 that scientists had isolated and cultured human embryonic stem cells (NBAC 1999b, 89).

After October 2001—Actions Taken

The events of September and October 2001 met with swift and far-ranging responses from the scientific community, federal government, and industry. Each response raises important ethical and policy questions.

Reaction of the Scientific Community

The international scientific community has long recognized the risk of biological weapons and encouraged involvement of scientists in several ways, from conducting research, assessing risk, and supporting policy makers, to lobbying for effective instruments banning the development production, and use of biological weapons (Heap 2001). Moreover, examples abound when science has spoken with one voice to express its outrage and condemn unethical use of tools or products of biological intervention for purposes other than advancing knowledge or treatment. When it is well organized, science can play an influential role in helping guide national science policy. Two meetings at the Asilomar Conference Center in the mid-1970s convened by biomedical researchers concerned about the biohazards of working with tumor viruses and of the use of recombinant DNA molecules, respectively, resulted in a set of safeguards for the conduct of research in these areas. The recommendations and guidelines were almost immediately adopted as interim rules by the newly established Recombinant DNA Advisory Committee at the National Institutes of Health (Cook-Deegan 1997). The Asilomar meetings remain an important example not only of how scientists took it upon themselves to restrict progress in a promising area of science, but also how the power of scientific knowledge can inform policy construction.

But scientific clarity is not a sufficient guide to national policy, even on matters of science policy. One need only look at the current debate about whether the federal government should support research on embryonic stem cells to appreciate how science alone cannot trump policy concerns whose moral values run deep. No one working in science today would disagree with the letter or spirit of the Biological and Toxin Weapons Convention, ratified by the United States in 1972 and in effect in since 1975, which expressly prohibits the use of biological weapons that are directed at people, animals, or agriculture. Article 1 states:

Each State Party to this convention undertakes never in any circumstances to develop, produce, stockpile or otherwise acquire or retain (1) Microbial or other biological agents, toxins or whatever their origin or method of production, of types or in quantities that have no justification for prophylactic, protective or other peaceful purposes.

Moreover, the scientific community is united in its condemnation of the use of biological weapons, and has taken important steps to make knowledge available that will help prevent future attacks and to treat illnesses caused. Many scientists appreciate that their work may have implications beyond the specific problem or topic on which they are focusing. They understand that science may be used for malevolent reasons. Much as they try to consider scientific knowledge to be morally neutral, and that such knowledge acquires moral content only when it is put to use by others, it is naïve to presume that scientists do not consider the implications of their work. They recognize that science can be social knowledge (Longino 1990), that the organization of science (especially its funding) is an inherently political activity (Greenberg 1967), and that there is a difference between *data, information,* and *knowledge,* and these differences are ethically important: choice of the research question, methods used to investigate it, interpretation of results, and degree of certainty one has about results, all have a moral dimension (Meslin 1994).

I suspect this is particularly true with respect to genetic knowledge. Try as we might to avoid treating genetic information empirically, epistemically, and ethically different from other medical information, it is understandable why we may think this way. In its 1999 report on the ethical issues arising from the use of information (including genetic information) contained in human biological materials, the NBAC Commission stated that there were reasons to acknowledge different risks of misuse; for example, learning information about a person from a genetic test result will provide information about that person's parents and children in ways that a cardiac test alone would not (NBAC 1999a). But how does this view of genetic information and knowledge square with the events of October 2001? Genetic knowledge as applied to turning anthrax or other organisms into weapons does seem to be empirically and ethically different from applying the same knowledge to a genetic test result. The same technologies used to carry out DNA fingerprinting of suspected terrorists, or to identify remains of those killed in the attacks on the World Trade Center, the Pentagon, or the downed plane in Pennsylvania (Lipton and Glanz 2002), can be used to design more sophisticated weapons. This phenomenon runs the risk of creating a genetic weapons arms race.

The best way of preventing such an arms race—including the prospect of technology being acquired by those who have no desire to comply with the spirit of the BTWC—is to halt all research in this area. A compelling argument for not engaging in research on biologicals was made by one of the world's foremost authorities on smallpox. D.A. Henderson maintained that among the reasons that all smallpox stores should be eliminated (besides contravening the BTWC), is the reduction in the risk of the stores being used to "define a whole new array of bioweapons, more awesome than any now known" (Henderson and Fenner 2001). It is no surprise that this issue has several sides, one of which is whether small-pox supplies should be retained, not because they can be used to design better defenses against the weapon version that Dr. Henderson worries about, but because of the need to design a smallpox-vaccination program, itself a controversial topic (Drazen 2002). But as with all applied science, the opposite risk—loss of research knowledge used to prevent, diagnose, and treat—must be assessed. It is not whether to do research, but what kind and under what sorts of controls.

The Government's Response

The federal government acted quickly and decisively in the days after the September and October attacks. In a November 2001 address that accompanied his 2003 budget proposal for bioterrorism defense, President George W. Bush said: "Disease has long been the deadliest enemy of mankind. Infectious diseases make no distinctions among people and recognize no borders . . . All civilized nations reject as intolerable the use of disease and biological weapons as instruments of war and terror."

Bush's budget request of $5.9 billion was an increase of $4.5 billion, a 319 percent increase from the 2002 level, focused on three areas[7]: building infrastructure to help state and local health care systems improve their ability to manage biological attacks; improving response to bioterrorist attacks (for example, to enhance the size of the national pharmaceutical stockpile); and to improve research and development efforts in publicly funded science. Evidence of this commitment to fund science came on March 14, 2002, when the National Institute of Allergy and Infectious Diseases, the lead agency of the National Institutes of Health, announced its "bioterrorism research agenda."[8] This plan combines directed research on specific pathogens likely to be used in bioterrorist attacks, with research on more traditional, but still devastating, infectious diseases. This agenda is a well-designed approach to infectious disease research: the tools necessary to combat bioterrorism can be deployed to attack diseases regardless of their mode of delivery. This is what federally sponsored science does best, so it came as something of a surprise when John Marburger, president Bush's science advisor, announced, "Only in a few areas would additional basic research be necessary . . . The deep and serious problem of homeland security is not one of science, it is one of implementation" (Marburger 2002). Marburger was quick to point out, "I do not mean to imply that the science role in the war against terrorism is unimportant," a statement one might take to mean that as a matter of policy, science must move in its own deliberate direction and not bounce from issue to issue. The point has merit, but it has several implications, two of which discuss mention.

Consequences to Other Health Priorities   Within a month of the first news of the anthrax tainted letters, scholars and public health officials perceptively observed that the United States response to terrorism would have a profound effect on the nation's other health and research priorities. In his videotaped presentation to the American Society of Law, Medicine, and Ethics, Chief Justice Michael Kirby of the Australian High Court warned, "enormous amounts of capital are being spent on the armaments of war" and that this "would likely take important funds away from public health" (quoted in Voelker 2001). Kirby is certainly right about the first claim, but the second claim is more difficult to assess. It appears that although the attention of the public health community may have turned toward bioterrorism preparedness and away from other health issues, this increased attention may have been long overdue. As recently as April 7, 2002, executive director of the American Public Health Association, Mohammed Akhter, was quoted in the *Washington Post* to put this in perspective: "Prior to 9–11 we were focused on the HIV-AIDS problem, focused on teenage pregnancy, focused on immunizing kids . . . Those things are now on the back burner" (quoted in Okie 2002). Bioterrorism preparedness now consumes a significant part of the United States health and research budget.

Secrecy versus Scientific Freedom   Researchers have long struggled with the issue of whether to make widely available or keep protected scientific information they develop in their laboratories. While a scientific principle expressly encourages data (or simply credit) sharing, the road to many discoveries is littered with examples of misconduct, acrimony, and lack of cooperation (Broad and Wade 1982). There are some notable exceptions. The National Human Genome Research Institute (NHGRI) had a long-standing policy of early release of sequence data so that researchers would be able to access the data through a public database. The policy, last updated in 2000, requires that all NHGRI grantees would deposit sequence in a public database within twenty-four hours of generating a sequence assembly of 2 kb or larger (NHGRI 2000). The National Institutes of Health's (NIH) Office of Extramural Research announced a draft statement pertaining to data sharing, the purpose of which is "to support the release of final research data from NIH supported studies for the use of other researchers"(NIH 2002). Among possible responses to the otherwise free exchange of information has been the possibility that scientists would be discouraged from publishing all data and conclusions that might be used to create bioweapons. George Poste, former head of research at SmithKline Beecham and now chair of United Kingdom's Task Force on Bioterrorism, was widely quoted for his criticism of the biology community's failure to anticipate and take action on the implications of their work. In an interview with *Nature*, Poste described a familiar dilemma about the freedom of scientific inquiry versus the need to restrict access to scientific information for national security purposes: "What I think is untenable is the status quo— just allowing highly sensitive information to enter the public domain," [but] "[e]qually dangerous would be a draconian legislative response" (Aldous 2001, 237). In other words, it is right to be cautious, and it is obligatory for scientists to take seriously their responsibilities regarding use of and access to knowledge that emerges from their laboratories, but it is wrong to use the blunt instrument of national legislation as a gatekeeper: too permissive, and information might be used by others for malevolent means; too restrictive, and important research may be unintentionally restricted. This position is not new: scientists may habitually be disinclined to have their research activities limited by government regulation, and government may be legitimately inclined to limit free flow of information when national security is at stake. In a previous time, the need to restrict dissemination of scientific information could have been posited solely on its merits (e.g., security or proprietary interests) since control of the information rested with journal editors, patent attorneys, and grants administrators. But now that information moves seamlessly through the World Wide Web, these arguments are not as simple to defend: is publication of an entire genome a national security threat of sufficient magnitude that it should no longer be permitted?

The Private Sector's Response

In the aftermath of September 11, many in the private sector recognized a new set of responsibilities regarding bioweapons design and testing. At a February 2002 meeting of European biotechnology companies, venture capitalists and others (called BioSquare) held a panel discussion focused on ethical, legal, and scientific issues arising in the wake of the bioterrorism threat. Among the questions addressed by the panel (of which I was a member), was the following: is it a sensible business model for biotechnology companies, already engaged in mapping and sequencing viruses, to shift their emphasis to preparing tests, antibodies, and vaccines for what is essentially a limited market? The "market" was the national pharmaceutical stockpile or the finite number of doses of vaccine necessary to ensure protection against smallpox, anthrax, or ebola virces. A related question was whether it would appear unseemly or opportunistic for companies to redirect their research portfolios from drug discovery and development to bioterrorism preparedness.

The private sector has adopted policy positions on this topic. For example, the Biotechnology Industry Organization (BIO), the trade association for U.S. biotechnology, released its "Statement on Ethical Use of Biotechnology to Promote Public Health and National Security and to Fight Against Bioterrorism" (BIO 2002). The statement both condemns the use of bioterrorism by reaffirming "its long-standing policy opposing to the use of biotechnology to develop weapons" and outlines its continuing support for biotechnology research "to promote and protect the public health and national security." In a related way, the Pharmaceutical Research and Manufacturers Association (PhRMA) released its own statement summarizing its official positions on compliance with the BTWC, including recommendations for strengthening the Convention (PhRMA 2002).

Like BIO, PhRMA's positions attempt to strike a balance between safety and security on the one hand, and to promote research and devel-

opment on the other. These responses, and those of individual companies, are important statements of commitment, and when they are backed
up by actions they are even more deserving of public support. The Eli
Lilly Company established a partnership with the CDC to train foreign
scientists in methods of diagnosing and treating infectious diseases
spread both by bioweaponry and natural means. Several companies
joined with PhRMA and the CDC to provide and distribute educational
materials on infectious disease and bioterrorism to health professionals.[9]
But walking the line between virtuous behavior and opportunism
requires skill. Writing in the January 2002 entrepreneurial trade journal
Start-Up, Deborah Erickson (2002) reviewed the risks and opportunities
for companies that were considering moving into the marketplace in
response to the September 11 attacks. Clearly a number of opportunities exist for both newly emerging companies considering biodefense as
their principal niche, and established companies considering redirecting
their resources and existing products. Although relatively unknown to
the general public, many companies have had contracts with the United
States government for years, principally with the Defense Advanced
Research Projects Agency (DARPA), which spent $168 million on bio-
logical defense in 2001 (Erickson 2001, 23). One example, Sangamo
Biosciences, a company developing DNA technologies to help speed drug
discovery, recognized that these same technologies may be opportunisti-
cally used for biowarfare studies. The CEO of Sangamo is quoted as
saying, "Now we're interested in showing DARPA that our technology
can be applied to biowarfare" (Erickson 2002, 29).

It is reassuring to know that business ethics and bioethics may find
common cause through bioterrorism, but much remains to be done.
National investments in research and development are on the increase,
and in some countries tax advantages (such as for research and development) are provided to private sector companies to encourage them to
stay in a region of a country, ostensibly to discourage them and the
potential revenue they generate from going offshore. Policy statements
such as those of BIO and PhRMA have to be set into operation. One
area of particular interest will be the development and testing of
products that will be used to prevent, diagnose, and treat diseases using
human volunteers. Inevitably, we will have to engage the ethical issues
arising from the use of human subjects.

Research Involving Human Subjects

Many have recognized the need to reform the federal system for protecting human subjects in research (Advisory Committee on Human Radiation Experiments 1995; General Accounting Office 1996; Moreno, Caplan, and Wolpe 1998; NBAC 2001). For example, NBAC recommended that the oversight system—one that does not cover all research supported or conduced by the federal government and does not cover all privately sponsored research—must be replaced with a single, comprehensive set of rules that cover both publicly and privately sponsored research and is overseen by a national office (NBAC 2001).

Research on the causes of, preventive strategies for, and possible cures for bioterrorist attacks present several problems in research ethics: how can vaccine studies be conducted ethically when the risks to subjects are so high (possibility of serious disease or death from agents being tested)? How can informed consent of volunteers be obtained? How, in light of federal research ethics rules that discourage institutional research boards from assessing risks to persons other than subjects involved in the study itself, can risks and potential benefits be fully assessed? Given experience with conscripted subjects for radiation experiments (ACHRE 1995), it will be harder to design phase I and II studies involving human exposure to toxic or lethal pathogens. This problem would be alleviated to some extent if proposed amendments by the Food and Drug Administration were adopted that would alter its new drug and biological product regulations as they apply to studies testing the efficacy of such agents to exclude human volunteers (Food and Drug Administration 1999).

It is likely that given the risks associated with such testing, most research will be carried out on animals, which presents its own scientific and regulatory issues. More important, however, will be the secrecy that will no doubt surround this area of genetics research. In the absence of clear policy regarding classified research in the United States it is difficult to see how federal oversight of protocols involving the testing of genetic bioweapons can be managed within the existing public oversight system of institutional review boards.

For reasons arguably similar to (but no less controversial than) those for convening military rather than public tribunals to try suspected terrorists, one can imagine that research protocols involving testing of genetically modified organisms running square into the dilemma faced by all classified research in an open society: how can public account-ability for federal research dollars be balanced against the state's inter-est in preventing unintended consequences of misuse of this research? Given that society has not settled the issue of whether it is ethically acceptable to test toxic pesticides on people, considerable attention will have to be directed toward the proper policy for testing products used to diagnose, treat, and cure diseases caused by organisms modified to kill people.

Concluding Thoughts about the Contribution of Bioethics

The issues discussed in this chapter demonstrate how complicated con-structing a policy response can be. What makes it somewhat unusual is that the topic forces society to confront a now-too-obvious point: tradi-tional lines between domestic and foreign policy, and among health, science, and defense policy, are blurring. Genetic bioterrorism reminds us of fears society originally had about recombinant DNA research, with one notable exception: in the early 1970s the principal concern was unin-tended release of a toxic pathogen into the environment; now the concern is with intentional use of this technology deliberately to cause panic, harm, and death.

Genetic bioterrorism may resist contemporary bioethical analysis not only because it involves military issues (bioethics and moral theology have the conceptual architecture available from just-war theory), and not only because it involves manipulation of genomes of people, plants, and animal (bioethics has spent the past twenty years preparing for this). Rather, the events of October 2001 signal a new set of challenges, requir-ing both immediate attention and long-term vision from some unlikely collaborators: the basic and applied scientific community, foreign and domestic intelligence services, national security and public health offi-cials, and biotechnology and pharmaceutical industries.

Consider just one problem: implementing effective national legislation, or constructing enforceable international conventions, guidelines, or dec-larations to prevent individuals or groups from deliberately using this technology. Some believe that simple bans, prohibitions, and criminal laws are the best method of preventing genetic science from being used for terror. It has proved difficult enough to create legislation to address the social concerns associated with human cloning, stem cell research, genetic discrimination, and reproductive genetics (Knowles 2001). It will prove extraordinarily difficult for bioterrorism.

Since the human genome project was started in 1989, 3 percent and later 5 percent of the budget of NIH's National Human Genome Research Institute has been devoted to the study of ethical, legal, and social implications of genetics research (Meslin, Thomson, and Boyer 1997). A similar effort is necessary to support an infrastructure of researchers to anticipate and address the same consequences of research, development, and policy in this area. Traditional bioethics scholars must be joined by those in political science, history, religious studies, and economics. But they will have no impact at all if this larger group is not joined by an even broader coalition of those who have the capacity to make a difference—public advocates, professional associations, civic organizations, environmentalist, private sector companies, and policy makers. If the threat of genetic bioterrorism is important enough to devote significant resources to understanding the science to prevent its misuse, it would be unfortunate if resources were not equally devoted to understanding the social, political, and ethical consequences as well.

Acknowledgment

I am grateful for research assistance provided by Sarah Martin on earlier drafts of this chapter.

Notes

1. Adam Roberts (2002) speculated about the possibility of clearly defining the term terrorism. Although he notes that its original use as described in the Academie Française in 1798 referred to a "system or rule of terror," including the use of terror by a government against its own citizens, and for many decades tended to be associated primarily with political assassination of political leaders and heads of state, it now appears in several varieties:

In the half century after the Second World War, terrorism broadened well beyond assassination of political leaders and heads of state. In South East Asia, the Middles East and Latin America there were killings of policemen and local officials, hostage taking, hijacking of aircraft and bombing of buildings. In many actions civilian became targets. The causes espoused by terrorists encompassed not just revolutionary socialism and nationalism, but also religious doctrines rejecting the whole notion of a pluralist world of states.

2. The account of this history is drawn from several sources, including Fraser and Dando (2001), Miller (2001), and Frist (2002). Frist's account, which is more for public consumption than as a scholarly review, includes Iraq, North Korea, and Syria as among countries that have or are asserted to have had such programs.

3. Still other researchers were working in agricultural biotechnology to map and sequence various plants. One of the most important scientific developments was sequencing of the rice genome.

4. In April 11, 2002, a judge appointed by the former apartheid government acquitted the former head of Project Coast, Dr. Wouter Basson, of forty-six counts of murder, fraud, and drug dealing associated with this program. Testimony from witnesses described Basson's program as one designed to develop antiinfertility drugs, poisoning, and stockpiling of human immunodeficiency virces, cholera, and anthrax (Nessman 2002).

5. The politicization of ethnogenetics took a new twist in late 2001 when the journal *Human Immunology* withdrew a paper accepted for publication that claimed to have explained the genetic origins of Palestinians (Klarreich 2001)

6. The facts and events that follow are from Miller, Engelbeg, and Broad (2001).

7. All of the information that follows comes from material released on November 1, 2001, by the White House and can be found at www.whitehouse.gov/news/releases/2002/02/20020205-1.html.

8. http://www.niaid.nih.gov/dmid/pdf/biotresearchagenda.pdf.

9. Available at http://newsroom.lilly.com/news/story.cfm?id=947.

References

Advisory Committee on Human Radiation Experiments. 1995. *Final Report of the Advisory Committee on Human Radiation Experiments*. New York: Oxford University Press.

Aldous, Peter. 2001. "Biologists Urged to Address Risk of Data Aiding Bioweapon Design." *Nature*.

Biotechnology Industry Organization. 2002. "Statement on Ethical Use of Biotechnology to Promote Public Health and National Security and to Fight Against Bioterrorism". Available at www.bio.org.features/200111105.asp (visited January 1, 2001).

Bloom, Barry R. 1995. "Genome Sequences: A Microbial Minimalist." *Nature*. 378: 236.

Block, S.M. 1999. "Living Nightmares: Biological Threats Enabled by Molecular Biology." In *The New Terror: Facing the Threat of Biological and Chemical Weapons*, edited by S.D. Drell, A.D. Saefer, and G.D. Wilson, 39–75. Hoover Institution, Palo Alto, Ca.: Stanford University.

Broad, William and Nicholas Wade. 1982. *Betrayers of the Truth: Fraud and Deceit in the Halls of Science.* New York: Simon & Schuster.

Cook-Deegan, Robert M. 1997. "Do Research Moratoria Work?" 1997. In *Cloning Human Beings.* Vol. II. *Commissioned Papers.* National Bioethics Advisory Commission, H1-52. Rockville, MD: U.S. Government Printing Office.

Drazen, Jeffrey M. 2002. "Smallpox and Bioterrorism." *New England Journal of Medicine.* 346: 1262–1263.

Erickson, Deborah, 2002. "Biothreats: Biodefense Bonanza?" *Start-Up: Windover's Review of Emerging Medical Ventures.* 7.1: 20–30.

Food and Drug Administration. 1999. "Proposed Rule. New Drug and Biological Drug Products; Evidence Needed to Demonstrate Efficacy of New Drugs for Use Against Lethal or Permanently Disabling Toxic Substances When Efficacy Studies in Humans Ethically Cannot Be Conducted." *Federal Register.* 64.192 (Tuesday, October 5): 53690–53970.

Fraser, Claire M. and Malcolm R. Dando. 2001. "Genomics and Future Biological Weapons: The Need for Preventive Action by the Biomedical Community." *Nature Genetics Online.* 29.3: 253–256.

Frist, Bill. 2002. *When Every Moment Counts.* Lanham, MD: Rowman and Littlefield.

Greenberg, Daniel. 1967. *The Politics of Pure Science.* Chicago: University of Chicago Press.

Heap, Brian. 2001. "Scientists Against Biological Weapons." *Science.* 294 (November 16): 1417.

Henderson, Donald A. and Frank Fenner. 2001. "Recent Events and Observations Pertaining to Smallpox Virus Destruction in 2002." *Clinical Infectious Diseases.* 33: 1057–1059.

Klarreich, Erica. 2001. "Genetics Paper Erased from Journal over Political Content." *Nature.* 414 (November 22): 38.

Knowles, Lori. 1999. "Primordial Cell Research: Implications for International Repulation of Assisted Reproductive Technologies." *Journal of Women's Health and Law.* 1: 31–58.

Lewis, Rikki. 2002. "Race and the Clinic: Good Science?" *Scientist.* 16.4: 16.

Lipton, Eric and James Glanz. 2002. "Limits of DNA Research Pushed to Identify the Dead of Sept. 11." *New York Times.* Full text available at http://www.nytimes.com/2002/04/22/nyregion/22IDEN.html (visited April 22, 2002).

Longino, Helen E. 1990. *Science as Social Knowledge: Values and Objectivity in Scientific Inquiry.* Princeton, NJ: Princeton University Press.

Marburger, John. 2002. "Science and Technology in a Vulnerable World: Rethinking our Roles." Keynote address, 27th annual American Academy of Acts and Science colloquium on Science and Technology Policy, April 11, Washington, DC. Full text available at http://www.ostp.gov/html/02_4_15.html (visited April 19, 2002).

Meslin, Eric M. 1994. "Toward an Ethic in Dissemination of New Knowledge in Primary Care Research." In *Disseminating Research/Changing Practice: Research Methods for Primary Care*, vol. 6, edited by E.V. Dunn et al., 32–44. Thousand Oaks, CA: Sage Publications.

Meslin, Eric M., Elizabeth J. Thomson, and Joy T Boyer. 1997. "The Ethical, Legal, and Social Implications Research Program at the National Human Genome Research Institute." *Kennedy Institute of Ethics Journal.* 7: 291–298.

Miller, Judith, Stephen Engelberg, and William Broad. 2001. *Germs: Biological Weapons and America's Secret War*. New York: Simon & Schuster.

Moreno, Jonathan D., Arthur L. Caplan, and Paul R. Wolpe. 1998. "Updating Protections for Human Subjects Involved in Research." *Journal of the American Medical Association.* 280.22: 1951–1958.

National Bioethics Advisory Commission. 1997. *Cloning Human Beings*, 2 vols. Rockville, MD: U.S. Government Printing Office.

National Bioethics Advisory Commission. 1999a. *Research Involving Human Biological Materials: Ethical Issues and Policy Guidance*. Rockville, MD: U.S. Government Printing Office.

National Bioethics Advisory Commission. 1999b. *Ethical Issues in Human Stem Cell Research*, 3 vols. Rockville, MD: U.S. Government Printing Office.

National Bioethics Advisory Commission. 2001. *Ethical and Policy Issues in Research Involving Human Participants*. Bethesda, MD: U.S. Government Printing Office.

National Human Genome Research Institute. 2000. "NHGRI Policy on Release of Human Genomic Sequence Data." Available at http://www.nhgri.nih.gov/Grant_info/Funding/Statements/RFA/data_release.html (updated December 21, 2000).

National Institutes of Health. 2002. "NIH Draft Statement on Sharing Research Data." Available at http://grants1.nih.gov/grants/policy/data_sharing/index.htm (visited April 17, 2002).

Nessman, Ravi. 2002. "South African Chemical Expert Acquitted of Apartheid-Era Atrocities." *Indianapolis Star.* April 13, A11.

Okie, Susan. 2002. "U.S. Health Care System Grapples with New Role." *Washington Post.* April 7, A3.

Pharmaceutical Research and Manufacturers Association. 2002. Summary of PhRMA's Position on a Compliance Protocol to the Biological Weapons Convention. http://srpuls.phrma.org/phrona/Jul.98.DLRMA.bwe.html (visited September 11, 2002).

Roberts, Adam. 2002. "Can We Define Terrorism?" *Oxford Today.* 14.2: 18–19.

Royal Society. 2000. *Measures for Controlling the Threat from Biological Weapons*. London: Royal Society.

Schumacher, E.F. 1975. *Sonael Is Beautiful: Economics As If People Mattered*. New York: Harper & Row.

Salama N. et al. 2000. "A Whole-Genome Microarray Reveals Genetic Diversity Among *Helicobater pylori* Strains." *Proceedings of the National Academy of Sciences USA*. 97: 14668–14673.

Tettelin, H. et al. 2001. "Complete Genome Sequence of Virulent Isolate of *Streptococcus pneumoniae.*" *Science*. 293: 498–506.

U.S. Commission on National Security/21st Century. 1999. *Road Map for National Security: Imperative for Change. The Phase III Report of the United States U.S. Commission on National Security/21st Century. Final Draft Report*. Available at www.nssg.gov.

Voelker, R. 2001. "Will Focus on Terrorism Overshadow the Fight Against AIDS?" *Journal of the American Medical Association*. 287.17: 2081.

Wilson J.F. et al. 2001. "Population Genetic Structure of Variable Drug Response." *Nature Genetics*. Advance online publication: October 29, 2001, DOI.: 10, 1038/ng761, 29: 265–269. Available at www.nature.com/ng/.

Index